AD PRIMERS

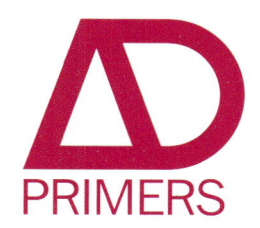

Scripting Cultures

AD PRIMERS

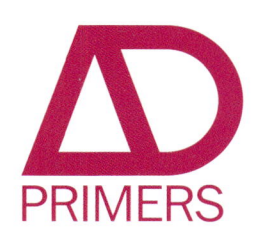

Scripting Cultures

Architectural design and programming

MARK BURRY

WILEY

A John Wiley and Sons, Ltd, Publication

This edition first published 2011
© 2011 John Wiley & Sons Ltd

Registered office
John Wiley & Sons Ltd, The Atrium, Southern Gate, Chichester, West Sussex, PO19 8SQ, United Kingdom

For details of our global editorial offices, for customer services and for information about how to apply for permission to reuse the copyright material in this book please see our website at www.wiley.com.

The right of the author to be identified as the author of this work has been asserted in accordance with the Copyright, Designs and Patents Act 1988.

All rights reserved. No part of this publication may be reproduced, stored in a retrieval system, or transmitted, in any form or by any means, electronic, mechanical, photocopying, recording or otherwise, except as permitted by the UK Copyright, Designs and Patents Act 1988, without the prior permission of the publisher.

Wiley also publishes its books in a variety of electronic formats and by print-on-demand. Some content that appears in standard print versions of this book may not be available in other formats. For more information about Wiley products, visit us at www.wiley.com.

Designations used by companies to distinguish their products are often claimed as trademarks. All brand names and product names used in this book are trade names, service marks, trademarks or registered trademarks of their respective owners. The publisher is not associated with any product or vendor mentioned in this book. This publication is designed to provide accurate and authoritative information in regard to the subject matter covered. It is sold on the understanding that the publisher is not engaged in rendering professional services. If professional advice or other expert assistance is required, the services of a competent professional should be sought.

Executive Commissioning Editor: Helen Castle
Project Editor: Miriam Swift
Assistant Editor: Calver Lezama

ISBN 978-0-470-74642-4 (hardback)
ISBN 978-0-470-74641-7 (paperback)
ISBN 978-1-119-97927-2 (ebk)
ISBN 978-1-119-97928-9 (ebk)
ISBN 978-1-119-97929-6 (ebk)

Cover design, page design and layouts by Karen Willcox, www.aleatoria.com
Cover image model: Mark Burry, scripting support: James Wojtek Goscinski, render: James Loder
Printed in Italy by Printer Trento Srl

Dedication

To my family

Acknowledgements

First and foremost I must acknowledge with gratitude the contribution of Andrew Miller who has steered the complex *Scripting Cultures* project to its conclusion having undertaken the initial background research with tenacity. Ensuring that the scripting represented in Chapters 6 to 10 was at industry strength I gratefully acknowledge the expertise of Peter Wood (Chapters 5, 6 and 8), Dr Wojtek James Goscinski (Chapters 7, 8 and 9), Daniel Davis and Alex Peña de León (Chapter 10). For rendering support I thank the indefatigable Grant Dunlop (Chapters 5, 6, 7 and 9), James Loder (Chapters 8, 9 and 10) and Daniel Davis (Chapter 10). I thank Adam Corcoran and Michael Wilson for their contribution to the various diagrams that support the scripting throughout the book. I thank Brad Marion for the fabulous rapid prototype in Chapter 9 photographed beautifully by Andrew Miller. Thank you Jane Burry and Andrew Burry for reading and positive commenting, and Tim Schork for early input.

Chapter 3 was based on the extraordinary generosity from over thirty early and recent scripting pioneers who responded voluminously to the set of short 'questions of the day' that I posed. I am sorry to have been able to include only loose gems from the basket of jewels amassed, but all the contributions have substantially influenced the contents of *Scripting Cultures*. My sincere thanks to my scripting cultural defenders: Acconci Studio (Vito Acconci), Francis Aish (Foster + Partners), Robert Aish, AKT (Adams Kara Taylor) (Sawako Kaijima and Panagiotis Michalatos), Biothing (Alisa Andrasek), CEB Reas (Casey Reas), CITA (Mette Ramsgard Thomsen), Pia Ednie-Brown, Cristiano Ceccato, Paul Coates, Evan Douglis, John Frazer, Mark Goulthorpe, Tom Kvan, Axel Kilian, Neil Leach, Kokkugia (Roland Snooks), Kyle Steinfeld, labDORA (Peter Macapia), Achim Menges, MESNE (Tim Schork and Paul Nicholas), MinusArchitecturestudio (Jason Johnson), Mode, MOS (Michael Meredith), Neri Oxman, Brady Peters, Nick Pisca (Gehry Technologies), Proxy (Mark Collins and Toru Hasegawa), Dennis Shelden, SOFTlab (Michael Szivos), SPAN (Matias del Campo), Supermanoeuvre, Martin Tamke, THEVERYMANY (Marc Fornes), Hugh Whitehead.

Key components of the project discussed in Chapter 10 were work in progress emerging from a collaboration between SIAL at RMIT University School of Architecture and Design in Melbourne, Australia, and CITA at the Royal Danish Academy of Fine Arts, School of Architecture in Copenhagen, Denmark. The project was led by me in my role as Velux Visiting Professor at CITA and Mette Ramsgard Thomsen, Head of CITA, in collaboration with Martin Tamke, Jane Burry, Phil Ayres, Stig Anton Nielsen, Alex Peña de León, Daniel Davis, Jacob Riiber Nielsen, Anders Holden Deleuran, Morten Winter, Aaron Fidjeland, Michael Wilson and Tore Banke.

I gratefully acknowledge the support of the Australian Research Council and their award of my Federation Fellowship without which this book would not have been possible. RMIT University School of Architecture and Design has provided the essential creative context for much of the work reported, and I acknowledge the Sagrada Família Church Foundation in Barcelona for the opportunity they provide to dig deeply into the less accessible reaches of Gaudí's later portfolio.

Finally I thank Helen Castle for her encouragement and insightful editorial direction and Miriam Swift and Calver Lezama for their patience and forbearance on what has inevitably been a lengthy and unscriptable project.

Contents

Chapter 1 Scripting cultures   008

Chapter 2 Contextual summary of computing,
scripting and speculative design   013

Chapter 3 Cultural defence   027

Chapter 4 Resources   072

Chapter 5 Dimensions   089

Chapter 6 Scripted productivity: Gaudí's rose windows   126

Chapter 7 Composition and form   152

Chapter 8 Simplifying complexity for fabrication   171

Chapter 9 Scripting narrative space:
Our World and The Third Policeman   190

Chapter 10 Performative scripting   224

Chapter 11 Cultural account:
scripting and shifts in authorship   246

Glossary   256

Scripting tools   260

Recommended reading   265

Index   267

Picture credits   271

1
Scripting cultures

Digital design is now fully assimilated into design practice, and we are moving rapidly from an era of being aspiring expert users to one of being adept digital toolmakers. This primer looks at this transition and acts as a first resource for all those curious about developing a higher-order engagement with the computer, but with an eye to critical enquiry rather than geekdom. *Scripting Cultures* considers the implications of lower-level computer programming (scripting) as it becomes more widely taken up and more confidently embedded into the 'design process'.

Scripting is a rather loose term by any definition and in this primer can be taken to mean computer programming at several levels. For the novice dabbling at the more accessible end of the user spectrum, scripting is the capability offered by almost all design software packages that allows the user to adapt, customise or completely reconfigure software around their own predilections and modes of working. At its most demanding for the emerging connoisseur, scripting can refer to higher-level computer programming where, in the 'open-source' environment, 'libraries' of functions can be combined with preconfigured routines (algorithms) as a means to produce manufacturer-independent digital design capability.[1] At its simplest, therefore, scripting affords a significantly deeper engagement between the computer and user by automating routine aspects and repetitive activities, thus facilitating a far greater range of potential outcomes for the same investment in time. Along with extending design experimentation, scripting can also be the antidote to standardisation forced by an ambition to lower production costs, rather than any more sophisticated motivation: the previously elusive opportunities for multiple versioning and bespoke production can now be considered more seriously through the use of scripting. This new territory combines with emerging affordable digital fabrication technologies taking advantage of the improving file-to-factory protocols. This has the potential to free up the designer to spend more time on design thinking. Authoritative customisation of the 'black box' affords the designer opportunities to escape the strictures inherent in any software – by definition in ways not thought of by the makers, otherwise it would be an existing capability.

Strictly speaking, to script is to write a screenplay or dialogue from which a play might be performed. Setting down the language from which others perform is presumably why the word 'scripting' has entered the lexicon of software users, and in computing, 'scripting language' is often synonymous with 'programming language': it is the means by which the user gives highly specific instructions to the computer with which they are interacting.[2] At a semantic level it is possible that the designer is less likely to flinch at the term scripting than they might at the term programming, for it is quite clear that most of the designers who use computers as a core part of their digital practice do not automatically turn to programming to form part of their repertoire. By not doing so users at once place their entire trust in the software engineers in the expectation that those anonymous collaborators have thought through all that might be wanted by the designers, just as they are conceding that what seems on occasion endless manual repetition is an acceptable use of their time when they could otherwise have been seeking some degree of automation. Software modified by the designer through scripting, however, provides a range of possibilities for creative speculation that is simply not possible using the software only as the manufacturers intended it to be used. Because scripting is effectively a computing program overlay, the tool user (designer) becomes the new toolmaker (software engineer).

Motivation to contribute to the scripting Zeitgeist

Why write a book on scripting in terms of culture when it may only be a passing 'style'?

Scripting is not new to design and was originally considered the task of a specialist; being taught to program computers in any way was not part of a design education. It is only recently that there has been a sufficient groundswell of interest to prompt change. Many designers are now aware of the potential of scripting, but it is still seen as a difficult arena to enter. This book joins the growing list of titles that have emerged over the last few years offering routes for designers into the world of scripting. This primer could treat scripting as a technical challenge requiring clear description, guidance and training, but instead leaves that task to others and focuses on motivation. Crucially, *Scripting Cultures* offers some answers to why the designer would script in the first place, and considers some of the cultural and theoretical implications along the way. Scripted code readily changes hands and, in terms of potential risks, it could become a cloning tool for less talented operators to mimic their masters. In contrast and in terms of opportunities scripting ought to be the opposite: a liberating design force unleashed by the Internet combining with the innate human desire to share knowledge; the *live hive* in which the collective critical mass is far greater than the sum of the individuals.

This book offers three important differences to other titles and seeks to provide complementary material rather than dig away at essential points of difference. Firstly, the predominant theme is 'cultural' rather than 'practical', 'computational', 'artistic' or 'generative'. It enquires into the cultural implications of scripting and asks what are the cultures of scripting as, emerging in myriad ways, they more conspicuously influence the designer's toolkit. Secondly, on an associated website hosted by Wiley, this book directs readers to substantial worked examples of code adopted in some of the most widely used modelling software for some of the project work described. In these samples, every parcel of code is provided for the reader with basic explanations as to what it does, and why it appears where it does in the script. Thirdly, for the designer who does not want to work on top of manufacturers' software packages, a worked example will be laid out as proof of concept using freely available open-source software, offering the experienced designer complete freedom in the way that they operate.

The book is organised in three sections. It commences by considering the fundamentals of computing and design as a means of capturing some of the spirit at the time in which I am writing. More critically still, the primer moves on to distil the thoughts of many of the current generation of key scripters into an action plan as first steps to deducting some kind of collective *'quo vadis?'*. As essential background for the aspiring novice, this is followed by a succinct consideration of what others have written on the subject and the principal choices of approach available to the scripter but not discussed in detail in this primer. The final section is a series of five commentaries around two decades of my own endeavours in the field. This is preceded by an account of a set of design preoccupations as the context for this personal line of enquiry. I hasten to add that I am not an expert scripter myself, but the longevity of my involvement has led to a series of insights shared here, to serve at least as provocations if not as an actual *modus operandi* for general adoption. The introduction to the five projects, 'Dimensions', covers my motivation to start scripting and commences the general theme around the primacy of first idea, then ideation, conceptual development and, ultimately, logical exposition. Technique, which could so easily have been foregrounded, has instead taken a back seat. Rapid changes in software and emerging alternative computational design approaches enforce this 'knowhow' reticence, not least to avoid the primer becoming obsolete soon after publication. The intellectual challenges of ideation and the logic of digital design discovery alone are sufficient motivation for an exposé of this kind, transcending any need for a developed discussion on the relative ease or difficulty of particular software or open-source opportunities in our current era.

Necessarily, I bring my own baggage to this account, but in conducting my research for the primer it became clear that my situation, that of an autodidact, is not the exception that I had perhaps assumed. This is one of two reasons why it is titled *Scripting Cultures* and not simply *Scripting Culture*; this is to say, innovative scripting designers do not want to be locked into a single defining culture. The other motivation to pluralise 'culture' is to reinforce the message that the book is not about identifying and tuning into the latest swarm phenomenon, and placing an umbrella over a 'new' design movement or style. Scripting, as an approach to computational design, offers access to whole new ways of exploring design, but design remains always at the core. It is clear to me that so long as coders follow their own leads, there will be many scripting cultures. Scripting is especially prominent now because of the difference between digital design pre scripting and digital design now, as scripting steps temporarily into the limelight as a burgeoning new creative force, as agents of change often are. Its assumed novelty will pass, no doubt, but we are still at the stage of largely uncritical engagement. This primer will play its part, I hope, in encouraging digital designers to take up scripting while still continuing to think for themselves as designers first, as they always have done.

References

1 At the highest level still (short of designing one's own computer) there is 'machine code', the actual machine operating language of a computer with which the user-engaged operating language negotiates. We will not be going anywhere near there.
2 Some software includes opportunities to engage through scripting at several levels of sophistication, from macro writing, scripting, and programming via a SDK (software development kit).

Contextual summary of computing, scripting and speculative design

2

At this point we are not at all clear about where we have arrived in the world of practical computing and speculative design and their full value, culturally as well as economically. This chapter considers computer engagement in practice and its assistance in automating practical aspects of office work at one end of the utility spectrum with digital design dreaming at the other. The focus of *Scripting Cultures* is more dreaming than dealing with immediate workaday practicalities, although in advanced architecture it is hard to separate the two. Design *speculation* is the primer's predominant subtext and quite what is meant by this term will unfold throughout the book.

There is tension between the design automation and digital speculation within a context of a residual undercurrent of general resentment over the computer's arrival in the first place (granted, barely perceptible now, but present all the same). Not only does one still come across ardent critics who perceive as sullying the computer's incursion into a world of practice uncontaminated for centuries by reprographic machinery of any kind, but there are several levels of nostalgia-based discontent over the choice of tools with which to inscribe our thoughts. At its most fundamental, such critics rue the passing of tracing vellum and pencils, compasses with nibs attached for inscribing circles, 'T' squares, French curves, traditional drawing boards, delicate watercolour washes, and the art of the perspectivist. While the majority adapted to the 20th-century instrumentalisation of architectural drawing, for instance, my propelling pencils, technical pens, and calculators were still regarded as retrograde distractions by some eminent architects who taught me in the 1970s.

For the last two decades the economic returns of using computers have been increasingly undeniable to nearly everyone, and few would disagree with any assertion that they are here to stay, but there remains the tension I refer to above, between the computer as practical *aide-de-camp*, and computer as digital design agent. I see merit in both schools of thought, and scripting as an effective mediator, but there are many who do not see it both ways. In my opinion scripting for effective building delivery, important within the general framework of construction economics, while technically a challenge, is not as directly interesting for the designer as design thinking and dreaming.

A brief history of CAD

For the younger reader entirely familiar with what computers can now do, it may be worthwhile to reflect on how much has changed and how quickly. Here is how design computation was approached as it was taught to us in a university at the forefront of design computation research in the late 1970s (Cambridge, UK).

I was lucky to have had Bill Mitchell as the person who introduced my class to computer-aided design. This was a real privilege as Bill seemed the kind of person who would help make the world become how he envisaged it, which he largely succeeded in doing within his sphere.[1] One does not meet too many people with this degree of infectious vision and capability. Someone else had the ambitious task of putting part of Bill's vision into practice for my class, and once a week for a semester we went down to the university's computer centre where we would do the maths and valiantly punch cards to input the computer with the necessary analogue binary data. At the end of the semester I had computer-drafted a cube that could be viewed in perspective; an inauspicious introduction to design computation. Possibly this was the reason that I took absolutely no interest in the field until encouraged by circumstance to do so in 1989. When I left my architectural employment at that point I suffered the ignominy of being replaced by a computer at exactly the same time as I was beginning to re-engage with a task that cried out for computational assistance. My interest had been sufficiently piqued to revisit the topic. How much had it advanced in a decade, I wondered?

Tracing the evolution of computers in practice is absolutely clear in contrast to attempting to map the support of speculative design by designers. 'Design computing' from Herbert Simon onwards has a proud history (principally around Artificial Intelligence – AI) with globally located key design research centres such as those at Carnegie Mellon, Strathclyde, Cambridge, MIT and Sydney Universities. Engineering specialists regard the challenges of porting building information from computer system to computer system as being core to business needs so they have been prominent drivers in the adoption of computers in practice. Worryingly, in terms of business that is, little has changed in four decades with regard to the ambitions of 'BIM', as it is now known (*Building Information Modelling*); it is as much in the forefront of large practices' priorities as it was back in the early 1970s when 'hospital design systems' set the 'computers in architecture' ball rolling. Central to these particular priorities is the management and sharing of large databases, integrated models, and relationships built between recognisable architectural objects. The problem is that the systems are still only coping with the more straightforward challenges with the inexhaustible optimism that interoperable comprehensiveness is just around the corner.

It is not at all easy to discern the design priorities here. Planners and facilities managers too have yet another set of priorities with which the agenda is forced, as do cost estimators. If the university were the last bastion for independent thinking about digital design, it did not present a convincing defence with academics largely insisting over the past two decades that the focus should be on teaching skills immediately useful to practice, such as Computer-Aided Design (CAD) as digital drafting, photorealistic renders and digital construction detailing and referencing. Then there is the whole information management and communications resolution always hustling for recognition.

Where has digital design speculation been throughout all this?

The answer is that digital design speculation has always been there, but supported more as a kind of counter-culture (through active engagement rather than by being merely tolerated) by relatively few institutions, notably the DRL at the AA and the Bartlett, London, SCI-Arc in Los Angeles, The MediaLab at MIT, ETH in Zurich, and the one I direct; the Spatial Information Architecture Laboratory (SIAL) at RMIT University in Melbourne. Consider the way these digital design research centres acquire odd names or unhelpful acronyms, almost as a subversive move to obfuscate what really goes on inside. I apologise to colleagues of the many burgeoning programmes worldwide that now support innovative digital design speculation through scripting: my list is representative of the pool of ambition generally, and the groups listed are relatively well established.

Scripting is as vital in all of the fields listed above as I believe is the case for its role in design. In fact, for many working in the technical areas, computer programming is a core activity without which nothing would happen. What helps account for why computers have had demonstrably less immediate impact in architecture (design) than in any other creative discipline is perhaps that 'computers in architecture' research has been biased towards many of the discipline's technical fields; unfortunately, computers and architectural technology can be in a relatively obscure consciousness zone for those whose focus is the speculative nature of design. This is the first of several paradoxes that pepper this book. In the discipline the majority of architects

Gehry Partners,
Beekman Tower,
New York, construction
March 2010.

are motivated more by design in architecture than the many associated and predominantly technical subdisciplines. The technical subdisciplines have dominated research into computers in architectural practice because, as a useful art, these areas will more immediately help the commercial aspects of practice than would design tools, and more conspicuously too. Architects, after all, can design with pencils anyway. Research money therefore goes into technical applications and productivity aids such as drafting software. The paradox is that for decades architectural software has striven to emulate the analogue working practice that architects developed over the past two centuries and, as a group, architects have not been especially motivated to assist lifting themselves out of the analogue design methods rut. I cover this in more personal detail in the following chapter.

Scripting, then, sits across all aspects of computer use in architecture but width is not the focus of this primer. The reason is that there is an abundance of material for would-be BIM scripters, the engineering scripter or in fact any area that attracts those with a strong technical bias, because the people attracted to these areas already have a bias towards skill acquisition as programmers. *Scripting Cultures* is therefore aimed more deeply, to nourish the less well fed, as it were; those who want to script for design because, in terms of factor of difficulty, this area has the most hurdles in front of it. The rapid ascendance of more user-friendly design software, easier scripting languages, a growing community of scripters and a gradual wearing out of the fuddy-duddy brake pads implied at the beginning of this chapter, all combine to make this a good time for newcomers to be primed up, ready to make their innovative contribution to scripting cultures.

The style question

Where have we been and where are we now?

The answer to the second part of this question is teased out more in the next chapter but I shall at least provide some hints here. What follows is a personal take on the lead up to what many regard as the current semi-seismic shift from scripting as counter-culture to scripting as a driving force for 21st-century architectural thinking.

I do not believe that there is any particular consensual understanding or appreciation of where we have got to now or universal enthusiasm for promoting digital design as having emerged as the dominant paradigm. Cecil Balmond is very explicit on the subject in his wonderful *Informal*:

> *We are in a time when anything goes and there is no basis for a manifesto – post modern has come to, ultimately, no meaning. With little understanding of the motivation of form, modernism runs into minimalist dead ends and by continuing to look to the outside the seduction with objecthood and architecture as art is perpetuated. Geometry is not invoked; no one peers within and asks questions about the archetypes of form. These are forgotten.* [2]

The actual level of success that prominent practitioner-educator-commentators such as Patrik Schumacher will enjoy in identifying and pushing *Parametricism* as the first real style since, and therefore successor to, the Modern Movement will be seen in the future by its take up as a manifesto force, or its possible rejection as a superficial overview.

> *We pursue the parametric design paradigm all the way, penetrating into all corners of the discipline. Systematic, adaptive variation, continuous differentiation (rather than mere variety), and dynamic, parametric figuration concerns* all *design tasks from urbanism to the level of tectonic detail, interior furnishings and the world of products.*[3]

Parametricism itself does not interest me particularly, especially as 'parametric design' is tantamount to a *sine qua non*; what exactly is non-parametric design? It is difficult enough getting to grips with parametric design from a number of points of view. In my university-based research group, we were early adopters of so-called parametric design software in 1991 as described in Chapter 5, but for the past ten years we have been doing our best to challenge its assumed authority. Others, too, such as Michael Meredith, express their reservations forcefully:

> *When something supposedly looks 'parametric' today, it's aesthetic (re)production—the repetition of quality and taste. The mastering of hi-tech engineering software is ultimately used to produce ornate architectural decoration.*[4]

The motivation for making such a claim as 'parametricism' does interest me however. My own view at the time of writing (2010) is rather ambivalent. I can see why it is important for individuals or groups to stand up from time to time as *provocateurs*, catalysing the debates that everyone else tries to avoid. But I was also getting comfortable with the fact that stylistic hegemonies had at long last died out, dinosaurs of an age when collectivism, suppression of individualism, obligatory conformity to *the* (rather than *a*) style, and dominant paradigms were at last deemed unnecessary cultural constructs. I have had at least 15 years to wallow in the freedom that pluralism brings to the individualist, the continuous reenergising and unprecedented connectedness that the Internet offers, and the pleasure that the 'local' has more importance than ever within the global village. Whereas the 'local' might be all that was known in not so distant times, today we know the local of any situation better because we have many views of the world in which to locate it. And now that we understand the local in terms of the global, with the gift of the Internet like minds can gravitate towards each other with sufficient critical mass to eschew automatic adherence to unnecessary global movements.

If we are in fact in an era of pluralism, as well as or instead of parametricism, it is a very interesting condition. The Modern Movement was the only cultural hegemony to have influenced the entire world simultaneously – little wonder at the interest in the question about what would follow it, hence Postmodernism, Deconstructivism, and then the void that digital design offers to fill.

Like all great radical movements, the Modern Movement would have a degree of preposterousness to it were it not for having been so great an influence in all cultural activity for at least two generations. Looking back over the period with the advantage of being a generation removed, its distinctiveness decreases in the longer view of history, that same illusion of distinctiveness that its promoters used to advance its cause: alleged breaks with tradition, modernity et al. It might have been only the accident of a combination of personalities and egos that took all the world into Modernism following the first International Congress for Modern Architecture (Congrès international d'architecture moderne, or CIAM), hosted in 1928 at La Sarraz (Switzerland). There, rather than the various routes offered by a number of unalloyed alternative movements that had emerged in the previous generation, standardisation became the new force. The alternative groups had been actively embracing:

> … *the exuberance of Expressionism, the mystical fanaticism of De Stijl, the bracing coolness of die Neue Sachlichkeit, the wild invention of the Constructivists, the brooding complexity of the Organic School, and the rationalism of the Purists.*[5]

Through what comes across as an unseemly suppression of the contributions of Hugo Häring it was made clear at the congress that new imperatives replaced such loose sentiment:

> The politics of launching a movement aimed to produce an orthodoxy of method, technology and language on an international scale could ill afford the sensitive and responsive approach of someone who pleaded, 'we want to examine things and allow them to discover their own images. It goes against the grain with us to bestow a form on them from the outside'.[6]

In place of such pleas, the delegates of that first CIAM declared that

> The most efficient method of production is that which arises from rationalization and standardization. Rationalization and standardization act directly on working methods both in modern architecture (conception) and in the building industry (realization).[7]

And this remained the dominant paradigm, the 'standard' for two generations of architects for the next half-century. The holism and philosophical underpinning of the discrete but empathetic groups of 'non standard' was sufficient grounds to justify the pejorative labelling of such wayward architects in the first CIAM declaration as 'academicians'. Paradoxically the elevation of the dullness of standardisation countered the most significant developments of the early 20th century including the potential impact of the move from Euclidean to non-Euclidean geometry, the arrival of quantum physics, and with it a more sophisticated role for the mathematician, all of which could have been especially influential for what would have been a unique breaking of architectural traditions. Culturally and socially too, there were developments, individuals and travesties as potential influencers that could have been so much more influential: mechanised war, moving pictures, flight, radio, James Joyce, Futurism, are examples.

Whatever was lost as an opportunity to radicalise architecture then has perhaps been regained in our time. It is an interesting conundrum: the history of architecture is dominated by the fundamental processes of architecture being sublimated by changes in its clothing – style. However reductionist the Modern Movement might have been in one sense, it was absolutely tied to that essential architectural tradition: espousal and implementation of a dominant paradigm. Scripting has the potential to consolidate the apparent fractures that were being willed in the first

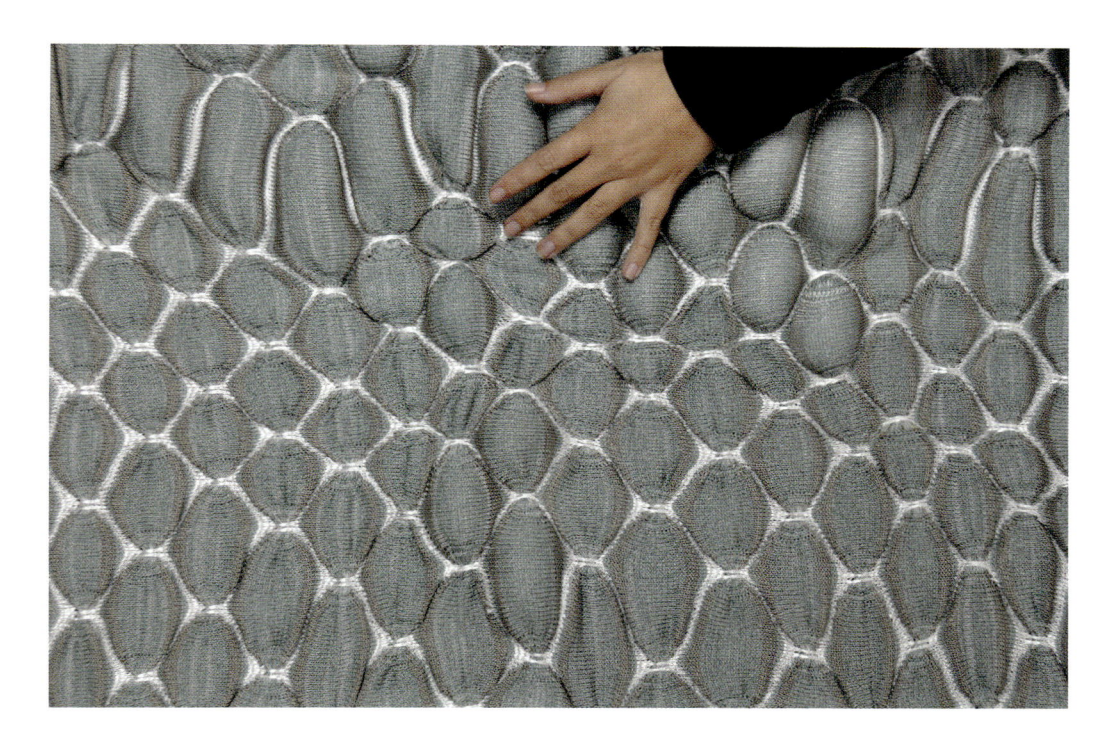

Mette Ramsgard Thomsen, CITA, CAD-CAM Knitting, Copenhagen, 2010.

quarter of the 20th century, and earlier even, threatening the established hegemonies and any that might be being promulgated in the wake of a vacuum following the 'death' of Modernism.

> The architectural field's current use of the parametric has been superficial and skin-deep, maybe importantly so, lacking of a larger framework of referents, narratives, history, and forces. Despite the contemporary collective desire to forget postmodern semiotic signification, everything visual eventually devolves into symbolic imagery. The recent architectural production has been dedicated towards a post-postmodern architecture of radical distortion as a way to escape signification and subvert semiotic legibility (twisted hyperbolic forms, stretched out shapes, extreme continuity of planes and surfaces, etc.). I would argue that the 'parametric work' being produced today fits within an evolution of so-called postmodernism, concerning the image and referent although the parametric is the tautological modulated image of quantity; the indexical referent is itself and analogous systems. To the extent the profession has utilized parametrics today, there is very little instigating complexity

other than a mind-numbing image of complexity, falling far short of its rich potential to correlate multivalent processes or typological transformations, parallel meanings, complex functional requirements, site-specific problems or collaborative networks.[8]

Parametricism or not, clearly we are on the cusp of an extraordinary shift in creative potential and priorities and with it architectural practice. The authoritative creative force in terms of published column inches within the architectural press can be identified, in the main, as a group of male designers of advancing years, the majority of whom are not digitally design literate regardless of how much use is made of the computer in their studios (nor how much pro-digital rhetoric emerges from their practice). Meanwhile, at this time when global financial crises have been curtailing economic activity, especially in the construction sector, a combination of 'design research' practices and highly innovative studio teaching is emerging as an unstoppable force. I am diffident about predicting any details of a future of new architecture or new practice. Through my own experience of two decades of a critical and vital uptake of the computer in my projects, I am acutely aware of how much architectural design thinking has changed for the relatively few pioneers, and how inevitably what were previously seen as exceptional ways of thinking will increasingly infuse the various design procedures and vocabularies with which all will no doubt operate in the future, not just an enlightened few.

The problem with rules

When I first started teaching design 15 years after being taught myself, I was discomforted by the changes in priority between my time as a student and those that informed my teaching on elevation to the other side of the lectern. When I was a student, design was presented didactically as a range of options, some right or wrong, some better or less good. It did not matter that there was confusion between a quasi-moral code and an ethically relativistic position attempting to coexist under the banner of Modernism; it was all shoehorned into a package. Our portfolios were assessed on this basis with aphorisms like 'you need to know the rules before you break them'. My instinctive response was, then 'why have rules?', but that was before finding out about scripting, and the need for precise language. This is my second paradox – design freedom apparently compromised by the inflexibility of (almost) all scripting languages. As designers, of course, we welcome the frisson that discovery of the viable workaround to scripting's inevitably highly precise coding always provides.

Over the years I have enjoyed studio teaching conducted on the basis of helping talented young designers hone what are sometimes only vestigial skills in critical judgement of their own creative output, primarily through engaging with their peers. It is about unlocking potential rather than guiding conformity to universally held doctrinal positions, so movements seem unhelpful to me in that regard. I will return later to this topic in terms of the lack of a 'Gaudí school', as it was put to me when I was a student, and a little more fully in Chapter 5.

The motivation to script is varied and none of the designers who have contributed to the territorial overview in the next chapter would claim to script for scripting's sake. Much of this book is a series of worked examples that provide the vehicle for the crux of my account: dissections of my own

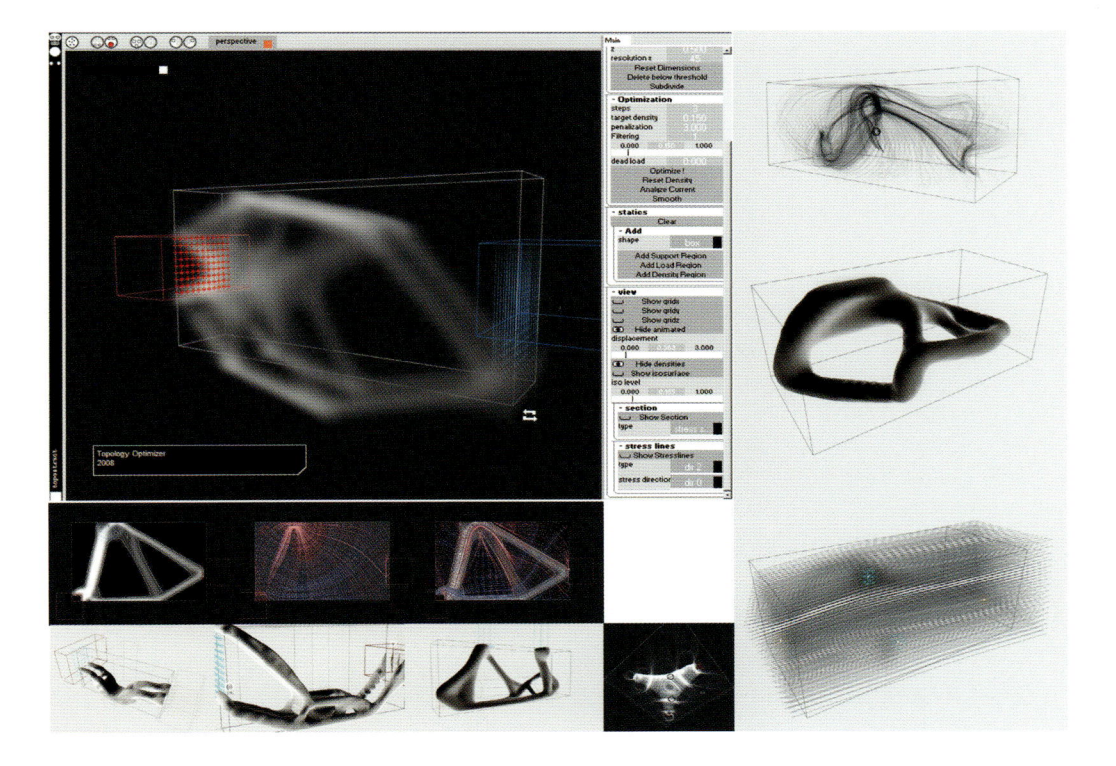

P Michalatos & S Kaijima, AKT Architects, Topology optimiser, London, 2010.

experience offered as primer source material and insights for readers to engage with. In this chapter I consider my own motivation from a generic point of view in order to declare my bias up front, and possibly to encourage others to shed any style shackles that might hold them back too.

I might have looked in detail at a wider set of design scripting approaches in order to discuss the full gamut of opportunities in the field in detail but, as I am sure my peers will agree, such a neutral comprehensive overview would inevitably be disingenuous given the personal investment that goes with scripting design. Scripting can be a design idiom. On this basis I will endeavour not to overly critique other approaches that I have not tried myself, as it would not place me on a sufficiently critical footing. Alternative approaches skilfully tried and tested by others but not by me will be remote descriptions only, and not serve any useful purpose here. In the final analysis, the selection of scripting approaches I have adopted myself over the years would indicate where my creative instincts lie, and the fact that I have not taken up some of the many other well-known procedures (algorithms and libraries of code samples that I refer to in Chapter 4) simply points to the fact that they have not seemed useful to me for my purposes. Others have clearly found them to be essential, and I will direct the reader to specific exemplars in the next two chapters as appropriate.

Last word on the school

We all come from a school of something. When I was a student in the late 1970s, for instance, we were warned off taking too much interest in Gaudí's oeuvre as 'there was no school' of the type I refer to above. In other words, he was so hopelessly idiosyncratic and self indulgent as an architect (my lecturer's assessment, not mine I hasten to add) that he had no long-term followers, and so his message died with him. Of course, such a statement was all that I needed as a provocation to find out more, and two of my five worked examples here come semi-directly from my work at the Sagrada Família Church in Barcelona; I have been working on the project to complete the building for the last three decades, endeavouring to untangle some of the important mysteries around Gaudí's way of working that would otherwise be lost from view. I cannot argue that my contribution to this task was only possible through scripting, but I can say that my research through scripting has significantly added to the discovery of riches.

In terms of 'what is my school', I come from the school of 'design is the mapping of an idea through to an intended outcome'. It does not involve a method nor does it heartily embrace the role of accident. Serendipity may play a part, but as a possible surprising influence rather than as a driver. The logic structures attendant in scripting suit me because I am happy to see design as a declarative activity rather than something vague or esoteric. There are many alternative schools, but the one I subscribe to is distinctive for placing the word *intention* centrally within the construct. This does not preclude intuition at all, but it does make generative processes a little difficult to embrace fully if any authorship is ceded to chance in a careless way. As I enjoy the company of friends and colleagues who profoundly disagree with this stance, it seems best to put my position on the role of intention firmly on the table from the outset.

Back to earth, these are still early days. We have a hunger for far greater computer power to allow the multi-parameter decision-making to take place in real-time, and many of today's scripters need to take off their gloves, define their goals more precisely, and think about coding from first principles as excitedly as adopting an algorithm designed for another context, before discovering any limitations. This primer is therefore priming the reader for an exciting sense of the future that might not have quite arrived. The next chapter trips back into the past with a personal account – every scripter has one, and they are all quite different it seems. It also picks up on the present and near future with a selection of extracts from the views of over 30 pioneer and contemporary scripting maestros who responded to a series of questions I put to them when researching scripting cultures.

References

1 Bill Mitchell died in June 2010. Author of many profoundly insightful and future-oriented books largely proselytising intelligent computer use in practice, he is profiled in my 'pioneers' pantheon' in Chapter 4. Readers will gain particular value from those of his many publications listed in the bibliography at the end of this book.
2 CT Balmond, *Informal*, Prestel USA (New York), 2007, p 15.
3 Patrik Schumacher, *Parametricism as Style – Parametricist Manifesto*, New Architecture Group (London), 2008. Presented and discussed at the Dark Side Club, 11th Architecture Biennale, Venice, 2008; http://www.patrikschumacher.com/Texts/Parametricism%20as%20Style.htm.
4 See projects by Michael Meredith, Aranda\Lasch, Mutsuro Sasaki in T Sakamoto, A Ferre, M Kubo, *From Control to Design: Parametric/Algorithmic Architecture*, Actar (New York), 2008, p 6.
5 Colin St John Wilson, *The Other Traditions of Modern Architecture: the uncompleted project*, Academy Editions (London), 1995, p 13.
6 Colin St John Wilson, *Architectural Reflections: studies in the philosophy and practice of architecture*, Butterworth Architecture (Oxford and Boston), 1992, p xi.
7 CIAM meeting, item 4 of section I (General Economic System).
8 Michael Meredith, 'Never enough (transform, repeat ad nauseo)' in *Parametric/Algorithmic Architecture: From Control to Design*, Actar (New York), 2008, p 6.

3 Cultural defence

In the previous chapter I considered two cultural conditions in parallel, and sought a connection: a short history of the use of computers in architecture, and the current question of 'where are we now?' in terms of a dominant paradigm in respect of 'movement'. As detailed in the previous chapter, on the one hand we have a position promulgated as 'anything goes' by a leading practitioner Cecil Balmond,[1] and on the other 'the next major movement is …' from Patrik Schumacher.[2] It is possible that both practitioners are arguing for the same thing from a slightly different trajectory, but what of the individual designer not necessarily at the height of their powers?

Every design scripter scripts design for the first time – but what are they joining: mainstream alternative practice, a club, a movement, a counter-culture? This curiosity was sparked by my own experience: in preparing for this book I reflected on how I myself started thinking about design and computer coding in the same thought space. It occurred to me that everyone moving into this excitingly different domain of practice might also have found themselves facing similar challenges with the same sense of joining a road without clear signposts. Certainly, when faced with students tackling scripting for the first time, there is a palpable sense of 'this could well be too difficult and beyond me, and how would I use it anyway?' It seems we are over the first hurdle – initiation – as there is considerable evidence of an emerging scripting generation with a host of committed pioneers who have trail blazed before them. Is this it: problem solved, scripting now mainstream, or near mainstream, or do we collectively still face a substantial journey? It is the combination of a personal sense of still being in *terra incognita* despite having left *terra nullius* that prompted me to correspond with a selection of current maestros and pioneers. In this chapter I lift the lid of my own experience in order to derive a series of 'questions of the day' to pose to my chosen correspondents.

How I came to script

My scripting adventure began in 1992. Investigating Gaudí's surviving plaster models for the Sagrada Família church (detailed in Chapters 6 and 7), I had reached a point at which I seemed to be devoting an inordinate amount of time to carrying out unremittingly repetitive tasks. The alleged efficiency gains using computer-aided drafting began to seem rather far-fetched, not least the preternatural tendency for CAD software to steer towards 2D drafting, which made excursions into 3D modelling rather awkward in comparison. I had thought naively that the 'D' in CAD stood for design, not drafting, which is how the software seemed to have been prioritised to me. Specifically, there were two particular tasks that were grinding me down: drawing 2D *hyperbola* curves from which to construct 3D *hyperboloids of revolution of one sheet*, and labelling hundreds of points with unique names combined with their coordinates. For the first of such wearying tasks, the hyperbola, I needed to produce several hundred mathematically derived curves to match sections extracted from the models Gaudí had composed principally from elliptical hyperboloids. At that time I was using AutoCAD™ and this task involved computing a *polyline* through sufficient points to allow the curve to be both smooth and mathematically precise. The trouble was that each point had to be derived manually using a scientific calculator and the formula for a hyperbola. Each point, and there were 15 required for each curve, was calculated then entered into 2D space manually by typing in via the command line. At the outset, I assumed that there would be a tool within the various CAD software packages that I had access to through which I could simply type in the formula, give values to the variables and surely the curve would appear magically inside my 3D modelling environment in the correct position and orientation. There seemed to be plenty of what are now called *applets* about that could do this just as I have described, but they were the products of computer science postgraduates who generously shared them in the public domain as stand-alone 'shareware programs'. I could find no such tool within my CAD software, nor any means of interoperating between the shareware and CAD.

I was aware that in offices at that time many users of AutoCAD™, for example, had access to customised versions that had routines written in AutoLISP, a language specific to the software. These routines had been prepared to minimise routine tasks, but none of my contacts had actually written them; they had been acquired informally with consent or otherwise through the normal networks. Extensive enquiries failed to furnish any such hyperbola routine to help me draw mine so, as is often the best possible stimulant in such situations, necessity mothered a drastically innovative approach on my part: learning to program the hyperbola myself.

Like so many who were conventionally trained as architects, programming was not in my blood. I knew no one in my circle who could assist me, and I assumed it would be way beyond me: if I was to tackle programming I would have to pick it up on my own, on that basis. Once I had settled to the task two aspects surprised me. Firstly, it was not quite as forbidding as I had expected and, secondly, there was no room for approximation or error: for an effective outcome that was both robust and consistent, precision was non-negotiable. Once I had succeeded in producing a routine that could be called up either in the command line or via a drop-down menu I had reduced a process that had been taking a significant fraction of an hour per hyperbola into a matter of seconds. Furthermore I could toggle each result to unique layers and names. With three points defining respectively an origin, a point where 'x' was a minimum, and a point defining the curve's asymptote, I had all that was needed for the hyperbola to be calculated automatically and drawn in an instant. After having this frustration settled, I tackled the other tedious task that had also been so energy sapping: marking points in space with unique names, extracting their coordinates from the database and listing them in an associated text file, and placing this information in 3D space next to the relevant points. With both time-consuming repetitive tasks sorted, I had developed a completely different view of computer-aided drafting at least, and probably the more elusive computer-aided design that interested me far more.

Both these undertakings were highly specific to my research at the time and it is not surprising perhaps that neither were available as ready-made options within commercial software. The effect of learning to script changed my relationship with the computer. Hitherto I had regarded it as a necessary adjunct to my work as an architect moving towards the 21st century. I had no love for it at all, and I probably resented the enormous gulf between my thought processes and whatever was happening inside the black box. Once

I had a handle on this coding caper, I could see then that I could attempt to transcend whatever limitations software might impose on me as a designer, guiding this electronic instrument with the same authority I applied to my pen and compass. At the outset, I realised that the stumbling block was not so much learning the code itself or the syntax required for its use as deconstructing the problem involved sufficiently well to represent it in code. If I could not get the logic right, no amount of syntactic precision with the code was going to compensate.

The two problems that had encouraged me to step outside my professional comfort zone of compliant passenger to become front-seat driver were stimulated by a need to rid myself of repetitive work that was not only numbingly boring, but also inclined to suffer from my human error, typically induced by any manual data entry that relies on reading from the screen, writing it down, calculating, then keying it back in a different context – there was no cut and paste at that time. Very quickly, however, I could see that a prime motivation for coding on top of software was to augment my design practice by allowing me to work in ways hitherto impractical, and so scripting became a medium of experimentation ahead of productivity gain.

Within a year, scripting had infiltrated my teaching, and in 1993 I instituted an elective course in which the participants had to come up with two pieces of code: a productivity tool (this was to appease my senior CAD teaching colleagues and satisfy the school's curriculum priorities) and a design experimentation script. In many ways that period was one of my more memorable teaching and learning experiences, as we all seemed to be in the same boat on a shared voyage of discovery. We would speculate as a class and variously seek solutions together in this mutual empty territory. Seven years later, as the decade culminated, the class had progressed from working as individuals unpacking unconnected whims through coding, to collaborating on an exercise addressing the same challenge in a combined script. I have drawn from this in detail for Chapter 9.

From 2001 onwards I have not scripted for myself in quite the same way, as a student base with different capabilities emerged (these I dub the 'scripting generation'), who had access to much better software environments and coding options plus the time to invest. This combined with a shift in my professional responsibilities to confine me rapidly to the role of pioneer relic rather than hands-on scripting maestro. This is not to say that I am now remote from scripting: quite the opposite. Today's scripters are working at a fundamentally deeper level than I was able to reach a decade ago, and I am able to benefit from their input (along with contributions from the various computer scientists and software engineers with whom I have collaborated subsequently), far more effectively than I was able to do travelling alone. It seems that there is an interesting potential paradox here: for a designer to work at the right level using scripting, they probably need assistance in code writing because of the time this can take, but this necessitates a degree of handing over. The benefits gained from working with someone who is writing code all the time exceed those from direct author-applier efficiencies, yet to work effectively with a scripting collaborator the designers themselves must know how to script. To avoid this paradox the trick is being able to retire from the front line gracefully, yet continue to enhance the cultures of scripting through the injection of wisdom born of experience.

This concludes the account of my journey into scripting but my baggage does not quite end there. Originally my motivation to contribute this book came from a sense of frustration around some surprising paradoxes in addition to the one I outline immediately above. The first is the prevalence of scripting universally in exhibited and published experimental work during the past 10 years yet it is still largely absent from architectural education programmes – with certain exceptions. The second is that despite the surge in opportunity with both hardware and software along with more user-friendly and more powerful scripting tools, the originality of the output has hardly kept up. Thirdly, instead of such powerful new media further pluralising the creative community, there seems to be a tendency to swarm towards particular approaches such as generative design using genetic algorithms, or agent systems, or some other 'system', usually from the same stable. Designers are appropriating scripting 'systems', not making them. Fourthly, the preternatural instinct of the senior designer is to be secretive, quite the opposite of the scripting generation, who willingly share their booty on the Internet. Such levels of generosity may mean that while wheels are not being reinvented everywhere as they were in the closeted ateliers of yore, young designers are more inclined to mash up each others' code rather than struggle away from first principles, which could potentially stunt creative growth. Finally, the fifth paradox is that of the potentially reduced level of creative free-flow, with the former reliance on the emergence of ideas, concepts and designs from the sketch at risk of being compromised through the application of the cold hard logic in a script. Such logic is required to distil the route to an answer to the problem, perhaps yet to be fully identified, using scripted code that foregrounds discovery rather than pre-empts 'the answer' that ought to emerge through its use. For me it is this paradox that is the most stimulating, for it pits the non-scripters against the scripters if we accept emergence as a principal opportunity within any design process. In digital design it seems obvious that if one scripts in a way that avoids painting the designer into a corner and, instead, provides opportunities for new bifurcations to be encountered along the way, far richer outcomes will be possible for the same investment of time than that which will be arrived at using software merely at face value.

Some alternative views

Looking through my own lens there are at least three scripting cultures, distinctive and not necessarily immiscible. The first is scripting for productivity, the second is experimentation by scripting a path to 'the answer', and the third is scripting for a voyage of discovery. The five worked examples in Chapters 6 to 10 are variations on this theme, but coming from a single commentator my view that there are several scripting cultures could nevertheless be seen as a single culture of simply 'scripting as I know how'. It is for this reason that I consulted widely among a group of young and not so young pioneers, practitioners and thought leaders. I have titled this chapter 'Cultural defence', as I was interested in investigating whether there might be any risk that scripting cultures are, in fact, tending towards a single trajectory. A scripted outcome forcing design authorship in directions that might threaten its richness such as the dilution of ideas, too much external machinist agency, or just being straitjacketed through code.

What follows is a distillation of a wider set of opinions that go beyond my own. I found the responses surprising in many respects, but very positive, and I imagine the care that every correspondent took to answer my enquiry, and the thoughtfulness of their replies will come across as extremely encouraging to the novice scripter. I believe that there is a strong shared sense that we are on the cusp of something different, and that the way in which we will work together as designers in the future, while still a little indistinct, is rapidly becoming clearer and therefore more tangible. I will first summarise my general impressions framed around my enquiry followed by quotes in answer to specific 'questions of the day'.

Correspondents consulted

Acconci Studio (Vito Acconci), Francis Aish (*Foster + Partners*), Robert Aish, *AKT (Adams Kara Taylor)* (Sawako Kaijima and Panagiotis Michalatos), *Biothing* (Alisa Andrasek), *CEB Reas* (Casey Reas), *CITA* (Mette Ramsgard Thomsen), Pia Ednie-Brown, Cristiano Ceccato, Paul Coates, Evan Douglis, John Frazer, Mark Goulthorpe, Michael Hensel, Tom Kvan, Axel Kilian, Neil Leach, *Kokkugia* (Roland Snooks), Kyle Steinfeld, *labDORA* (Peter Macapia), Achim Menges, *MESNE* (Tim Schork and Paul Nicholas), *MinusArchitecturestudio* (Jason Johnson), *Mode* (Ronnie Parsons and Gil Akos), *MOS* (Michael Meredith), Neri Oxman, Brady Peters, Nick Pisca (*Gehry Technologies*), *Proxy* (Mark Collins and Toru Hasegawa), *SOFTlab* (Michael Szivos), *SPAN* (Matias del Campo), *Supermanoeuvre* (Dave Pigram and Iain Maxwell), Denis Shelden, Martin Tamke, *THEVERYMANY* (Marc Fornes), Hugh Whitehead.

Initiation to scripting

Some of my sample group have been introduced to programming as early as primary school, others at senior school, but it appears that almost all did not begin scripting in earnest until college. The clear majority are autodidacts too, which is encouraging news for any reader concerned that only nerds can enter the fray. I was interested in an in-depth enquiry into the personal circumstances of the scripters ranging from expert amateurs to creators of scripting 'languages' that have subsequently been widely taken up by others. I enquired about the age at which they first scripted and which of the languages they had been drawn to.

I also enquired into whether as accomplished designers/educators/exhibiters they script themselves today or do they in fact brief others to script for them? I was curious to learn whether they have ever actually scripted for themselves or only through collaboration in the past. Were my correspondents responsible for all their own scripting, I wondered, curious about their productivity being so high given all the other demands on their time?

I had expected a veil of unshareable intimacy around this particular stream of my investigation – 'did you paint that yourself…?' Initially I found it odd that this question had raised itself, but this is not information that is volunteered in routine conversation I have found. An insight here, however, might reduce the timid designer's perceived degree of difficulty – those who are attracted to entering the coding terrain but are familiar only with software straight out of the box. This group can be discouraged by what they imagine to be an unbridgeable gulf to a world of impossibly high achievement. I have not found this to be quite such an issue when seeking to encourage just as tentative and equally unpractised novices to adopt more manually applied creative skills. A student who has never sculpted before can pick up a hammer and chisel and apply it to a piece of wood, for instance, taking on the challenge with enthusiasm because they can quickly assess the degrees of difficulty relative to their experience. Subsequently they can readily evaluate where their innate skill lies in comparison with the work of an expert. Where the skill being acquired appears to be deeply intellectual, as is the case with computer coding, a wall seems to place itself rudely separating the possible from the apparently impossible. Perhaps the scripting world's mysteriousness to the uninitiated suits the initiated – 21st-century tradecraft to be protected?

My correspondents reveal two interesting commonalities that dispel any notion that all scripters are natural born coders. The first is that they have almost all coded to a sophisticated level at some point in their careers even if they are not doing so now – they have developed their skills to a high standard of application. Some continue to work at the hands-on level, but a surprising number admit to only having enough time to *pseudocode*:[3] it seems that as careers progress, as my correspondents move forward from being struggling up-and-coming *arrivistes* to accomplished professionals, the corollary is insufficient time to indulge in coding. Many admit to coding being time-consuming even when they are experienced at it. The nature of the design envelope-pusher means that they are just as energetic in scripting beyond any obvious horizons as they would be burning the midnight oil designing by any other route.

In terms of design, the principal difference between scripting oneself and briefing others to script is not clear-cut. When an accomplished designer-scripter is working with others who are doing the lion's share of code writing there are three alternative pathways to follow. The first is via studio teaching where the give-and-take arrangements are quite clear: the maestro shares knowledge and, in some cases, pieces of code with their protégés who, in turn, work on a project with a complexity beyond what they would be likely to address on their own. The studio along with the project benefits from the insight brought to the mix by the project leader's experience. This model is probably the most prevalent, but carries the danger of the 'flocking towards familiarity' syndrome – moths drawn to a bright light, or even straightforward design cloning: a shared vocabulary or a sole signature that may not offer individuals sufficient sense of shared authorship. If this is an assertion it clearly risks coming across as a polemic, given that to some cloning can be read as sharing a creative voice with others. Whether this leads to a risk of a cultural impoverishment through the suppression of individual identities will depend on how critical owning a design actually is in the age of Web 2. I investigate this potential polemic, that is the supremacy of idea over the scripting process, in the conclusion to this book.

The second collaboration path is working closely with an expert programmer whose background is code writing, not design. This can be fraught with unexpected issues when the computer science-educated code writer has an outlook fundamentally attuned to an analysis of a situation or condition, and turns this distilled knowledge into a logical procedure. Unless the designer in the team can, in turn, completely attune their creative synthesis to the proposed logic, the relationship could be one of eternal disconnect with neither party feeling that they have achieved what they set out to do.

The third collaboration path is a variation of the second, where a symbiosis operates between designers and coders. In these teams the designers are experienced (usually former) scripters who can drill down within their design strategy to a logical basis. They can do this sympathetically as the code writer is sufficiently 'design aware' in terms of understanding the implications of creative synthesis not to lock their script into predefined and therefore inevitable outcomes. From experience, this represents a perfect partnership, but they are relatively hard to come by – certainly many of my correspondents describe this kind of relationship as being their ideal. Put at its simplest, 'talented designer seeks clear-headed coder writer' is not in itself an automatic success if an intellectual partnership cannot be assured.

I was interested to learn the extent to which scripting is seen by others as primarily a productivity tool compared with its potential to assist design exploration. I was motivated by my early experience in forcing a split between the two (productivity versus experimentation) in what one of my contributors described as a 'false dichotomy'. In my circumstances, and this seemed a global situation during the 1990s at least, CAD was taught as a productivity tool. The teachers of CAD were drawn from that pool of inspired individuals who had previously taught 'drafting', 'technical drawing', 'detailing', 'representation', *et al.* Relatively few teaching staff that I came across at that time tried to uncover any digital design potential and, in the main, students did not seek to experiment with software in the studio beyond visualising the completed project with obligatory fly-throughs. With the exception of Form Z™ I could see little in architectural CAD software to tempt students to be more playful. In that context to script with CAD software was to find ways to automate the mundane, as I described at the beginning of this chapter – this applied as much to my architectural practice as it did initially to my design research, and for this reason I initiated teaching scripting with both productivity and exploration as two distinct approaches.

Consulting a combination of preeminent and up-and-coming designers may not seem the most scientific means to elicit a categorical distinction between the two, but it served to establish a consensus all the same. Hardly anyone proposed that the motivation to script was founded exclusively on one or the other of the two poles – productivity and design exploration – with almost everyone describing a mix of the two, but with proportions that varied. The question obviously causes a pause for thought for many: even if design exploration via scripting is not a time saver in itself – in other words, if the same time is invested in the design as would have been without any scripting – through scripting the eventual outcome will be that much more sophisticated. Indubitably, in such terms, scripting is a productivity tool even if the scripter is more inclined to direct their coding towards a speculative investigation than simply to ensure complexity is untangled to guarantee a more manageable and affordable project. The differences between scripting for productivity (in the pragmatic sense) and more fluid design exploration are explored in depth in Chapters 8 and 9.

Software and scripting language choices

There is a very long list of scripting tools available. The list in the table here is distilled from my 34 correspondents.

Adobe ActionScript
C, C#, C++
Generative Components script
Html
Iron Python
Java, JavaScript
LUA

> Mathematica
> MATLAB
> MaxScript
> Maya (Maya Embedded Language (MEL) and Python)
> Objective-C
> Perl
> PHP
> Processing (Java)
> Python
> RhinoScript (VB, Grasshopper (VB), Python)
> RhI
> VB, VBA

Not surprisingly Maya, Adobe and Rhino appeared in the lists of at least half the group. Among my correspondents there is a cluster of initiates commencing around the year 2002, the time when several packages combined thrilling levels of 3D modelling with associated scripting languages, principally Maya™ (using MEL for scripting), and Rhino 3D™ using Rhino VB. A little more surprising is the fact that over half use languages such as C#, Python and VB, demonstrating real commitment to the task. *Processing* (shareware), written by Casey Reas (one of my correspondents) and Ben Fry, is used by half my sample. The power and simplicity of Processing point to the phenomenon of an emerging generation of scripters who wish to focus their intelligence on sorting out the logic of their design approach rather than on hitting obstacles with obscure coding syntax. Processing is a language designed by a designer to help other designers leapfrog over the lack of ease of use that characterises many programming languages.

To script or to brief others to script

I was surprised by the admission of several correspondents that they are no longer in a position to take up any new programming environments as their careers have moved on to leadership roles with associated time constraints. Others will not relinquish their direct pivotal role in design scripting at the highest level on the basis that as designers they need to be pulling, not pushing.

Many of those consulted have had access to expertise that can vary from straightforward assistance to (as in my case) input to coding at a level I would never have reached by myself, certainly within the timeframes of the projects concerned.

Challenge or breeze

With only a single exception everyone consulted sees programming as a hard-won skill, not acquired with ease. A few ventured that their teaching experience reveals that some students are more naturally able to assimilate the rather unusual aspects of code writing (compared with all other design activities) than others. Some suggest that on the one hand scripting is a vital opportunity but on the other, the required logical approach is challenging for designers more familiar with freer ways of thinking. There is evidence of people who, while they 'get' scripting, and despite scripting very ably, still struggle with it. With unusual candour some of my correspondents admitted to struggling themselves, all the more astonishing when their top-drawer output is compared with a self-assessed lack of facility – another instance of hope for the reader who might suspect that they too are a potential struggler. Most replied that it gets easier as they progress and, as with any high-level skill, constant practice is a necessity. The comment I enjoyed the most in this regard was that scripting is easy until you get to the first bug.

Design productivity and design exploration

I was also curious to learn the motivation of the designers I approached – what attracted them to scripting? The responses were satisfyingly varied:

- reaching beyond analogue processes;
- capturing material logic and computing performance;
- being playful;
- exploiting generative processes;
- seeking deeper access to the imagination;
- engaging with complexity;
- inducing rapid iteration and variation;
- grappling with the performative;
- toying with the unexpected and delving into the unknown;
- being forced to be explicit;
- discovering novelty;

- localising intelligence;
- investigating self-organisation principles;
- studying phenomena;

… and of course going for good old task automation.

Hardly two responses were the same, which is a circumstance I explore in a little more depth in the book's conclusion.

I received a similarly wide and perceptive range of responses to my enquiry about potential dangers in scripting such as contributing to 'the death of the pencil sketch', 'enfranchising the amateur', or design becoming 'automated'. In some it provoked a response bordering on irritation – as if this were an absurd proposition – while others went to the other extreme, positively welcoming an end to the supremacy of design skills being framed entirely around mind–hand–eye coordination. Several made comparisons with the arrival of cheap high-definition still and movie cameras, which they noted had not necessarily reduced the quality of top photographers and filmmakers: talent always shines through. This is an optimistic view perhaps, as one considers the implications of the architectural equivalent: amateur house designers given tools to create their own home; can we really compare an album of poor photos with a landscape blighted by properties built from poorly understood design principles? Is this even a scripting consideration?

There is at least a niggle that a designer who has appropriated the use of someone else's script to create 'interesting effects' might end up with the credit for something for which they are not the complete author. Again, this is the dilemma of tool or process versus outcome. When scripting there is a further dilemma that comes from the typical need to begin encoding a design at the outset compared with new ideas emerging through intuition from the undirected sketch, as it is hand drawn or modelled along the way. But in scripting a design, a logic has to be investigated up front, which for many can be seen as an opportunity, not a hindrance. Any argument that scripting leads to standardisation can be countered by the fact that it affords highly wayward and idiosyncratic designers the opportunity to innovate in ways otherwise not possible, which segues into my next line of enquiry: new design avenues.

Essential scripting and its value

When I asked my correspondents what they could design through scripting that they could not reasonably produce otherwise, and with what added value, I received a highly spirited response with as many unique suggestions as respondents. Firstly, the ability to work with large data sets, proceeding in many directions simultaneously, and working beyond our perceptual capacity were prominent responses. While scripting might veer towards the complexification of otherwise quite simple things as well as deal with still more, several pointed out that scripting can do the exact opposite, and be used to look for simplification. Others enjoy the opportunity to capture specific know-how, encoding it with tacit knowledge rendering it more declared and shared. A proportion of my correspondents also pointed to the link between scripting and fabrication, which is something that I deal with in detail in chapter 8.

Achim Menges and Jan Knippers, ICD, ITKE research pavilion, Stuttgart, 2010.

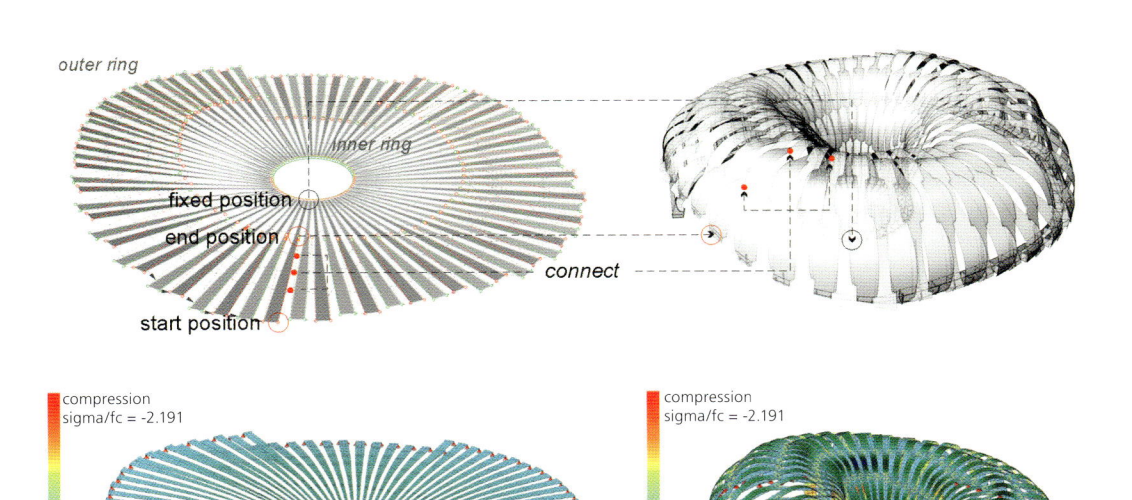

How stuck would scripters be without the opportunity to script elicited replies ranging from not being able to do any of the things that particular individuals or practices currently undertake to do, to only being inconvenienced, forced to spend more time than would otherwise be necessary, and possibly being forced to work with a reduced set of inputs.

Scripting education

In this chapter I have covered the origins of my own interest in scripting, and I have opened up the subject a little by anonymously reporting the opinions of a group of experts who have responded to my request for additional insights.

My motivation for writing this book includes the proposition that one generation on, scripting seems to be here to stay. So what does this mean for the education of architects? I conclude this chapter by incorporating the views of my correspondents listed earlier to enrich what ought to be a very vigorous debate in every school of architecture and all practices still relying on traditional ways of working in the face of a wider uptake of scripting.

The need for prior knowledge

I am impressed by the way that architects' professional organisations in many countries have worked hard to ensure that a school that is highly experimental and culturally focused is professionally accredited on the same basis as a school with a strong technical focus, for example. Correspondingly, entry requirements seem to vary considerably. I have worked in schools where maths proficiency at senior school level was a core requirement and others where no such condition of entry is made. Given that almost all those I have consulted see scripting skills as being hard won, should the schools that include scripting at an elective if not fundamental level seek some computational skilling as a prerequisite to coding? If this comes across as an unusually draconian proposition, readers who have tried to involve in their scripting studio a student with no maths beyond early senior school basics in a class otherwise full of those with a good level of maths, will appreciate the dilemma that prompts this question. For anyone nervous that compulsory scripting skills for pre-university initiates is a secret agenda within scripting cultures, the selected responses that follow will help allay any such fears, while still provoking some discussion all the same.

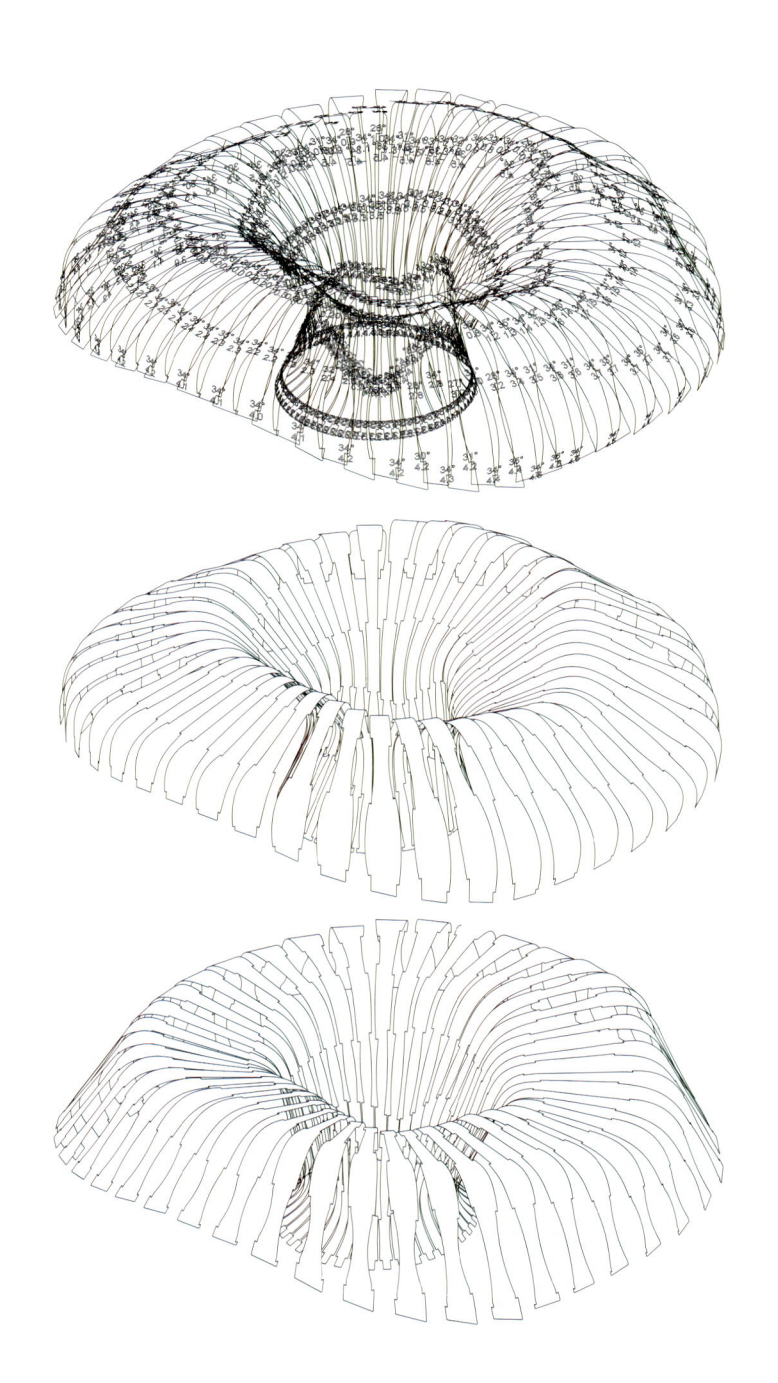

Achim Menges and Jan Knippers, ICD, ITKE research pavilion, Stuttgart, 2010.

The question does open up a broader educational issue, for instance the assertion that scripting might contribute usefully to what is taught in many disciplines well before college.

> *Scripting should be taught in high-schools (will elementary schools follow) as general culture: scripting for architects & designers, scripting for mathematicians & biologists, scripting for dancers & musicians, scripting for poets & moviemakers & dramatists.* (Vito Acconci)

There are also assertions that procedural literacy has an increasingly vital role to play:

> *Yes, absolutely, I think the education system should start teaching procedural literacy from the beginning. Students should then build on these skills and focus them within the context of architecture.* (Casey Reas)

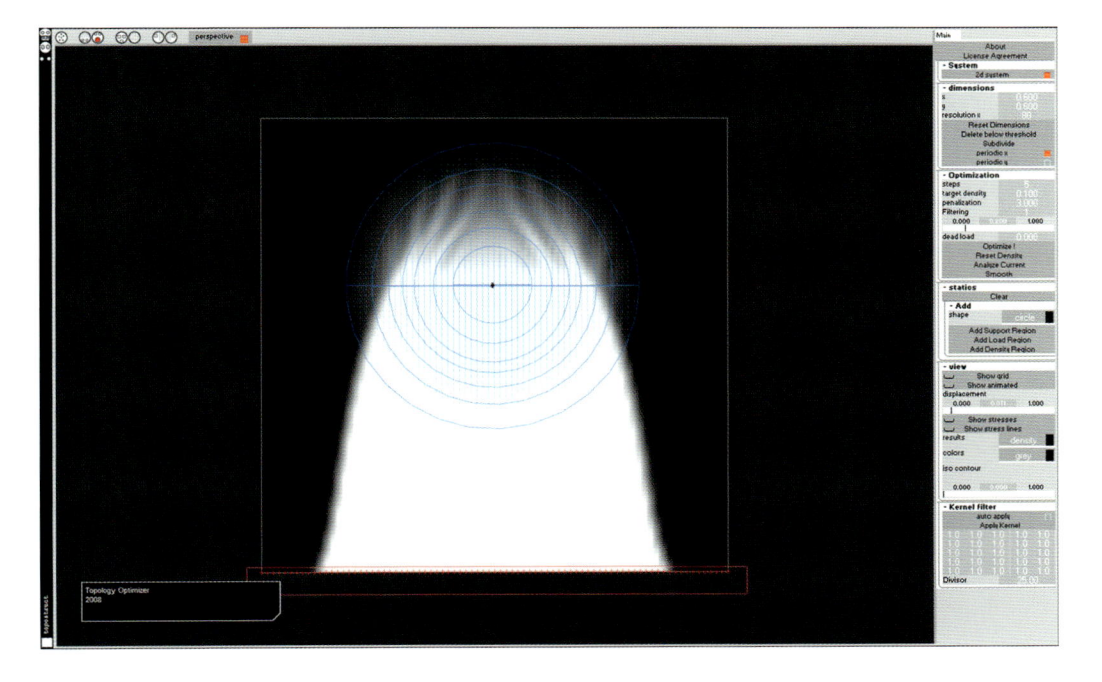

Panagiotis Michalatos & Sawako Kaijima, AKT Architects, Topology optimiser, London, 2010.

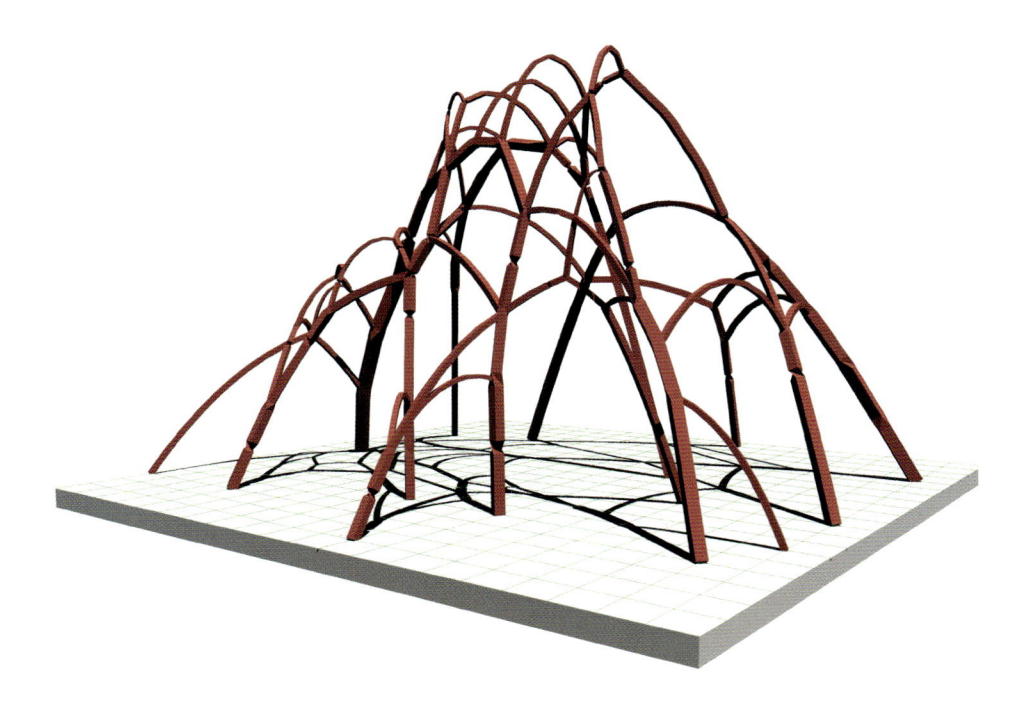

Axel Kilian, Vaults, particle spring library Simon Greenwold, MIT, 2004.

This level of affirmation is not universal with a call for sufficient scope to accommodate the unexpected perspectives that innocence often brings to the mix:

> *It is useful but not necessary at the moment. People with no skill or interest in digital media may bring a different and often needed perspective or experience.* (Panagiotis Michalatos & Sawako Kaijima, AKT Architects)

Crucially, many argue the case for prior training in thinking procedurally rather than for arriving with prior coding ability:

> *What is far more important than the mechanics of scripting is for students to be able to think algorithmically. One question might be: Should this be taught at high school or at University? We then might consider the subsequent issues as to whether algorithmic thought should be taught abstractly or as applied to a specific subject (of interest to the student)? Therefore linking the algorithmic thinking to the subject of architecture might make it more attractive to some students who might not respond to the abstract form.* (Robert Aish)

There are also those who are happy to work with all comers; note the bravura registered with the following two comments:

> *Not necessarily. They can 'mutate' very fast. It is often better to learn scripting and abstraction layers directly on design problems.* (Alisa Andrasek)

> *No, it's OK for them to learn it there – it's part of a culture. And those that have familiarity through another education have to retrain themselves anyhow.* (Peter Macapia, labDORA)

There is potential for a debate here: the hacker and masher getting by versus the highly skilled writer of elegant code working with the benefit of thorough learning. As useful as the latter context might be for skilled grounding, it is not deemed essential by the community, nor is it likely to become the norm.

Scripting as part of an architectural education

Although there was ambivalence about prior learning, almost all my correspondents are quite emphatic about the need to integrate scripting into the curriculum, although 'learning by doing' through direct application in

Biothing, Fissure – Agent Wall, London, 2010.

the studio is seen as an appropriate environment by many. As shown in the selected extracts, some proponents of the teaching of scripting in college are quite emphatic about this.

> *Architects are ultimately choreographers of systems, and the benefits of teaching programming in an architectural context are manifold. If architecture wants to survive as a discipline, it needs to engage the culture of innovation and computing.* (Mark Collins & Toru Hasegawa, Proxy)

Scripting can be seen as offering an alternative view of creativity:

> *An algorithmic understanding of creativity – that the act is not a flash in the dark, a blessing from heaven but the result of hard rigorous thought which*

Biothing, Seroussi – Mesonic Fabrics, London, 2009.

Evan Douglis, Helioscope, New York, 2008.

can in many parts be represented algorithmically – that is the important step. Right now, scripting is a very useful paradigm but it is not exclusively so.
(Tom Kvan)

And a call for scripting education to be subsumed in a wider intellectual framework:

To the extent that it is framed within the intellectual development of language, writing, mathematics, etc. and understood for what it is, not mythologized.
(Mark Goulthorpe)

These are still strange times for architectural pedagogues settling down from the previous tensions between analogue as opposed to digital design

Evan Douglis, Helioscope
New York, 2008.

practice, who now face another unscheduled cultural shift. While we are moving well into an era of digital design acceptance, we nevertheless operate within a legacy that includes many educators who have no idea of how to do anything beyond the basics with their computers. If we obsess about the need to teach coding skills we will repeat the errors of the 1990s when CAD equalled drafting. Those who want to script need to be taught by designer scripters and not by 'computer people'. More crucial still is the need to focus beyond 'scripting' to the meta topic: an appropriate approach to learning about the emerging systems in which scripts operate; culturally, and as an emerging theory.

Scripting critique

Given the wealth of opportunities that scripting offers to shift design practice in new directions, can we anticipate significant shifts in architectural culture and its critique, or will scripting simply be subsumed once the novelty has gone?

Since the cultures of scripting are evolving they are not yet fully formed core design constructs, hence my investigation into cultures rather than probing into 'scripting' as if it were some kind of *Zeitgeist* movement. Two

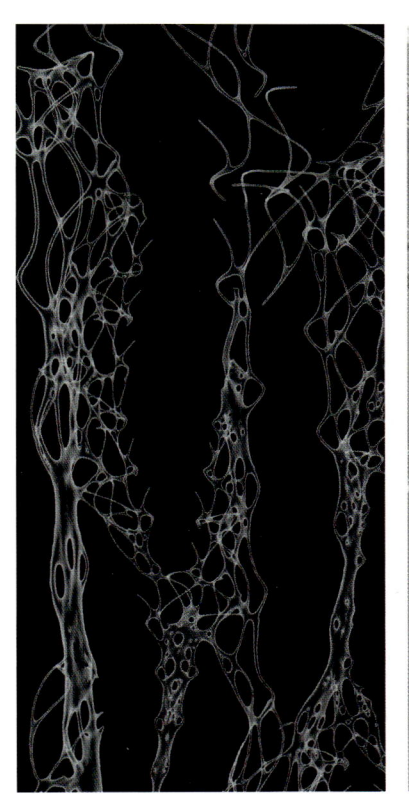

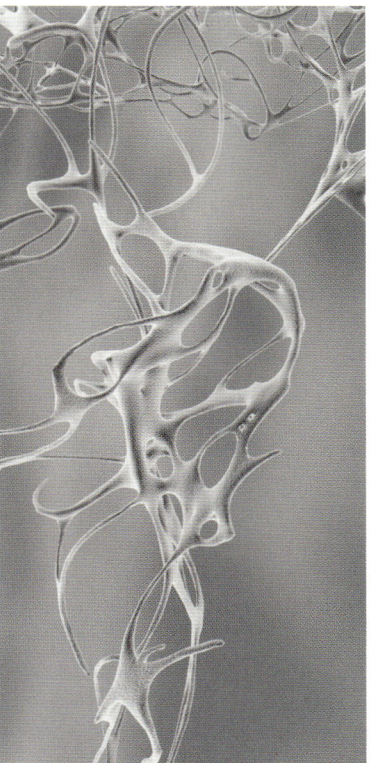

Kokkugia, Swarm Matter, New York, 2010.

Kokkugia, Micro, New York, 2010.

generations on, the pioneers from the 1970s and '80s might decry current output as not having met expectations that their early work had pointed to, but would this be a fair criticism? Have we truly made the best use of our opportunities, and what has been the value attained anyway? I have my own opinion on this, which I develop in the conclusion, but here are some thoughts from others.

Inventiveness

My perspective is that too many scripters are cloning from one another under the banner of contemporary legitimacy. Many instinctively swarm to consolidate a dominant paradigm such as the swarm itself, agent-based modelling, this particular algorithm or that, potentially fogging up the zone. Who is fundamentally inventing new strategies and approaches? Whose radars are the most highly attuned to spot emerging talent and aid in its proselytising? Who discovers then generously shares with others? And how many are plundering from here and there without acknowledging their sources, or have we arrived at a new epoch where worrying about authorship in this sense is completely old fashioned?

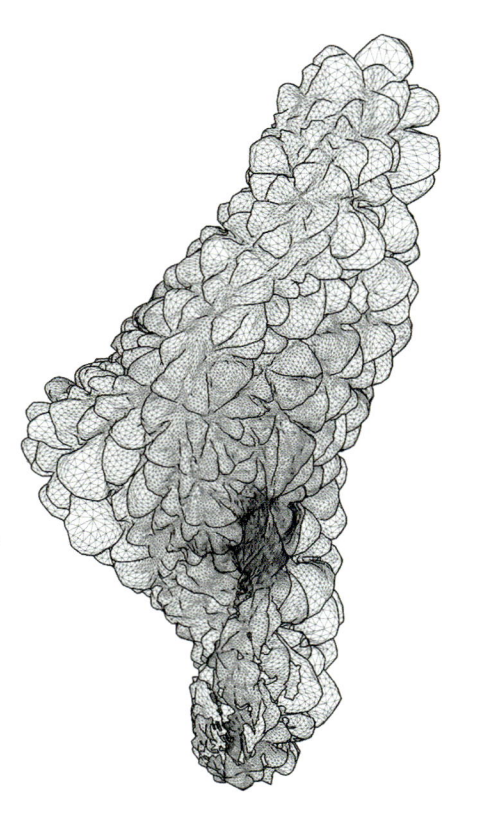

Had I been looking for so negative a perspective I should obviously have consulted a different group of experts and educators, as most of the responses to this enquiry were largely positive, signalling a bright new future, although some replies did carry a caveat that we could do better but need more time. I did not confine my enquiry to a group with similar interests who would talk up scripting as I also sought pioneers who would, no doubt, still consider themselves among the vanguard of design computation protagonists, progressing the cause but wondering all the same whether a sea of copyists would prove a more prominent legacy than the inventors they themselves had been. I had a variety of reactions from this group, too.

In order to capture a snapshot of where we are in 2010, I have extracted some of the more provocative and sceptical opinions. The first quote points

LabDORA, Gross topology tower, EFTEPillow, New York, 2010.

to the means of sustaining a new cross-discipline dialogue:

> *Where we see interesting work occurring is in the development of interfaces between different software applications that enable designers to further test architectural ideas that bridge across related disciplines such as engineering and construction.* (MESNE)

While the next three suggest an awareness of a polarity between inventiveness and uncritical uptake:

> *There's more bad scripting going on than ever before. But, at the same time, there's extraordinary innovation happening. The bar is rising.* (Casey Reas)

> *In terms of production very [inventive] – in terms of creating new models for design less so – meaning a lot is done with the same underlying models over and over again.* (Axel Kilian)

> *Still very few are truly inventive. We are at the very beginning of this process and very few designers are already virtuosic [sic] and highly creative. Many are still vertiginously propagating other people's inventions. This condition is changing with maturing of scripting cultures.* (Alisa Andrasek)

John Frazer's response, a pioneer whom I discuss in a little more detail in the next chapter, is absolutely clear about what he perceives as neither a lack of forward movement in much of contemporary engagement with design computation nor any tangible connection with the priorities of the pioneer years which he contends remain extant today:

> *If we talk in terms of Inventors, Masters and Diluters (as Ezra Pound classifies inventive activity), then we saw most of the Inventors in the early 60s, the Masters in the early 70s and then we got the Diluters in the mid 90s – who I have to say include a significant proportion of today's scripters.*

> *Just look back to the Cybernetics Serendipity exhibition at the ICA in 1968 which celebrated an incredible array of inventive energy: Norbert Wiener, Stafford Beer, Karlheinz Stockhausen, John Cage, Edward Ihnatowicz, Gustav Metzger, Gordon Pask – poetry, music, art, sculpture, dance, film, even architecture. That exhibition set the agenda for the next 50 years.*

> *It is perhaps difficult for today's scripters to realise how difficult it was to do*

Foster + Partners,
Smithsonian Courtyard Roof,
Washington DC, 2007.

anything at all with a computer in the late 60s. When I struggled to generate the complex geometrical drawings for my final year project at the AA in 1967–69, I had to write all the programs myself and that included the basic graphics instructions to draw just one line, never mind a wireline perspective, and they had to be output to a flatbed plotter with no graphics preview! And when I finally had access to a graphics display device at Cambridge University in 1970 I had to write the generative instructions in Atlas Titan machine code, and if you don't know what that is then you don't know how lucky you are!

But my main point is that we went to all this effort in order to solve real social, environmental and technical problems where we believed a computer could significantly assist. But now that there is massive computer power and software cheaply available, most scripting has become nothing more than an onanistic self indulgence in a cozy graphics environment. Endless repetition and variation on elaborate geometrical schema with no apparent social, environmental and technical purpose whatsoever. (John Frazer)

Frazer's pioneering work of the 1960s and '70s was synchronous with Archigram (publication of *Archigram* I: 1961). I attended the celebration of Archigram hosted at the Bartlett in 2003. There I heard Jan Kaplicky (1937–2009) make the same observation. Kaplicky, with the absolute credibility supported by his subsequent success through his practice Future Systems, noted that if in the 21st century work that drew on Archigram's four-decades-old speculation was being built for the first time, who was doing the future thinking now? This was more than a 'well, in my day …', aggrandising of a faded golden age of innovation; rather, it is a very powerful questioning around the inventive scope of what is being done today, and the scale of its ambition. Contemporary commentators echo this concern:

Today's scripters are inventive; however, scripting is a relatively new technique for the exploration of architectural designs and designers are still figuring out new potentials for using scripting as a design tool. (Brady Peters)

'Invent' is a loaded word. Most young computational designers are ignorant of the history of algorithmic design and think they invent everything. If you

Martin Tamke and Jacob Riiber, CITA, Lamella Flock, Copenhagen, 2010.

are coding now, and you think you invented something amazing, I guarantee you someone at MIT or SIGGRAPH in the 60s, 70s & 80s has already done it. (Nick Pisca, Gehry Technologies)

This is an impossible question. I think most scripters are trying to produce effects of complexity. These effects become less and less complex and interesting as they become more and more known. Corporate offices have scripters pumping out patterns for them. (Michael Meredith, MOS)

The issue of what it means to be inventive needs to be explored, and how it might be further drawn out, too:

There is a huge range. Some rely too much on the work of others, and some develop their own scripts. I think that it is important to have people teaching scripting who can teach students to write their own scripts for themselves. (Neil Leach)

Being 'inventive' really relates to the designer's ability to consider their tools in a way that adds value to the design product or process, somewhere across this range. Today, more than ever, more emphasis should be given to the intellectual foundations of this 'know-how'. Being a scripting digerati is simply not enough. (Neri Oxman)

MESNE, Resonant Frequency, Melbourne, 2008.

Today scripting is learnt through the practice of sharing code through web based platforms and open source. As such it holds the danger of being repetitive. When looking at student practice this is very evident. However, I think what perhaps holds students back is a real questioning of the concepts and potentials of scripting rather than it being just a matter of copying. (Mette Ramsgard Thomsen)

They can only become inventive to the extent that their scripting practice confronts other practices and processes. (Pia Ednie-Brown)

My conclusion is that there is a reluctant acceptance that much of the fizzy work we see grabbing attention today is not seeking to innovate enough. There is a duty, surely, for all in a position to influence design education through scripting to be part of a deeper enquiry and the quest for discovery of new goals and ways to reach them.

Variety relative to opportunity

With this question I am really trying to find a distinction between leaders and followers. A 'sufficient variety of outcomes' signals taxonomies of scripting; insufficient variety points to a scripting style. The majority view points to scripting within mainstream practice as being in its infancy, but there is optimism about a far more significant role for design computation as it becomes less of an exception within practice. Many referred to a need for greater computer power to realise the outcomes envisaged conceptually yet not able to be computed with existing technology. Real-time optimisation remains elusive for complex and conflicting relationships between data sets, for example.

Scripting is powerful, but not powerful enough. And our computers are entirely too slow to demonstrate the diversity and potential that scripting can bring. But that's not all, we're blocked conceptually as well as technically. (Casey Reas)

The main challenge of the scripting generation is the move from the creation of inventive articulated patterns, and the small-scale installations to the full scale architectural projects where scripting can unleash an entire universe of opportunities for architectural space. (Matias del Campo, SPAN)

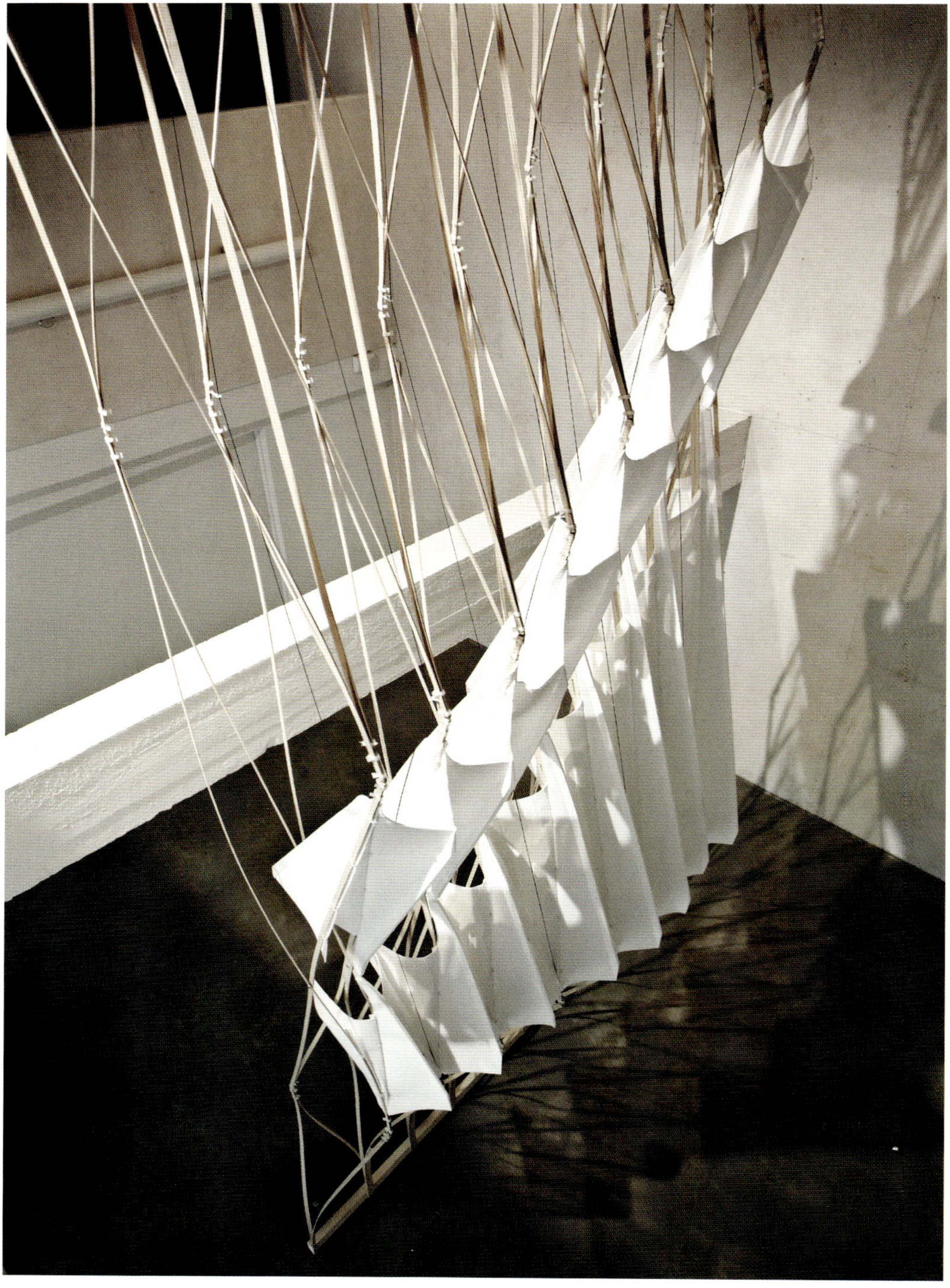

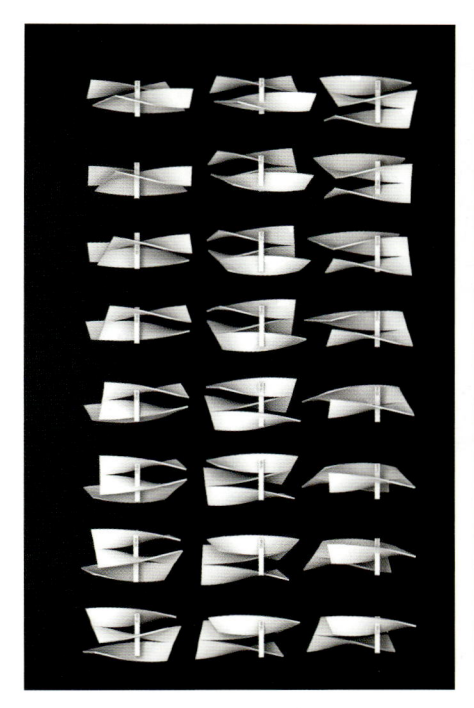

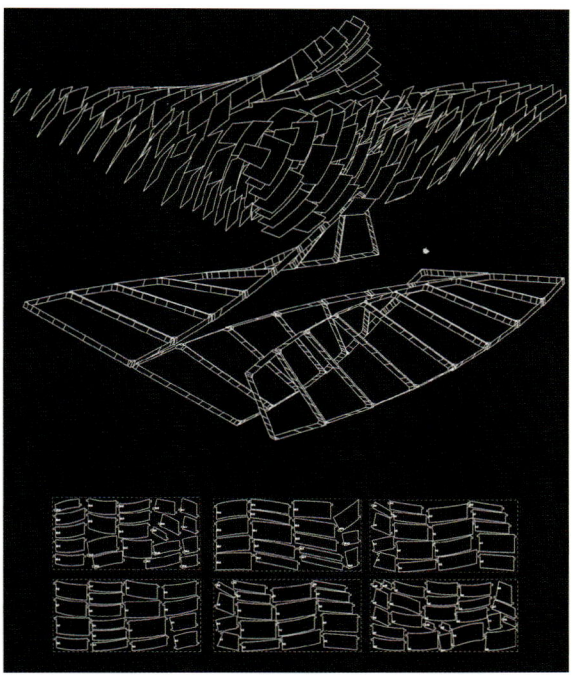

MinusArchitecturestudio, Catch&Release, USA, 2007.

There are concerns for the emergence of a style over substance:

> I think the outcome is extremely varied, but unfortunately it seems like scripting has started to become a style, as a result of the use of the same ubiquitous techniques. (Michael Szivos, SOFTlab)

> No, not enough probably, as the underlying mathematical and computational models are too similar – the products differ of course but more based on in which context they are deployed and not so much conceptually. (Axel Kilian)

> Certainly not. Too many projects share the same 'wiring', and there is a tendency to perpetuate the skills-based pedagogy of the previous generation. (Mark Collins & Toru Hasegawa, Proxy)

> Surprisingly a lot of the scripting work looks similar to me, so this cannot be an outcome of the tool itself but a desire for specific types of fantastic spectacular and wonderfully naive building forms. (Michael Meredith, MOS)

Mette Ramsgard Thomsen, CITA, Thaw, Copenhagen, 2010.

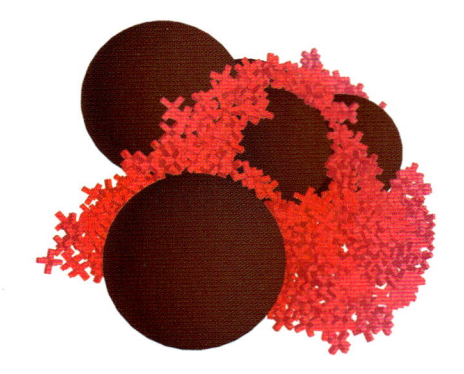

Variety cannot arise by the use of scripting alone. To the contrary scripting can go viral. Meaning that once something is shown to be done easily it gets endlessly repeated. (Panagiotis Michalatos & Sawako Kaijima, AKT Architects)

MOS, Sand, New York, 2009.

New modes of operation are identified as the emerging opportunities rather than scripting itself:

The effective employment of a broad set of computational methods is still ahead for architecture. (Martin Tamke)

Our interest is in how an algorithm, loaded with design intent, emerges from the design problem rather than simply the architecture emerging from a known algorithm. (Roland Snooks, Kokkugia)

The most radical way in which scripting has affected the field of design is not the outcome of a particular script or set of scripts, but rather the collateral effects of participating in such a design model. (Mode)

The extracts illustrate a 'still early days' consensus; it is interesting that no collective bombast emerges from the responses to this question, and on the contrary quite a clear challenge for design scripters to engage conceptually with greater ambition.

A role for mathematics

Some aspects of design such as variety and intricacy become far more interesting when mathematics is engaged at a fairly high level; a mathematical background provides the computational designer with a conceptual and philosophical edge. It would be a mistake to consider mathematics only as a problem-solving ingredient, but how essential is mathematics in offering creative assistance to scripting? The dictionary definition for mathematics, however, suggests that we might use the word too loosely for situations where we are probably referring to 'computation'.

> *Originally, the collective name for geometry, arithmetic, and certain physical sciences (as astronomy and optics) involving geometrical reasoning. In modern use applied, (a) in a strict sense, to the abstract science which investigates deductively the conclusions implicit in the elementary conceptions of spatial and numerical relations, and which includes as its main divisions geometry, arithmetic, and algebra; and (b) in a wider sense, so as to include those branches of physical or other research which consist in the application of this abstract science to concrete data ...*[4]

There is a dichotomy between the 'modern' use of the term and how it was used originally. Programming for a computer is a text-based language (an artificial language), precise and pedantic, and for use in architecture it involves a combination of logical expression and numerical input. Strictly speaking, mathematics uses a symbolic language to form abstractions of spatial and numerical relations. Probably designers are thinking of only 'the collective name for geometry, arithmetic, and certain physical sciences' when

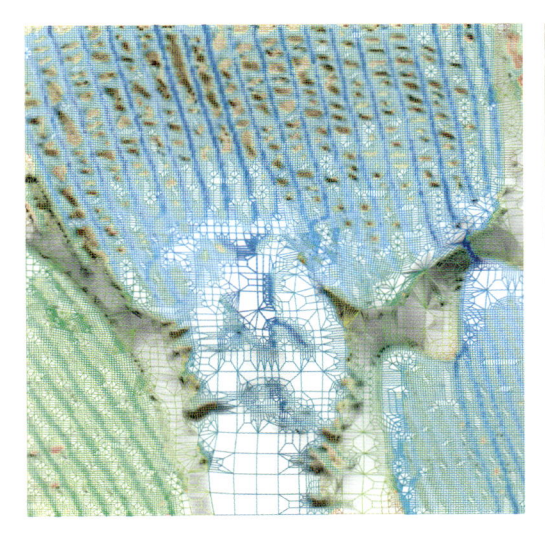

Neri Oxman, MIT, Subterrain, 2008.

Neri Oxman, MIT, Carpal Skin, 2009.

using the term in relation to using the computer. In posing this question I was not sure at what level of significance mathematics would be assumed. Here are the opinions of others, ranging from 'essential' to 'helpful'. No one claimed that it was optional, but nor am I necessarily claiming this as an exhaustive enquiry:

> *Essential. Mathematics is a necessary vocabulary – when we code we are implementing a possible universe, which can only resemble our own to the degree that we are able to describe it.* (Mark Collins & Toru Hasegawa, Proxy)

> *In our own practice we consider mathematics and geometry as a crucial point of departure for the development of a project, whether it be topology or specific forms of tessellations, it is always a core issue of the design.* (Matias del Campo, SPAN)

Other commentators suggest that it is useful:

> As an intellectual rigour, very helpful, but I suspect rhetoric would be useful too if we still taught it. There is little different from the expectations of classical education – clear thinking, articulation of ideas so that others can understand them. (Tom Kvan)

> In pure terms Mathematics is a cerebral activity which does not have any inputs or outputs that are sensory. Potentially these connections can be provided by scripting environments but only by re-thinking the concept of interface to design tools. The ability to interactively rewire plug-and-play dependencies is just one of many possible starting points. (Hugh Whitehead)

> Architecture has the potential to be informed by maths, but first the university tutors have to understand the relationship between maths and design in order to help the students make the connection. (Robert Aish)

> If you consider logic a subset of mathematics, then math is essential. An average coder would only need to know algebra for basic scripting and

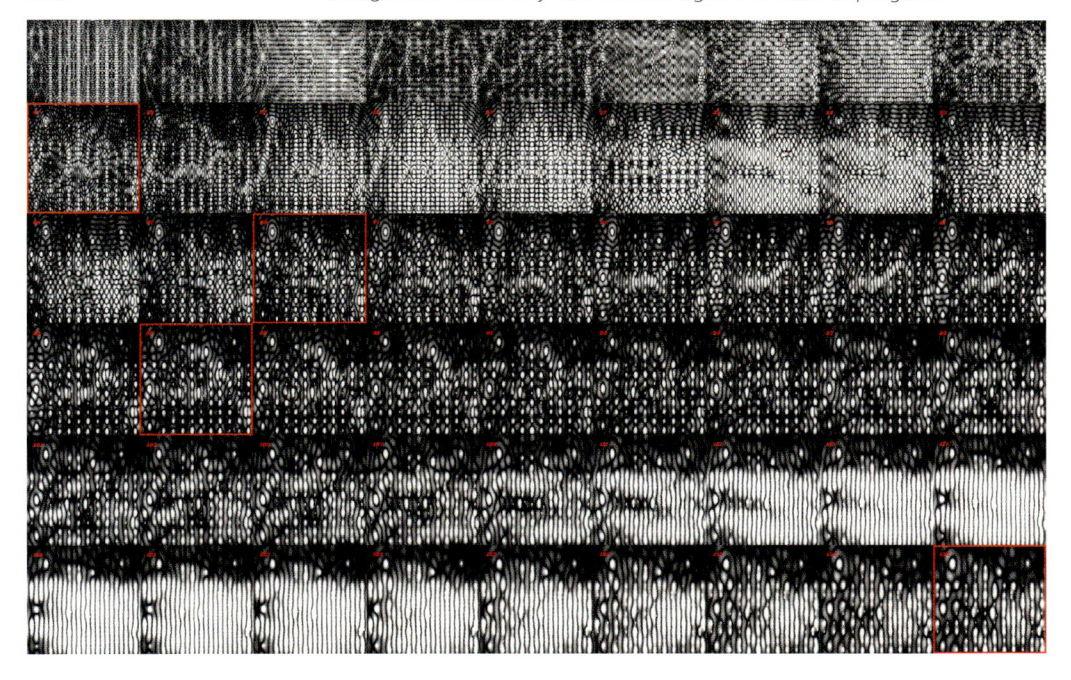

Proxy, Stabile, New York, 2009.

trigonometry for 3D. (Nick Pisca, Gehry Technologies)

Others are not convinced at all:

I try to keep it as simple as possible; maths is a Victorian hangover. (Paul Coates)

Computer programming can be largely logically based requiring minor numerical input, or it can be mathematically driven in the sense of a pure (conceptual) and applied (practical) mathematical input. The scripter has a choice between working with a systems approach and avoiding high-level computation, especially when they are relying on code snippets precompiled by others, or they can hook-in to mathematics' conceptual or abstract take on space, and roll up their sleeves. It seems we are at a time when we need to be quite clear about the distinction between computation and mathematics. The more intensive the computation enacted by the computer, the more likely that the output will be innovative. I suspect that if we seek more certainty in originality of output, the next generation of design scripters will benefit from engaging more profoundly with mathematics in its modern sense, given above.

Cristiano Ceccato, Form Evolution, Rome, 2010.

Likely future changes

I wondered whether the extraordinary developments in computers and software during the past decade had helped my correspondents predict any shifts in the next 5 to 10 years. In recent years we have seen fundamental shifts in accessibility into scripting for the architectural design arena such as the emergence of Digital Project™, Generative Components™, Processing, and Grasshopper with Rhino 3D™, to name a few of the paradigm shifters. Personally, I have always been surprised by the friendliness of Max/MSP™ in the sound design and music arena, and I wondered when it would cross over into visual design as it comes across as a much more natural way for designers to assemble a logical argument through programming. I have also been surprised at the effectiveness, fluency and integration of software dealing with the physics of materials into the games and movie industries: why have the architectural software companies been so complacent in this regard? Of course, that is a question that hardly needs answering, and in part it has been the lack of opportunity for creative design within conventional software that has forced scripting to start off by being a counter-culture. Successful counter-cultures eventually become part of orthodoxy, and judging from the relative lack of sparks by my correspondents around this question, I imagine that this could be a sign that scripting has already reached an appropriate level of usefulness and applicability.

One set of responses sums up my own view quite succinctly:

> *I anticipate new powerful simulation environments to grow emergent complex dynamic systems as a way of developing 3D morphologies – rather hoping to design one myself.* (Paul Coates)

> *Languages will become more compact, expressive, and comprehensible. After a period in which the mental effort of focussing on the script may have distracted designers from focussing on the design problem, scripting will become more natural, more integrated into design process, less of a distraction.* (Robert Aish)

> *I would like to think that in the next 10 years we will have succeeded, and we will have a new conceptual environment for creative thinking and without the*

SOFTlab, Alice, New York, 2009.

SOFTlab, Shizuku, New York, 2009.

need for scripting. If all we have achieved is to replace drawing with typing then we have achieved nothing! (John Frazer)

While some purists will stick to rigorous old school methods of working with code, many will want to bypass code and work through more accessible pictographic forms of automation. (Neil Leach)

A future direction is to make this library of design tools less platform dependent. The concepts contained within these scripts are general design principles and could essentially be applied in many different platforms. (Brady Peters)

I guess most of us want scripting software to be more intuitive, easier to write and more visually integrated with other software, easier to find the bugs, and with a trend to a common language not tied to any particular packages. Most look forward to harnessing the greater power of the next generation of computers, with the ability to model conflicting performative aspects of architecture in real time to assist our design decision-making, and not necessarily through typing in code. Some express the hope that we evolve new languages, move from scripting to programming and, the most plaintive cry of all: that we start to write our own discipline-specific algorithms instead of 'stealing' them from other fields. I believe that particular desire, if it were fulfilled, would lead to a double-edged sword, one where originality through targeted architectural solution seeking is compromised by architectural reinvention of wheels already in use elsewhere.

Miracle scripting environments

It would seem that most of my correspondents are happy enough with what we have already. I received very few suggestions for higher-order virtual reality suites for an immersive coding experience, no new tangible interfaces were called for, no yet-to-be-designed collaborative tools for shared 'what if…?' interaction desired. Are we broadly happy with what we have already, patiently awaiting improvements in speed and accessibility? Some indicative responses follow.

> *I would be waiting for an interface that allows the seamless integration of multiple other environments.* (Achim Menges)

> *An environment is missing that integrates representation and simulation based approaches. It could, for example, connect modelling with physics-based behaviour, scripted elements and the generated structure could still communicate as a whole to external environments.* (Martin Tamke)

StudioMode, Parsing Populations, New York, 2010.

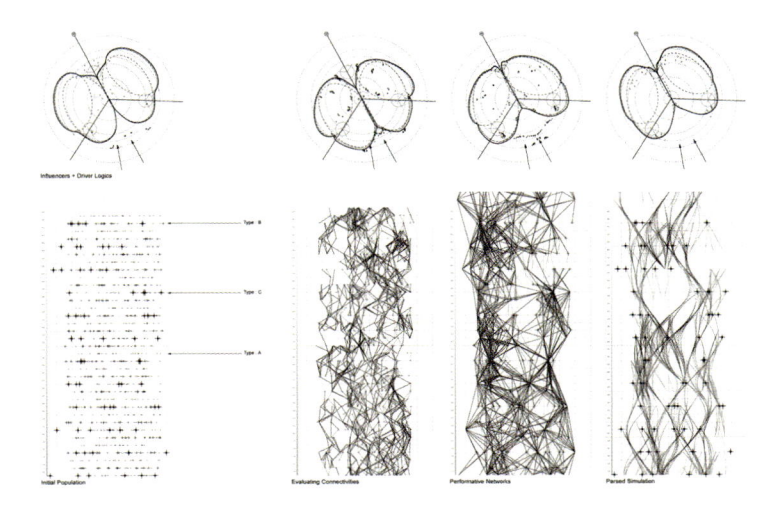

A universal scripting language that allows me to communicate with the entire array of software in our studio, instead of having to learn a new language every now and then. (Matias del Campo, SPAN)

Definitively not one single environment doing everything – please keep the platform multiple but as light as possible – speed is key when a large population or massive variations are involved. (Marc Fornes, THEVERYMANY)

Ben Bratton once commented that we are still in 'the silent movies' stage of digital techniques. Of course things will improve. We have hardly started yet. (Neil Leach)

Babel Script, vocal. (Mark Goulthorpe)

Design agency

As part of a cultural defence I was curious to learn from other scripting designers their thoughts on control, or loss of it to the algorithm, and on the formulation of solution seeking by 'others' not directly implicated with the problem at hand. By cultural defence, I mean defence of scripting as

StudioMode, RK4Tile3, New York, 2010.

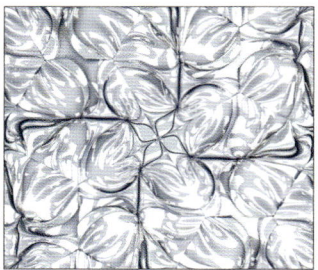

RK 4 Tessellation Field Centroid

RK 4 Fields

RK 4 Fields

RK 4 Tessellation Tile Prototype

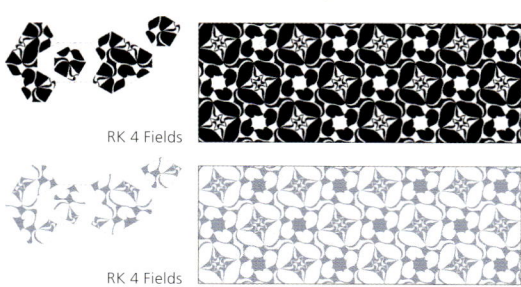

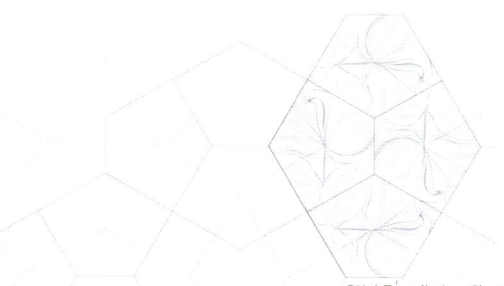

RK 4 Tessellation Cluster

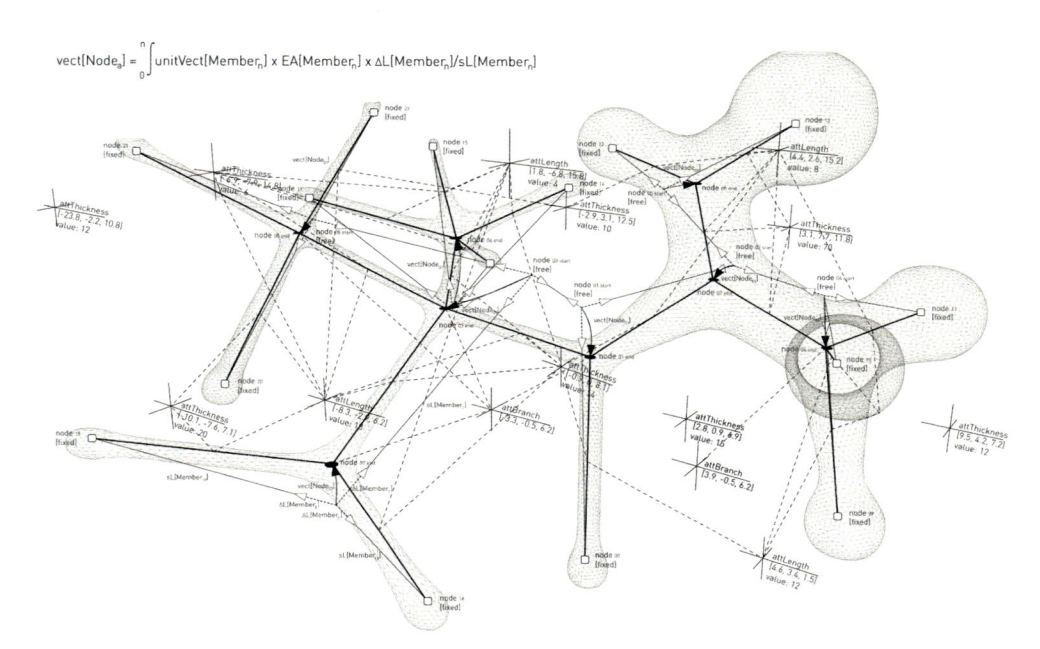

$$vect[Node_a] = \int_0^n unitVect[Member_n] \times EA[Member_n] \times \Delta L[Member_n]/sL[Member_n]$$

Supermanoeuvre, Protosynthesis, New York, 2009.

culture(s), not just a fad or a style. While some views point to an ascendancy of generative processes:

> I believe that all generative processes hold the designer to account. They should be seen as prostheses to the architectural imagination. But we need to lose the old fashioned notion of the architect as some top-down demiurgic 'designer' and reconfigure the architect as the controller of processes. (Neil Leach)

the majority view is one of designer as driver, regardless of the tools in their hands:

> Good question. Designer is accountable for all, and it's an important aspect of how the logic of authorship is changing. I hear a lot about networked intelligence and so on and it's there, but it isn't in my opinion going to produce, say, a great building. The cultural features behind making a building have their own forces. (Peter Macapia, labDORA)

> The designer who wants to be completely in control of the results must be in control of the process. To be in control of the process, the designer must be in control of the tools. The tools are computation, therefore a designer who

THEVERYMANY, Echidnoids, New York, 2009.

THEVERYMANY, Echidnoids, New York, 2009.

wants to be in control must also be a scripter (or suffer the consequence of the unseen influence of using other people's tools). (Robert Aish)

… the mind is versatile in evolving new media in response to its intuitive needs, and doubtless the crudity of current man–computer interfaces will increasingly become symbiotic with our evolving thinking. (Mark Goulthorpe)

Programming is useful in handling information beyond our perceptual capabilities. (Panagiotis Michalatos & Sawako Kaijima, AKT Architects)

Ultimately the designer should always be held accountable. The agency within a design process is on the side of the designer, not the other way around. (Mode)

With this final probe we have closed the circle of this chapter. I commenced with my account of what tempted me to script in the first place – most of

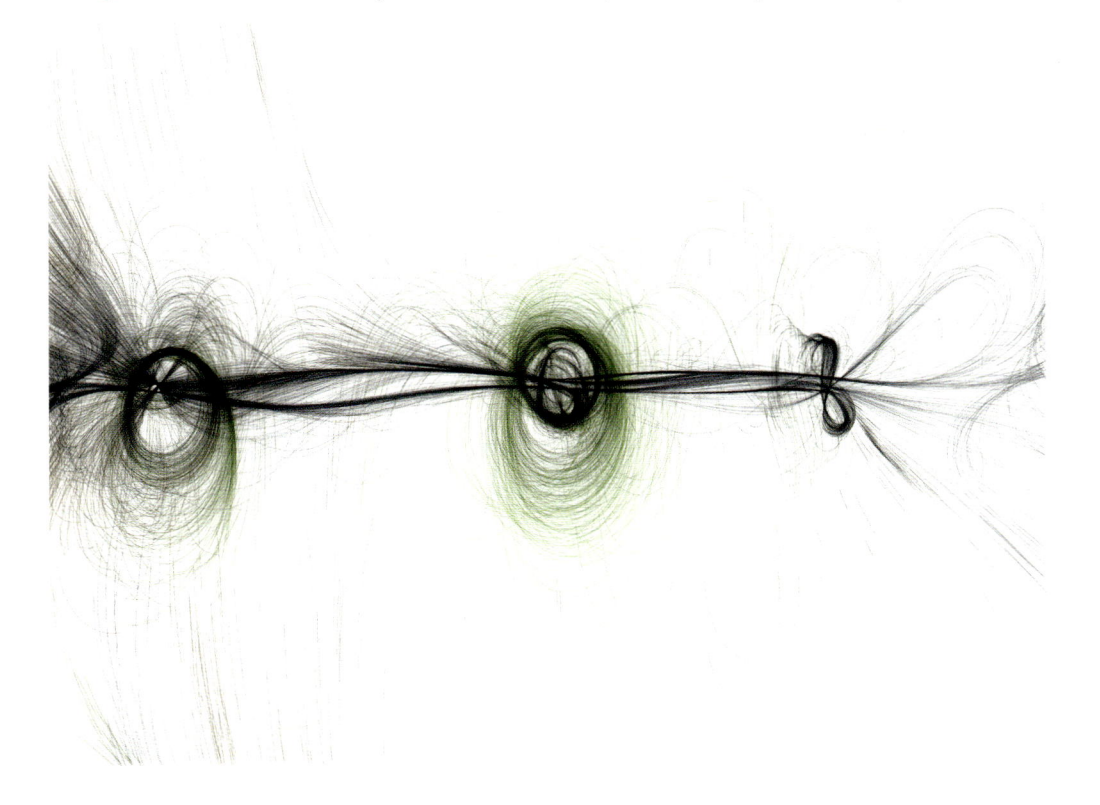

Casey Reas, Tissue-B01, Los Angeles, 2002.

us come to scripting from architecture rather than the other way around, and have unique stories to tell. Mine is one of being forced out of my comfort zone to confront the inadequacies of the tools I had available relative to my tasks. In the process of doing so I found that that I had to open Pandora's black box, but the bogies fled leaving me exposed to an unexpected world of opportunity offered through creative coding. From my early incursions into computing (as opposed to scripting) in the 1970s as part of my undergraduate architectural education I was made aware of logic programming, but it did not resonate with me in any tangible way. I would admit to having almost no enthusiasm then, as the dreary examples that were meant to excite our interest in fact had the opposite effect on me. I simply had a distaste for anything that sought to dampen the influence of what I regarded as the most precious design input afforded to us as humans: our intuition. Others will argue that this is evidence of a very closed mind for which my albeit weak riposte can only be: such may be the vicissitudes of youth.

Casey Reas, Process6_Puff_4, Los Angeles, 2005.

References

1 Cecil Balmond with Jannuzzi Smith, *Informal: the informal in architecture and engineering*, Prestel (Munich), 2002, p 14.
2 Patrik Schumacher, *Parametricism as Style – Parametricist Manifesto*, New Architecture Group (London), 2008. Presented and discussed at the Dark Side Club, 11th Architecture Biennale, Venice, 2008; http://www.patrikschumacher.com/Texts/Parametricism%20as%20Style.htm.
3 Pseudocode is natural language imitating computer programming language used as a means for a code commissioner to communicate to a coder, for instance: *'if green then make square else make round'*.
4 'Mathematics', *The Oxford English Dictionary*, 2nd edn, 1989. CD-ROM.

4 Resources

In this chapter I will pay brief homage to a small selection of pioneers from my scripting pantheon and identify some key texts that will expand my account as a prelude to a discussion of what has particularly motivated the approaches I have taken to scripting design and why in the following chapter. Here I identify what some scripters regard as core material, giving some reasons for why I have not included it in this primer along with some advice on where the reader might go to find out more. Although in the second half of the primer I focus on what I have actually experienced rather than merely been made aware of through reading and visiting exhibitions of the practice of others, it would be remiss of me not to refer at least in passing to some of the other markedly different scripting positions that can be taken.

I have used a general chapter title of 'Resources', and this can be taken in two ways. Firstly, I mean to imply that there are many approaches to design that one might take through scripting, and many ways to make one's own path. As discussed in the previous chapter, the proto-scripter can be taken as needing to discover these paths largely for themselves, as there are diverse scripting cultures in which one might originate, or at least participate. Secondly, there are considerably more scripting designers who now offer a critical mass and a diversity of practice, encouraging newcomers to experiment for themselves with confidence, rather than feel that they should align with a particular software, scripting language or approach. The majority of the contributors in the preceding chapter have exhibited and published widely and, through their practice, have become the maestros; essential contemporary catalysts with a role that is slightly different from that of the pioneers. We have all moved on.

This chapter is in two parts. I commence with a brief commentary on the 'state of play' as I read it in practice, noting along the way the essential literature and software available both to fledgling scripters and to the more experienced coders who might want to be shaken out of their scripting comfort zone a bit. I follow this with a brief overview of approaches to scripting that are current in practice, but not made explicit in my worked examples. This overview complements the contextual summary in Chapter 2, and the state of contemporary scripting assessed in Chapter 3.

Missing from scripting cultures: some pioneers and some alternative approaches

There are several important scripting streams and their concomitant cultures that have not been considered in depth in the examples that follow in this primer. In their stead here are some sources of information to follow up. There is a select bibliography and software list at the end of this book, which should also help orient the reader disappointed by my necessarily limited choice of examples.

The most obvious absentee stream is scripting for graphics and 2D animation. In this regard I introduce the first and youngest member from my pantheon of pioneer scripters, John Maeda, formerly from the Aesthetics and Computation Group at the MIT Media Lab, and now President of the Rhode Island School of Design. Maeda is the most conspicuous guru in this area; he has not only exhibited and published comprehensively, but has also contributed a host of scholars and practitioners who have been emerging from his studio for well over a decade. He has been assiduous in getting his message across, principally on the humanising of technology through art practice. Any practical contribution from me would be enfeebled in this context.

The work of Maeda and his protégés holds an interesting position in the recent history of scripting, because although it is framed strictly as electronic arts practice, much is made of the relationship between artist and expert computer user – electronic arts require expertise in both, an almost universally held view. It is also interesting to note that the focus of this group is on 2D graphics, or graphical representation of 3D, rather than on 3D space crafting. Two of the more prominent offshoots from his studio, Casey Reas and Ben Fry, went on to produce Processing in 2001, an open-source programming language that specifically targets both electronic arts and visual design, but has recently been taken up by the architectural, engineering and product design communities. Their 2007 publication, *Processing: A Programming Handbook for Visual Designers and Artists*,[1] by its very title determines the target market, but typically spatial designers have appropriated it to their own unique challenges. Using Java as its base language, Processing sits on top of it and sets out to simplify coding to the extent that the completely uninitiated can commence programming encouraged by instantly viewable results placed on the screen as they proceed. Its simplicity is a touch beguiling, and were readers to access the 3D example 'cube to pyramid to cone to cylinder' in the 2007 publication *Processing: Creative Coding and Computational Art*,[2] and compare this with the first part of Chapter 9 in this primer, they might wonder why I took so much trouble over such an apparently trivial spatial morphing 'problem', compared with the comparatively simple few pages of Processing code. In the conclusion I delve a little into 'depth of enquiry', and the difference between the unquestioning technical versus the philosophically and culturally motivated provocation, and I'll leave it there for now.

John Maeda contributed the introduction to the Reas and Fry book, from which I quote:

> *It is said that the greatest compliment to a teacher is when the student surpasses the teacher. This corner was turned quickly after I began to work with them, and the finishing blow came when Ben and Casey created Processing. They prominently elevated the call for visual experimentation with their timely mastery of the Internet to engage at first tens, hundreds, and then tens of thousands of hybrids all over the world. Wherever I might travel, young technology artists are always talking about Processing and ask me to pass on their thanks to Casey and Ben.*[3]

An astonishingly humble admission from a guru; one that it behoves all high performers to take on board. It echoes some of the replies that I received from my correspondents referred to in the previous chapter: no one can do everything, and some are more adept at some things than others.

For their part, Reas states in the preface to their book:

In 1997, during my final year of undergraduate school, John Maeda gave a lecture at our program. It was overwhelming for several of us, including one friend who sat mumbling 'Whoa, slow down ...' as we watched from the back of the room. In the presentation I finally saw the intersection between design and computation that I couldn't figure out before. It was a different perspective than building tools, which sounded mundane, or building interfaces, which also left something to be desired.[4]

The second oversight that might be alleged for this book would be failure to cover evolutionary generative coding in all its guises. This apparent omission is much harder for me to defend: I have not dabbled a great deal in an area that many others set great store by, and I have a number of difficulties with adopting this approach as core to my activities. I regard generative processes as having introduced some yet-to-be-resolved complexities, but I confess to having found relatively few who hold the same view as I do on the subject. What makes me slightly nervous is the transition between an idea and a design, and the design of that design. The view that I am most comfortable with is that of an idea being propagated in the mind and substantially worked into a design through purely intellectual processes, which may or may not involve direct computational support. This is subtly different, in my view, from an idea being developed through a computationally generative process or, worse, an idea being computationally generated. I am, however, particularly attracted to the situation where computational support is used to steer the design towards *simplexity* being enlisted as an external agent to counter the human tendency towards *complexification*. This concept is further discussed in Chapter 5.

In Chapter 2 I looked at the relationship between design and intentionality. If one simply enlists the random function, for example, stopping only when a defendable solution suggests itself, has the design come from a designer, or has the software writer or algorithm structure contributed to the design in a way unconnected to that in which the design task was originally authored? More acutely still, has the black box produced the design with the minimum of human intellectual agency other than the remote and anonymous computer and software designers?

This situation is not as absolute as I have painted it. A designer working in this way would at least claim that they exercised judgement and helped steer the process if not actually writing the generative algorithm themselves. They have addressed the 'stopping problem' with flair. And even if they did not call a halt to the generated options using their own judgement, they might at least have steered the process towards the optimal solution that meets exacting criteria with an intelligent selection of constraints. It is not something that I feel religious about. It is a view possibly framed more by my instinctual comparison between designers whose work I admire and am particularly familiar with, who would not seek to use a generative process as a driver for their work, and those who do. I fully expect to read back over this statement in the future and find myself admitting I was in error. I might be a bit purblind within this territory, but I genuinely think it is too early to be taking strong positions either way.

In my experience, it is never useful to argue against the use of generative scripting with hard-core generative design enthusiasts. There is a semantic obstacle to arriving at a consensual definition of 'generative' that can range between a soft and loose definition (probably my position) and that of a computer scientist who knows exactly what the term means, when it should be applied, and why the practice should be widely disseminated. In Chapter 9 aspects of a generative process are implicit in my account, but not foregrounded. Put to the fore here, however is reference to the next member of my pantheon of pioneers: John Frazer, formally of the Architectural Association (AA) in London, and now research professor at Queensland University of Technology (QUT) in Australia. Frazer's seminal account of his work since the 1960s and the philosophies that have informed it are set out in his 1995 publication, *An Evolutionary Architecture*.[5] I remember thinking as I read it just after publication: 'All the things I am interested in exploring, but here they are, already done!' Without exception every one of my postgraduates has added it to their reading without ever being prompted by me to do so. The book is perhaps appropriately immodest in its ambitions, something very clearly spelt out in its preface written by Gordon Pask and reinforced by the author throughout:

> The fundamental thesis is that of architecture as a living, evolving thing. In a way this is evident. Our culture's striving towards civilization is manifested in the places, houses and cities that it creates. As well as providing a protective carapace, these structures also carry symbolic value, and can be seen as being continuous with and emerging from the life of those who inhabit the built environment.[6]

Frazer argues that nature's design, the tendency to invest nature with 'vitalist forces' as represented in both science and poetry, is a term of convenience whereas, through the projects in his book, 'design' is applied as a 'new model with purposeful intent':

> *To us the connotations of the term 'design' are very different from the norm: when we 'design', we are clear in our intentions, but perhaps 'blind' to the eventual outcome of the process that we are creating. This 'blindness' can cause concern to those with traditional design values who relish total control. It can alarm those who feel that what we are proposing might get out of control like a computer virus. However we remain convinced that the harnessing of some of the qualities of the natural design process could bring about a real improvement in the built environment.[7]*

The architectural model espoused in the book is one of 'artificial life':

> *In nature it is only the genetically coded information of form which evolves, but selection is based on the expression of this coded information in the outward form of an organism. The codes are manufacturing instructions, but their precise expression is environmentally dependent. Our architectural model, considered as a form of artificial life, also contains coded manufacturing instructions which are environmentally dependent, but as in the real world model it is only the codescript which evolves.[8]*

An evolutionary architecture is founded on a fundamentally new model for architecture, and necessarily involves a generative technique. Frazer concedes that adopting generative systems is potentially problematic:

> *An essential part of this evolutionary model is some form of generative technique. Again this is an area charged with problems and controversy.[9]*

Former Frazer students who now carve their own trajectories such as Cristiano Ceccato are unstinting in their praise and positive assessment of their time with him:

> *I went through the entire AA School's Diploma Course from First Year through the Fifth Year. I had quite a hard time navigating very different unit agendas in my early (undergraduate) years, but John's unit was an incredible intellectual climax for me, in that it allowed me to combine something that I was profoundly familiar with since my late childhood – logic, computers and programming – with my interests in nature, form and structure, and provided a framework with which to integrate these two. I felt vindicated, after many*

years of struggle and persistence, to have found a vehicle – a modus operandi – that I could make my own during my studies.

Clearly the lasting legacy for me has been the 'forma mentis' imparted by John's teaching. In other words, the clarity of thought, and the ability to analyse a problem and formulate a logical solution in the simplest and most expeditious way possible.

Confronting the 'forma mentis' from the heady days of Dip 11 with the broader context of contemporary theory and global practice is, as one might say, part of growing up and getting a few more grey hairs.[10]

As one last sample from what is a highly charged book, here is the potential *quid pro quo*:

If taken much further, this could contribute to the understanding of more fundamental form-generating processes, thus repaying some of the debt that architecture owes the scientific field. Perhaps before the turn of the century there will be a new branch of science concerned with creative morphology and intentionality.[11]

The timeline might be a little overstated, and the target date for the new branch of science is optimistic with respect to fiercely independent disciplines, but in many other respects a quiet revolution is already playing out within science. While architects cluster not so quietly around biomimetics as Frazer's 'new model for architecture', I have been quite surprised at how open the sciences are not only to a contribution to architectural thought, but to the way creative thinking around addressing the 'wicked problem' has gained currency. As global environmental issues become manifestly inconvenient, a new field of enquiry (if not a new branch of science) is visibly emerging, one where designers, technologists and scientists come together in areas of mutual interest far more effectively than we have probably seen since the Renaissance. The prescience of *An Evolutionary Architecture* in this regard cannot be overstated, and even if the message is not fully subscribed to by all, it can be a model for comprehensive intellectual enquiry around computational architecture. Unfortunately, so much of what is regarded today as novelty is linked to emerging digital capability, yet the pioneers had already gone over much of the ground several decades ago, especially the hard thinking. Looking back they seem to have been only marginally limited by distinctly more primitive programs, as *An Evolutionary Architecture* demonstrates. The grandiloquent claims for novelty come today from some boosters, who fail to reference earlier, very valuable, hard-won and genuinely innovative thinking. A sense of this disconnect can be discerned in some of the commentaries recorded in the previous chapter, not least by Frazer himself.

Evolutionary design thinking is naturally tied to the importance of the algorithm; a piece of code which takes instructions as an input providing answers that satisfy stated conditions. This becomes very interesting if the algorithm is set to determine the best possible result against given criteria, such as evolutionary algorithms and their highly popular optimising subclass, genetic algorithms. This is the third major scripting stream that may seem underplayed in this primer relative to opportunity and its currency. 'Algorithm' now rolls off everyone's tongue with a facility that gives the lie to the notion of the word's almost total obscurity to designers barely a decade ago.

The dictionary definition of algorithm is 'A process, or set of rules, usually one expressed in algebraic notation, now used esp. in computing, machine translation and linguistics'.[12] Dabbling in computer science here makes for a very weak definition (from a computer science point of view), prone to being a circular argument when we contrast actual scripts with idealised algorithms. I touch on this a little more in Chapter 5. In its most benign sense, the algorithm in a design process is the problem-solving route conforming to a set of rules guiding towards a satisfactory or 'good enough' solution. The problem is that 'good enough' might satisfy (or, more accurately, satisfice), without being an exceptional outcome. For this reason, rather sophisticated algorithms have been developed, many of which, such as the genetic algorithms referred to above, seek to model natural systems. According to its advocates, the closer the genetic algorithm is to mirroring a natural evolutionary process,

John Frazer, flat-bed plotter drawing of Frazer's final-year project at the AA (1967–8), believed to be the first student design project ever drawn by computer.

the more likely a design resulting from the algorithm's application will tend towards being entirely satisfactory. I note that designers attribute a richness and complexity to genetic algorithms as design-oriented solution seekers. Mathematicians do not necessarily echo this acclaim to quite the same extent.

As contemporary architectural discourse moves from object thinking to system thinking (noted in Chapter 10), the genetic algorithm offers the generative designer a powerful *amanuensis* attuned to lessons gained from the natural world. Whether back to Charles Darwin (1809–82), or forward to D'Arcy Wentworth Thompson (1860–1948), even more recent serendipitous discovery (Alexander Fleming, 1881–1955), or James Watson, Francis Crick and Maurice Wilkins's paradigm shift in 1953 with their base pairing of nucleotides within an account of DNA, there is a perceptible convergence between natural systems and alternative ways to think about architectural design. Our algorithms speed up design discovery, but always tuned to the logical processes enshrined within, and are often modelled on nature. In my own work, genetic algorithms have been an essential route to a particular type of problem solving (but hardly as a design agent), which I touch on in Chapter 6. At the lowest level possible, I have applied the algorithm in a genetic sense to the project '*Our World*' described in Chapter 9. Others have made it a core focus of their life's work. One such is Paul Coates who teaches and researches at the University of East London in the UK.

Also in my pantheon, Coates, whose career is contiguous with John Frazer's, has been a maestro in algorithmic design. In his 2010 book, *Programming. Architecture*,[13] Coates offers a comprehensive history of computing and computational design. In his index and glossary, Algorithm (and Programming too) has as its first definition '*what this book is about*'. The book is a

John Frazer, circular cathode ray tube at Cambridge, 1970. The first generative project is shown developing on the screen.

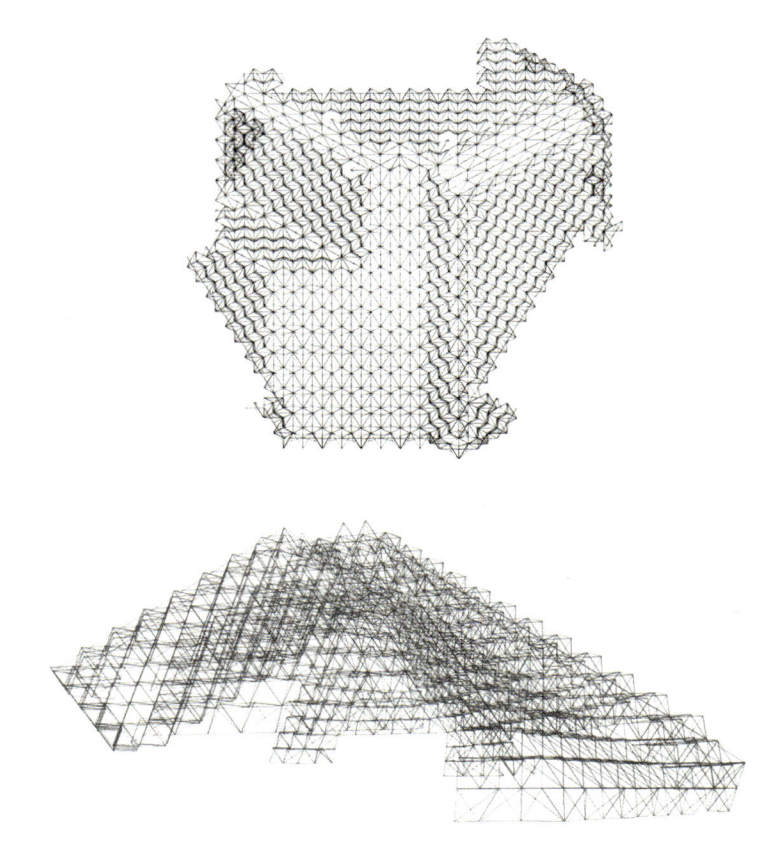

John Frazer, plotted output of a structure entirely generated from just a seed, 1971.

provocative synthesis of the history, theory and practical application of algorithmic design using computers. In the pursuit of emergence, Coates argues that the computers have an advantage:

> ... *in order to build the morphological system, you have to define it in a formal language (define an algorithm) which brings the structure and meaning of the model proposed into the realms of expression and debate (and also conveniently allows it to be programmed for automatic execution). This use of formal languages in modelling should provide a basis for the development of a theory of form and shape, which has more chance of being adopted and discussed than the conventional discursive art historical method because all the underlying assumptions are clearly laid out, not hidden by conventional approaches and the nineteenth-century idea of creativity.* [14]

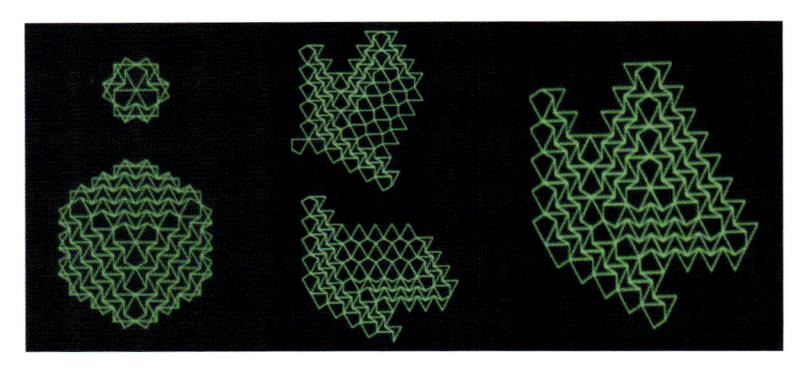

John Frazer, seeds growing and mutating on the screen under control of generative algorithm, 1971.

I first became aware of Coates's MSc in computing and design at the Association for Education and Research in Computer Aided Architectural Design in Europe (eCAADe) conference hosted in Glasgow in 1994, when two of his postgraduates stunned me with the sophistication of their use of AutoLISP™ (referred to in the previous chapter): it was just after I had been teaching myself to draw hyperbola curves using the same programming interface. It was my first introduction to using the computer to pursue a design outcome little different to what I would be doing in my sketch book: the relatively little prior exposure I had had made the subject seem not only dry but distinctly avoidable. Like the two other pioneers already mentioned, Paul Coates is a generous sharer of his considerable knowledge and experience, and his demeanour strikes me as much more that of a co-conspirator with his Masters students than as anything more formal.

The last in my pantheon of pioneers, also typified by an abundance of generosity, energy, and what always struck one as boundless optimism, is the late Bill Mitchell (1944–2010). A prolific author, he was a highly inspirational teacher at Cambridge in the UK and Yale before accepting leadership roles at UCLA, Harvard and, ultimately, MIT. His ambition was always to improve the world through better design, and to make design better through creative and intelligent use of computers. The book of his that most affected me (when a few years later I read it again, this time somewhat less critically than I had at the time of its publication in 1990) was his *The Logic of Architecture*.[15] The book was the first to touch on the relationship between what has motivated architects from the beginning. It delves into cognition, formalism, shape grammars and shape recognition and, very sympathetically, into the role of composition and a definition of architectural language as a helpful alignment with computer languages. The point is to offer insights into how designers with a deep understanding of the logic of architecture can more effectively engage with the ruthless logic of the computer. It was very well reviewed in 1992 by Ulrich Fleming:

> *Mitchell succeeds splendidly with respect to his first motivation [the formal models underlying computer-aided architectural design systems (if they are based, in fact, on a rigorous foundation) or to suggest such a foundation for systems in need of one]: He lays it all out for readers who are interested in being more than an appendage to a machine whose inner workings they do not comprehend, who want to understand what computer programs are able to do and want to use them (or criticize them) intelligently, and, perhaps most importantly, who want to make suggestions for improving the available software and take part in the development of computer programs that are more responsive to their needs or desires. All of this requires a basic familiarity with the mechanisms described by Mitchell.*[16]

I admire the unpacking that the book represents, but as with all efforts to make connections between architectural logic and computer logic, so vital if designers with the primitive machines of the time were to make the most of their opportunities, conformity was singularly important. However, I, for

Paul Coates, Shape Grammar, 1993.

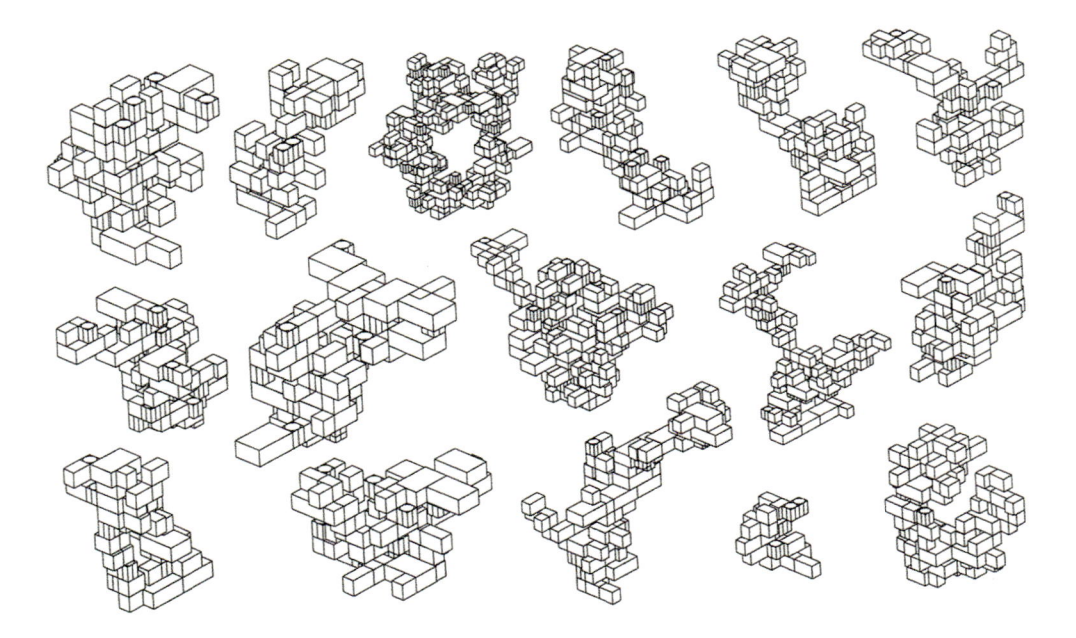

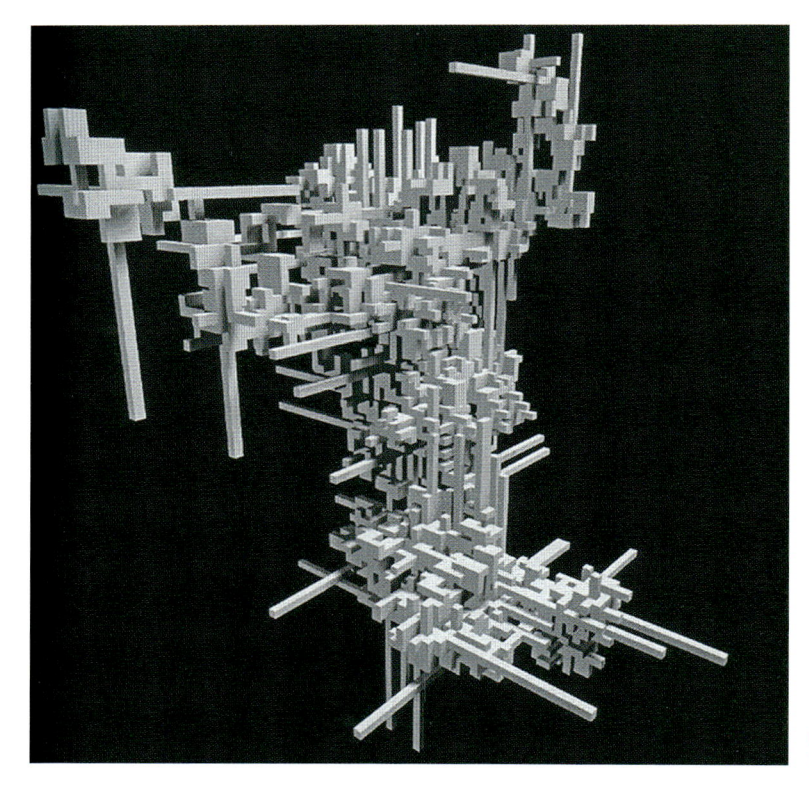

Paul Coates, Shape Grammar, 1993.

one, thrive on the wisdom of the maverick, the atypical and the exception, which is another version of the same old paradox: computers demand logic in programming but not all designers think, behave, or design logically.

Maeda, Frazer, Coates and Mitchell are among the top of my list of essential authors. This is not to say that they necessarily represent a natural alignment with my own views. Rather, it is for their original thinking, their cross-over role in that design-computation gulf that persuades me to single them out. From the pioneer generation I would also suggest that newcomers look at the published work of Christopher Alexander, Ulrich Flemming, Chris Yessios, Tom Mather, Alan Bridges, Chuck Eastman, George Stiny, Terry Knight, John Gero, Ranulph Glanville, Phil Steadman and Lionel March. The hardier could reach back even further to Gordon Pask (1928–96), Gerard de Zeeuw, John von Neumann (1903 – 57), and Alan Turing (1912-54). Then there are the pioneers such as Ivan Sutherland who with 'Sketchpad' in 1963 prepared us for the user interfaces so taken for granted today. It does not matter, in my view, whether their material elicits an empathetic response from their readers; the issue is to look into the originators who have already contributed through doing the donkey work. I am not convinced that everyone today is making this basic and ultimately time-saving effort.

Moving on

Bill Mitchell / Tom Kvan, an early scripted illustration of an office layout shape grammar in which exception is seen, early 1980s.

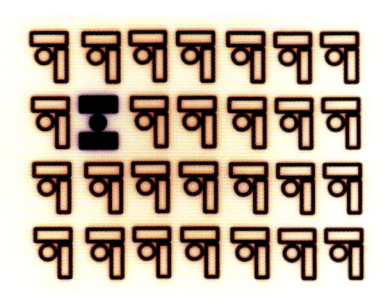

Bill Mitchell / Tom Kvan, an early three-dimensional script of a Charles Rennie Mackintosh Willow Chair, 1985.

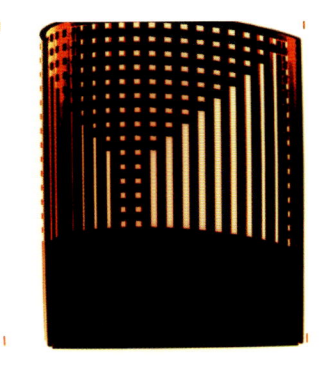

At the time of writing, many are flocking to the *swarm* as a source of inspiration At the time of writing, many are flocking to the swarm as a source of inspiration, and not necessarily with the pragmatic purposes of digitally modelling the behaviour of a crowd in response to a sudden event such as an emergency using 'agent-based swarm intelligence'. This is rapidly becoming a crowded space. I find the idea of a digital flock truly fascinating, although I have never had reason to experiment with the requisite algorithms. Coates covers them well. Swarming algorithms also model nature, first being applied to the behaviour of flights of birds. The theory is deceptively simple and the results surprising and often informative. The algorithm responds to three guiding principles. The first is separation: maintaining a suitable distance from immediate neighbours. The second is cohesion: not losing contact with neighbours also working within defined limits. Thirdly, alignment: this is the driver. It might be a terrain for mutual (potentially chaotic) response, or it might be leadership – defined or emerging, or it might be the tension that arises from competing leadership. Once a flocking algorithm is specifically tuned to a context and a narrative overlay, the results can only be extraordinary, unlikely to be contrived by human imagination without the assistance of a digital agency. The scripter has an ocean of choice here, limited only by their imagination I would suppose, never having been there myself.

There is no better way to illustrate how complexity can erupt from many local interacting decisions than flocking. The individual elements might be plants and animals in an ecosystem, vehicles in traffic, or people in crowds. If one considers the city a dynamic in which systems of flow – such as traffic, circulation of goods, or crowd behaviour – can be applied to any urban transformation, then flocking provides a vital model of complex coordination that describes these material shifts.[17]

It strikes me that in terms of engaging a narrative through code there is plenty of potential here, hence the current uptake. We might be seeing just the beginning of its potential being explored, especially as the majority taking up 'behaviour agents' are grabbing the code of others, rather than coming up with their own.

Agency itself, of which swarming is a sophisticated example, is also an interesting approach. An agent is an autonomous unit of code with inbuilt behaviours. The agents can be sent out to look for data with precise instructions about what to do with the data once accessed. From the scripting point of view, this is obviously very rich territory; if a design is set up as a defined desirable outcome, and a set of variables established as possibilities and initiators, appropriate agents can be deployed to look for information, respond to it, synthesise and sponsor a suitable response. An example would be urban morphology: 'given what we know about, say, city X, should such and such occur, what would be a viable architectural response?' With an eye to a future in which sensors become more numerous and actuators cheaper and more effective at the same time, buildings might be encoded with agents sufficiently sophisticated to allow continuous active response to circumstances as they change.

Before finishing with a brief overview of alternative scripting approaches, I should like to draw attention to the many other ways of looking at design computationally with a view to a design intermediary working between conceptual thinking and the digital tools to hand. At the dry end of the spectrum are shape grammars and object recognition, across to more mathematically located themes or 'tools' such as packing, tiling, patterning (such as Voronoi), weaving and blending and, my favourite, Boolean operations. Then there are the emerging opportunities for rapid prototyping and digital fabrication: deposition technologies versus subtraction. There are a lot of alternatives, many of which are not mutually exclusive.

To program, to code, to script, to borrow, to mash, to avoid?

At the end of this primer, most of the main software options for the scripter are listed. What should be taken up, and what is risky?

Here is a list of pointers that I think will help the initiate avoid spending many hours learning a program or language that ultimately proves to be the wrong one.

1 Listen to what your closest confidants, colleagues and teachers tell you, but always look beyond them. It is very easy for them to proselytise what they are familiar with, and teach you what they know.

2 Get a sense of your own aptitude. If you find the learning and practising achievable (note that only one of my 30-plus correspondents thought that coding skill is anything less than hard won), then consider learning a generic coding language ahead of a proprietary language tied to a particular software.

3 If you appear to be gifted then write your own, as has been referred to above (Processing).

4 Be generous – share rather than try to hide your code.

5 Keep an eye on the future … probably best done by considering the past a bit more closely.

6 Do not be slave to a technique, pre-packaged algorithms, copiable code unless working with someone else's prior knowledge that fits your preferred approach exactly. Leave the learning mother ship as soon as possible or risk being a clone.

7 Collaborate.

8 Most crucial of all: hone your critical judgement skills, look at what you have achieved as if you were looking into a mirror. Can you see yourself (intellect) in your work, or the uninvited contribution of anonymous others? Or, even more crucial, work out if this even matters in the 21st century.

To finish with a quote from Mitchell, Liggett and Kvan's classic *The Art of Computer Graphics Programming*:[18]

When it is viewed in a broad cultural perspective, computer graphics seems still to be at a stage, characteristic of infant media, in which the development of technique has far outstripped the ability of artists to understand its true potentials and to use it in a mature way. There are early Greek cut stone buildings that imitate the forms of still earlier wooden constructions, there are early photographs that imitate oil paintings, and there are early films that imitate stage plays.

Published in 1987, their observation still stands as a salutary challenge for scripters today.

References

1 C Reas, *Processing: A Programming Handbook for Visual Designers and Artists*, MIT Press (Cambridge, MA), 2007.
2 I Greenberg, *Processing: Creative Coding and Computational Art*, Friends of ED Academic (New York), 2007, p 657.
3 John Maeda in ibid, p xix.
4 Casey Reas in ibid, p xxiii.
5 J Frazer, *An Evolutionary Architecture*, Architectural Association Publications (London), 1995.
6 Gordon Pask, introduction to ibid, p 6.
7 Ibid, p 12.
8 Ibid, p 14.
9 Ibid.
10 Extracted from Cristiano Ceccato's letter to the author, dated 22 August 2010. Currently Lead Designer at Zaha Hadid Architects, Ceccato was formerly at Gehry Technologies, and was at the AA in the early 1990s.
11 J Frazer, *An Evolutionary Architecture*, p 20.
12 'Algorithm' Def. 3, *Oxford English Dictionary*, 2nd edn, 1989, CD-ROM.
13 Paul Coates, *Programming. Architecture*, Routledge (London and New York), 1st edn, 2010.
14 Ibid, p 167.
15 William J Mitchell, *The Logic of Architecture: Design, Computation, and Cognition*, MIT Press (Cambridge, MA), 1990, illustrated edn.
16 Reviewed work(s): William J Mitchell, The Logic of Architecture. Design, Computation, and Cognition, *Journal of Architectural Education* (1984–) vol 46, no 2 (Nov, 1992), pp 104–6. Published by Blackwell Publishing on behalf of the Association of Collegiate Schools of Architecture, Inc Stable URL: http://www.jstor.org/stable/1425204.
17 Benjamin Aranda, *Tooling*, Princeton Architectural Press Pamphlet Architecture, 2006, p 65.
18 William J Mitchell, Robin S Liggett and Thomas Kvan, *The Art of Computer Graphics Programming: A Structured Introduction for Architects and Designers*,Van Nostrand Reinhold (New York), 1987, p 524.

5 Dimensions

Up to this point we have formed a working definition of scripting, reviewed the contemporary context, referred to the principal software choices and literature resources available at this time, presented some influential opinions of pioneers and maestros, and located scripting within architectural education and practice today. This chapter precedes what I have positioned as five examples taken from my own portfolio of projects. The first three examples draw from my experience in practice and consider scripting for increased productivity, experiments in form, and links to fabrication. The fourth and fifth examples are thought experiments, hypothetical designs arrived at through scripting. This chapter provides a little more detail about some of the turning points that helped shape my portfolio; these are not offered as formulae for others to take up, but rather as pointers to some of the creative relationships that link scripting to design.

Design space between geometry, mathematics and computation

Ultimately scripting is anything but rigidly formulaic in application however much scripters might flock to this or that fashionable problem-solving algorithm at any particular point of time. Scripting can be engaged purely to speculate, and even working from an historiographical perspective, future gaze. The range of techniques I describe here are limited somewhat to what I can do myself framed around what I have actually wanted to do over the years. There is an absolute connection between the two. The key message in *Scripting Cultures* is not the techniques so much as the creative inclinations at work. In looking for an umbrella to place over all five examples I have settled on 'dimensionality' in all its meanings – a longstanding interest which I will detail as I proceed. Less figuratively than the word 'dimension' might initially suggest, it is precisely the frustratingly complex and therefore difficult dimensionality of space and its associated narrative potential that has guided all the projects presented here.

Through a combination of good luck and timing, a passionate interest in Antoni Gaudí (1852–1926) led to an interview in 1979 with two of Gaudí's octogenarian successors who were directing the small team completing the Sagrada Família church (1882 – ongoing); they had been young apprentice architects during Gaudí's final years. I was requesting material for my undergraduate thesis and I had two principal questions: where was the authority to complete the building coming from when so little of the building had actually been completed, and much of Gaudí's design models and all of his drawings destroyed during the Spanish Civil War (1936–9)? And how, precisely, were instructions given to the master masons charged with actually building so complex a construction? Their answer was to point me to boxes and boxes of model fragments with the suggestion that all the secrets lay within. I have been engaged as an architect and design researcher studying these models ever since.

My intimate introduction to Gaudí at the commencement of my career has coloured everything I have done. I hasten to add that this is not a stylistic connection – as if any pretender could succeed with such vainglory. The attribute I discovered in Gaudí's work that captured me was his dimensional thinking, evidently one of the principal drivers for all that he accomplished. He wrote nothing at all about his architectural theory in a career spanning 48 years. In order to gain insights into one of the most creative and technically competent architects ever, we have to unravel the mysteries of his work itself, which sets us all a number of significant challenges.

Any discussion about dimensionality here in words alone will probably lack prospects, and the projects that follow will take on the main thrust of this task. Let us begin with the *Oxford English Dictionary*'s (*OED*) definition of 'dimension' – at least the one that principally interests scripters. Here is the *OED*'s third definition:

> A mode of linear measurement, magnitude, or extension, in a particular direction; usually as co-existing with similar measurements or extensions in other directions. The three dimensions of a body, or of ordinary space, are length, breadth, and thickness (or depth); a surface has only two dimensions (length and breadth); a line only one (length). Here the notion of measurement or magnitude is commonly lost, and the word denotes merely a particular mode of spatial extension. Modern mathematicians have speculated as to the possibility of more than three dimensions of space.[1]

This is the mathematical and geometrical definition. When we add the other entries for 'dimension' as a noun to the mix, we see how bountiful the word is for spatial thinkers. The *OED* includes 'The action of measuring', dividing notes in music to shorter ones as measures of time or rhythm, spatial 'extent', a measure of time, 'any of the component aspects of a particular situation' citing 'an attribute of, or way of viewing, an abstract entity' as an example. We find that the definition of 'dimension' ranges between a measure, spatial extents such as 'thickness', mathematical, geometrical and algebraic properties, and the descriptive part of a compound noun such as 'dimension line'. Designers can call on all these definitions; some are more immediate than others, but overall the dimensional language of the architect is probably much easier to work within design than as written language. When we apply the word to what we do, however, and try to link it to mathematical concepts, we can quickly get into hot water. Here are some examples.

Beyond 3D space

Let us start with one dimension. Convention would have it that points lying on a straight line describe a single axis, and represent a dimension. In fact, we tend to use the word 'line' when we should say 'curve', and we do not use the word 'vector' and instead refer to a 'straight line'. By using mathematical terms freely, that is to say without precision, and not engaging with the underlying mathematical concepts, we help perpetuate the myth of space being a 3D construct: limited to the first dictionary definition of 'dimension' posited above, *'modern mathematicians have speculated as to the possibility of more than three dimensions of space'*.

My impression is that spatial thinkers are comfortable with space as an abstract concept, intuitively think spatially, but end up being the equivalent of tongue-tied when it comes to representing space conventionally rather than purely through design. Ordinarily or, more accurately, in earlier pre-digital practice, a sculptor could get away with never abstracting their work as a set of coordinates, for instance. An architect working with a simple repertoire of vertical and horizontal plans could abstract their work in reasonably simple sets of projections. Crucial exceptions, however, have always been with us whether it is Francesco Borromini (1599–1667) describing the roof of San Carlo alle Quattro Fontane (1638–41), the French mathematician Gaspard Monge (1746–1818) consolidating the principles of descriptive geometry that he had invented, or Gaudí and his hanging model for the Colònia Güell chapel (1896–1914). Whatever their elaborate methodology for successfully describing spatial complexities to their colleagues, they were geometrical, not mathematical instructions.

Our recent aspirations have tended towards designing spatially complex architecture. As an example of our new ambitions in this regard we can compare Foster + Partners' magnificent dome over the British Museum Court and around the Reading Room (completed 2000) with IM Pei's relatively straightforward glass pyramid that performs a similar function at the Louvre courtyard in Paris (1989). The British Museum courtyard roof is rapidly becoming less of the exception than previously the case, being neither simplification to a convention of Cartesian coordinates set along planes and right angles nor the elegant post-Enlightenment geometrically descriptive approach by which the museum building itself would have been made. Ironically, scripting requires us to be algebraically and geometrically explicit using spatial and vectorial calculations to negotiate digitally with the computer; yet allowing these conventions to reign removes us from mathematically exciting space-warping concepts that define the glazed canopy above. This paradox is also a mark of tension: what exactly does it *mean* to be an architect today?

Lest we persuade ourselves that complexity is a goal worth striving for, a very elegant case is made for 'Simplexity' as an antedote by Sawako Kaijima and Michalatos Panagiotis:

> *Simplexity is a term in system science which describes the emergence of simplicity out of intricate and complex sets of rules.*
>
> *In recent years there is an increasing trend in architecture to exploit the ability of algorithmic design to produce complex forms by implementing relatively simple and easy formulas. This often results in the addition of unnecessary*

layers of complexity to a project just for the sake of production of seemingly more complex forms. This in turn can degenerate to computational decoration and after taking into account all the layers of information, the resulting algorithms seem little different than a complicated random number generator.

In contrast there is a whole class of algorithms that deal with simplification which are usually more complex and difficult to implement. This is partly the result of the fact that multiplication and proliferation can be easily implemented via iterative function calls and local simple operations over parts of a system.[2]

The demonstration of the strictly relative and conventional rather than absolute nature of the Cartesian coordinate system, and thus its fallibility, is a simple one. Imagine that instead of three intersecting *xy*, *xz* and *yz* planes, each of the planes is in fact a gently arced surface similarly oriented as the adjacent Cartesian planes and intersecting in the same sense at the same origin. Coordinate values given as *x*, *y*, *z* could be the same in both constructs and have the same meaning, but would the point be in the same location? It is therefore a touch risky referring to *time* as the fourth dimension, when mathematically it is not: I am certainly guilty of helping perpetuate this lazy little simplification. We should use the term 'Euclidean space'

Diagram to show the convention of Cartesian space as defined by three coordinates drawn from three intersecting surfaces (planes). If the three surfaces are not planes, the coordinate can still be defined, but without spatial meaning.

instead of 'Cartesian space',[3] and be aware that by the late 19th century mathematicians, commencing with the German Felix Klein (1849–1925), were establishing themselves for their work on non-Euclidean geometry, challenging the millennia-old hegemony (of Euclidean geometry).

We should also be aware that this is not a recent post-digital interest in the creative sector, but one that has been in the artistic consciousness since at least the early 20th century. In 1924 the Dutch artist, writer, poet and architect Theo van Doesburg (1883–1931) was quite explicit about what he saw as new potentials for architecture, as can be seen in the following extract from his manifesto *Towards a Plastic Architecture*:

> *The new architecture is open. The whole structure consists of a space that is divided in accordance with the various functional demands. This division is carried out by means of dividing surfaces (in the interior) or protective surfaces (externally). The former, which separate the various functional spaces, may be movable; that is to say, the dividing surfaces (formerly the interior walls) may be replaced by movable intermediate surfaces or panels (the same method may be employed for doors). In architecture's next phase of development the ground-plan must disappear completely. The two-dimensional spatial composition fixed in a ground-plan will be replaced by an exact constructional calculation – a calculation by means of which the supporting capacity is restricted to the simplest but strongest supporting points. For this purpose Euclidean mathematics will be of no further use – but with the aid of calculation that is non-Euclidean and takes into account the four dimensions everything will be very easy.*[4]

Is this being a little pedantic? Not if we wish to engage more seriously with the mathematics of design, and to avoid the conceptual limitations of computation framed around Cartesian data input scripted into the black box. In the following two chapters I will show that conceptually Gaudí was working multi-dimensionally beyond Euclidian space. In Chapter 9 I also consider the futility of tying the word 'dimension' to 1D *lines*, 2D *planes* and 3D *volumes* by demonstrating that we can derive situations with many more dimensions than cardinal axes. Again, how relevant is all this to architects who have both feet on the ground?

Long before I became aware of a culture clash between Euclidean and non-Euclidean space dwellers, I was happy to consider time as a fourth dimension, which it is if we think of dimensions as attributes rather than absolute spatial delineators. As an example of *dimension* being an attribute rather than a coordinate let us consider the following situation:

> *Move!* (instruction) *4 paces forward* (first dimension), *turn right at right angles!* (instruction), *3 paces forward* (second dimension), *grab the vertical ladder* (instruction), *climb 5 rungs* (third dimension), *drop off the ladder* (instruction), *measure how long it took to drop* (fourth dimension).

This is the essence of numerical control (NC), which is first-order cybernetics,[5] not Cartesian geometry *per se*. Numerical control is the data stream with which we control our fabricating machinery and is, of course, our main currency as matters stand, as it is by these means that we can fabricate our fantasies reasonably economically. Many complex fabrication tasks can now be taken on that could not have been realistically undertaken until quite recently. It is another of the several digital design paradoxes that are sprinkled throughout this primer. In this case it is the four minimum streaming data inputs that allow NC machines to work their magic: three instructions around placement (forward, right, up), and one about action (displacement in a direction) versus design computation based on mathematics and not

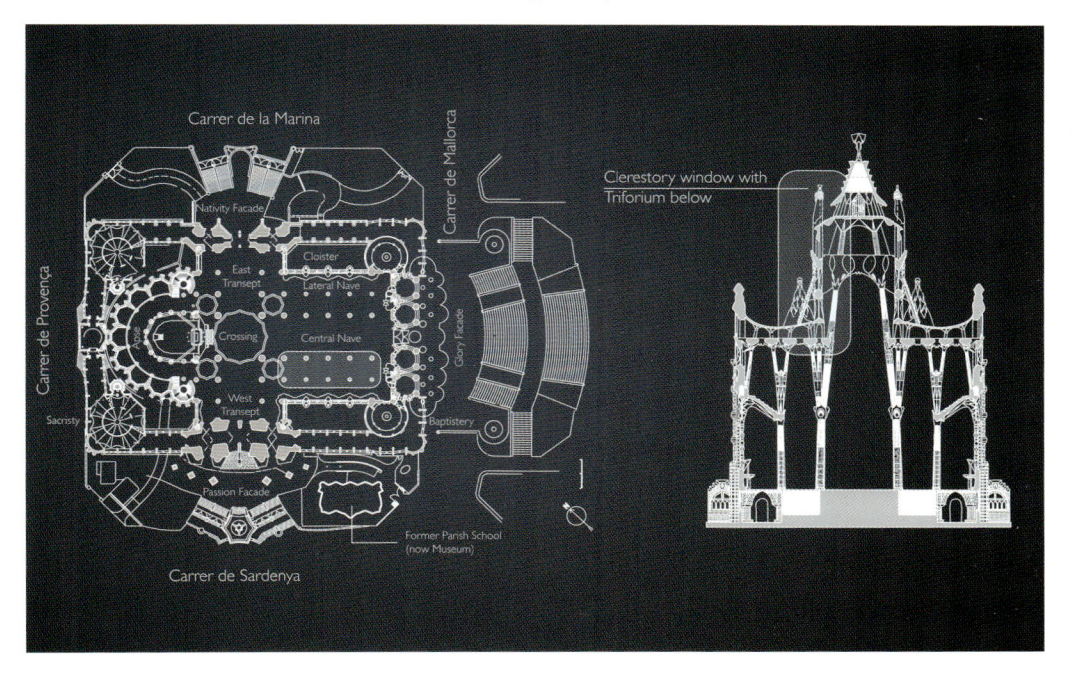

Antoni Gaudí, Sagrada Família church, Barcelona, 1882–ongoing: plan and cross section.

Antoni Gaudí, Sagrada Família church, Barcelona, 1882–ongoing: 1:25 scale model of Gaudí's final version of the nave design restored after being smashed during the 1936–9 Spanish Civil War.

the limitations of machine logic. The tension between iterations of shape, for example, without shifting location (which is animation), and iterations of shape while moving are interesting as tests for the delineation of architecture. My interest has always been drawn to architects who embrace this tension as part of their repertoire. For the rest of this chapter I am going to signal key moments along my own journey where greater architectural potential has been discovered, realised, or invoked through scripting with a 'time or displacement dimension'. In all cases, scripting has driven an important architectural advance that would not otherwise have been made.

Life, growth and granite: sequences through serial division

Antoni Gaudí, Sagrada Família church, Barcelona, 1882–ongoing: three prototype columns made by Gaudí during his last twelve years. The left-hand column is the earliest version, a single helical rotation. The other two are two counter-rotated helical columns, the mid one a Boolean union, and the right-hand one a Boolean intersection.

In 1991 I started to look at the computational logic behind the geometry of Gaudí's columns for the nave. We know from comments captured by his young colleagues on site that he conceived the entire volume of the Sagrada Família church as being inside a forest with the nave ceiling a great canopy soaring 45 metres overhead formed from tree branches, fronds and leaves supported by great stone trunks: slender columns all leaning axially into their load paths. The crossing, the central part of the church where the main body, the nave, intersects with the transept spaces on either side, completed and finally cleared of scaffolding in 2010, appears as a woodland clearing 60 metres above the altar.

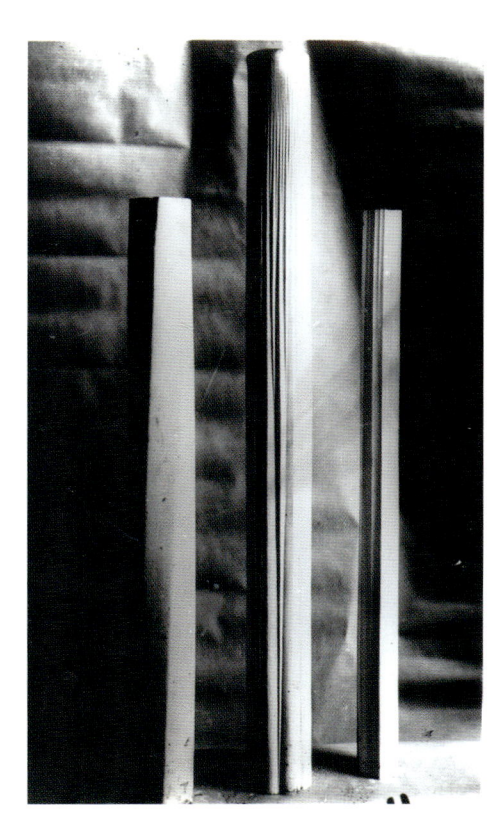

Gaudí himself never saw any of this beyond a large 1:10 scaled model of the nave, but at that scale he considered every detail, not least the columns. When the nave columns are studied closely, they appear as remarkable hybrids, or amalgams at least, referring to both Greek and Gothic column language: Doric in part due to the characteristic Greek-order fluting emerging halfway up, and organicist too especially at their bases. The term organicist is appropriate both philosophically in terms of the tree-scape metaphor being read as an organic whole, and in the biological sense when we see the base of the trees as a system rather than an artful composition. When it came to building the first column as a prototype in the 1960s, before the wonders of today's CNC machinery, the approach taken was based on a model fragment that had survived the rigours of the Spanish Civil War, when Gaudí's former studio on site was trashed and burned. This particular 1:25 scaled model has cross section zinc templates along its length at every metre equivalent – 40 millimitres actual size, with the column surfaces interpolated between each horizontal template. Unfortunately, in my opinion, the model read in the way I have just described suggests a different explanation from what was probably in

Mark Burry   Chapter 5 Dimensions

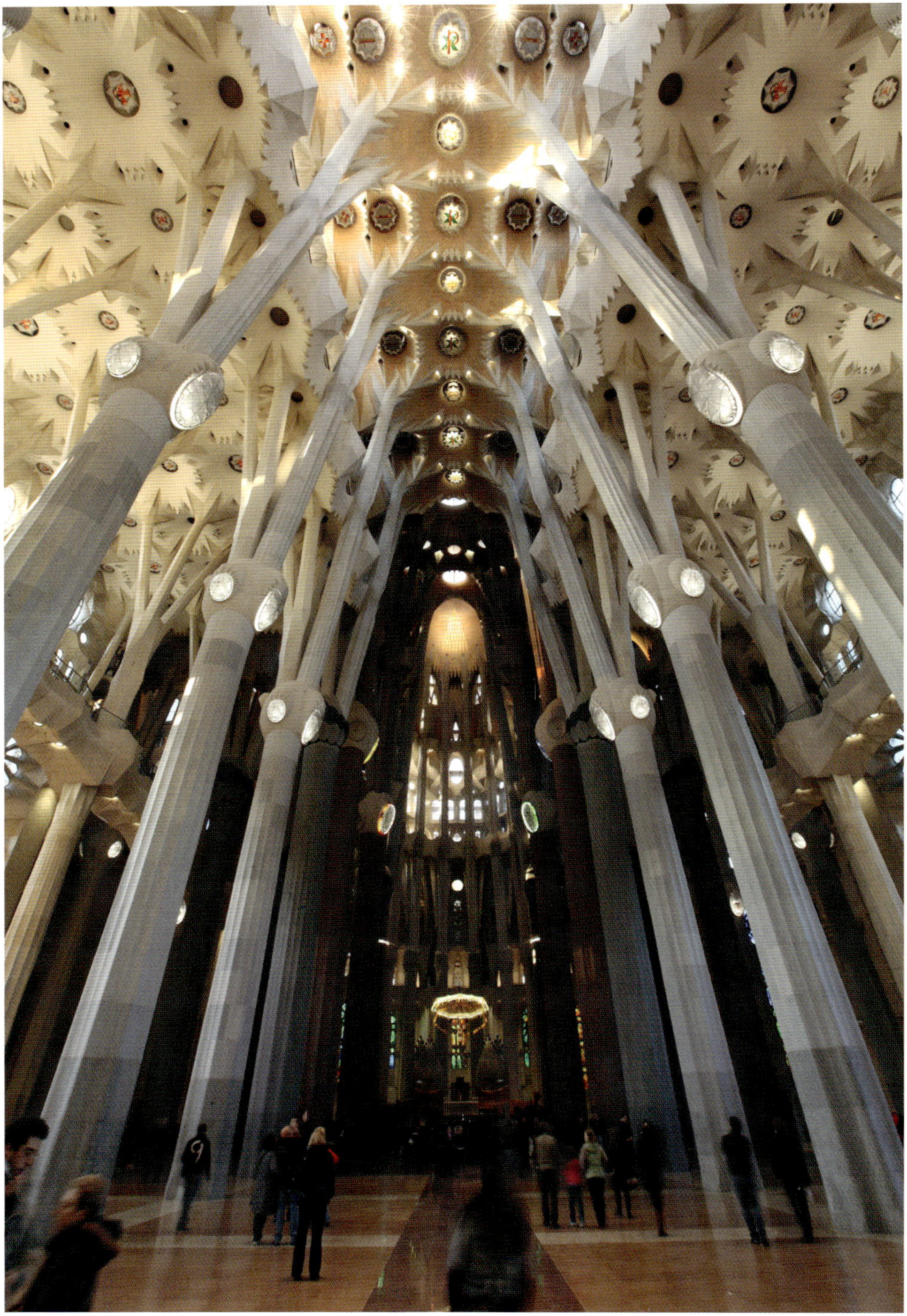

Antoni Gaudí, Sagrada Familia church, Barcelona, 1882–ongoing: view of the nave close to completion (2011).

Antoni Gaudí, Sagrada Familia church, Barcelona, 1882–ongoing: view of the apse ceiling vaults nearing completion (2010).

Antoni Gaudí, Sagrada Familia church, Barcelona, 1882–ongoing: view of the nave close to completion (2010).

Gaudí's mind, for initially the column has been conceptually unpicked from this model, built as a prototype, and then extrapolated into a *modus operandi* for the subsequent automated cutting. This has had no adverse effect on the viability of the column as an object, but until we could script an alternative story, it proved to be very difficult for some commentators to conceptualise what was really going on. Gaudí had in fact invested the column's morphogenesis with a natural life story.[6]

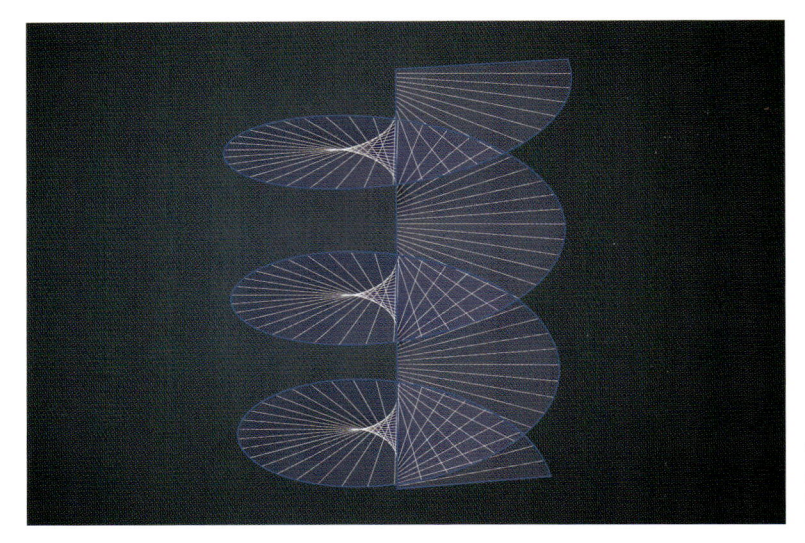

The helicoid, a ruled surface and the conceptual base of all Gaudí's columns designed in his final years.

Using mathematical parlance, the conceptual route to the completed column form is a Boolean intersection of two solids. Taking the main columns for instance, the two constituent solids are sticks of barley sugar, Solomonic – twisted just a few degrees clockwise for one, and anticlockwise for the other. When superimposed the columns share the same profiles at their bases. As they rise in height they rotationally twist in the opposite senses to each other until eventually their profiles intersect again. We will call this one phase. Gaudí arrests the process at half phase, a point where the columns have twisted around as far from each other's path as possible, at a point from where they start to swing back in if the rotation continues unabated. At this arrested midpoint the profile shows the characteristic Doric serrations. Here Gaudí now conceives the base profile as being directly re-implicated.

This is clearly about displacement as the fourth dimension; let us consider the description of the generation of the column slightly differently. The curvy organic profile at the base is formed from cotangent concave and convex parabolas. Conceptually, these profiles ascend the column counter rotating with respect to each other as they rise. At any point of the displacement, the actual column profile at that position is the intersection of the two counter-rotated base profiles – the bounded surfaces common to each. At the point that the rotational symmetry is halted exactly out of phase, the two profiles now have to duplicate such that we have the two existing profiles continuing on their path, and the two new duplicates

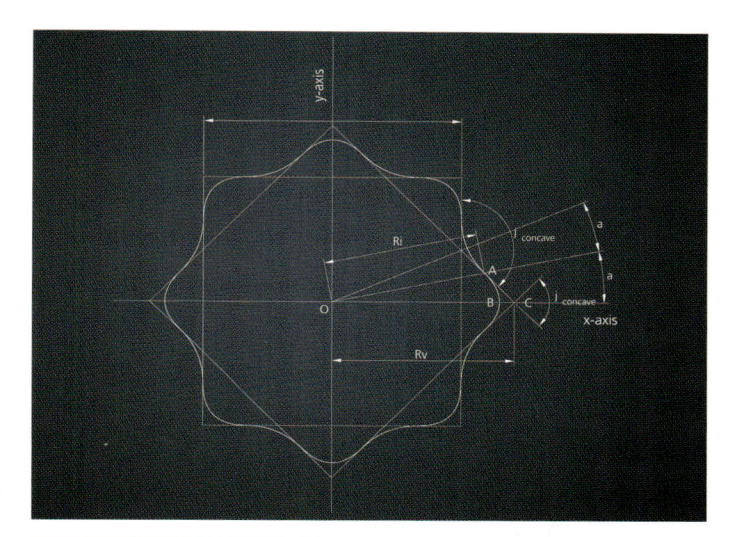

Base section profile for eight-sided nave column for Antoni Gaudí's Sagrada Família church, Barcelona, showing cotangent concave and convex parabolas.

Overlaid horizontal section profiles for 8-sided nave column at 1-metre intervals, for Antoni Gaudí's Sagrada Família church, Barcelona.

counter-rotating back in the opposite direction until the next mid-phase point: four similar profiles all exactly out of phase with each other. This occurs at half the height of the original event. The four profiles then duplicate to make eight, and so the process continues at half the last rise, a quarter of the original, at which point they duplicate to make sixteen in total. For the central nave columns (made from granite), the heights are as follows: 8 metres before the two profiles become four, a further 4 metres

6-points inside two equilateral triangles

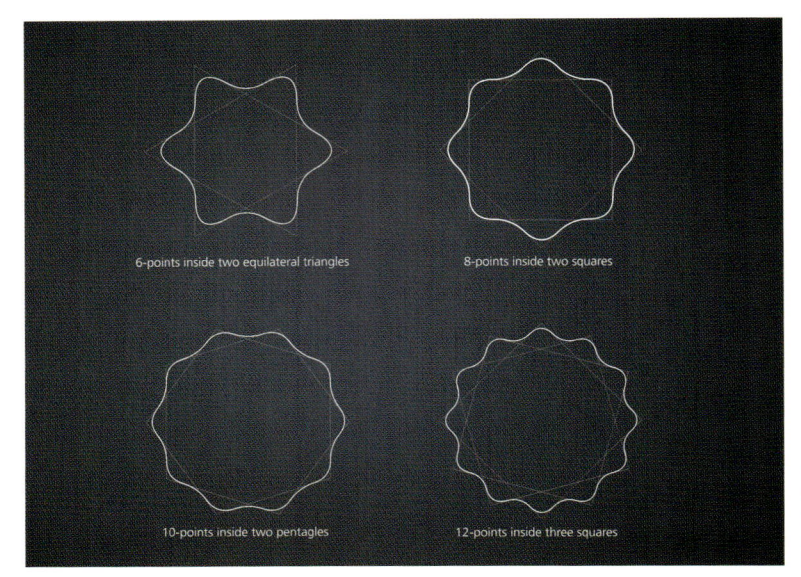

8-points inside two squares

10-points inside two pentagles

12-points inside three squares

Base section profiles for the four different column types at nave floor level in Antoni Gaudí's Sagrada Família church, Barcelona.

Section profiles taken through eight-sided column at 1-metre intervals, for Antoni Gaudí's Sagrada Família church, Barcelona.

for the eight profiles, and another 2 metres before there are sixteen, at the top. There is no need here to labour the parallel to morphogenesis and cell division cycles. The same life game is being played higher up in the volume of the church whether the columns have a square, rectangular or any other shape as their progenitor profile.

We have to build what Gaudí has designed with unequivocal interpreted fidelity and accuracy in terms of its physicality. With no written record made by Gaudí, how we interpret this intellectually is entirely up to the individual. Joan Bergós (1894–1974), an architect and artist who collaborated with Gaudí in these last years and who subsequently wrote several influential books about Gaudí and about his own experience visiting the Sagrada Família church, quotes Gaudí as having stated:

> Man's intelligence can only act in one plane, with two dimensions. He can solve equations with one unknown, of the first degree. The angels' intelligence is three dimensional, acting directly in space. Man cannot act until he has been

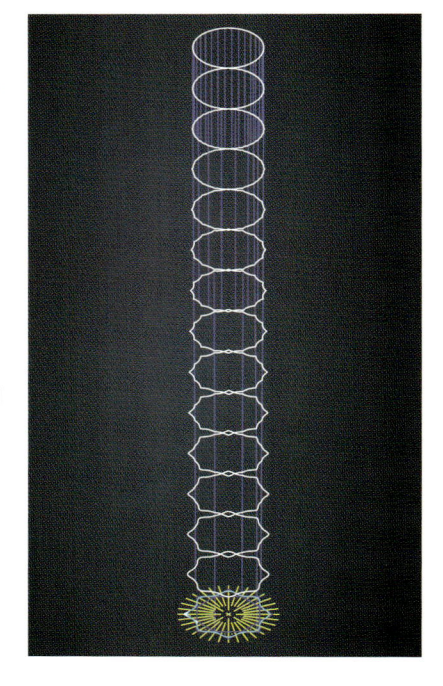

presented with the whole fact: at the outset, he can only follow paths, lines on a plane.[7]

The multi-dimensional qualities of the column, the product of Gaudí's uniquely creative mind, would by his own definition place him in the realm of the angels. The various attempts made in print to reveal all the intellectual and spatial qualities of the column that otherwise elude ready analysis can be brought together more effectively in one single visual environment: multimedia.

Scripting the narrative outlined above seems crucial if we are to animate the sequence and afford more general intelligibility. This story cannot to be told any other way, and even a video of the model-making machine (invented by the model makers on site after Gaudí's death) apparently defeats clear interpretation of the game being played by some who watch it in use.

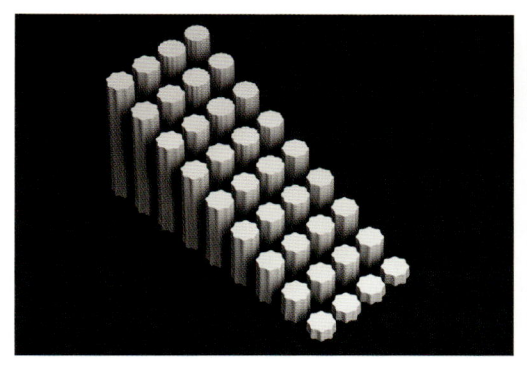

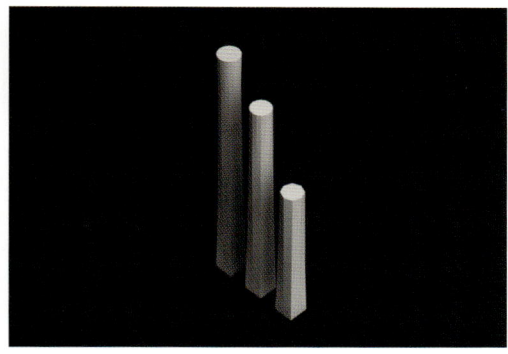

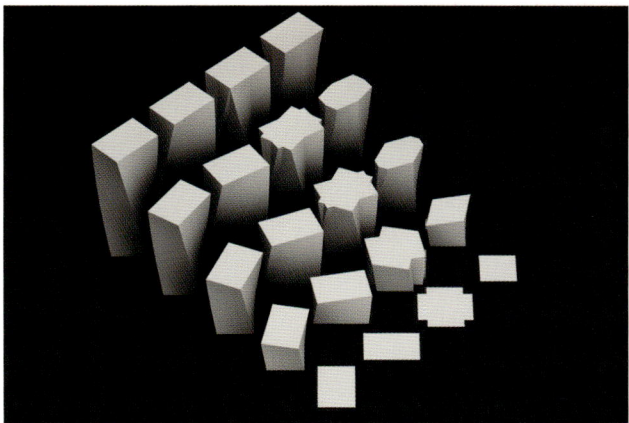

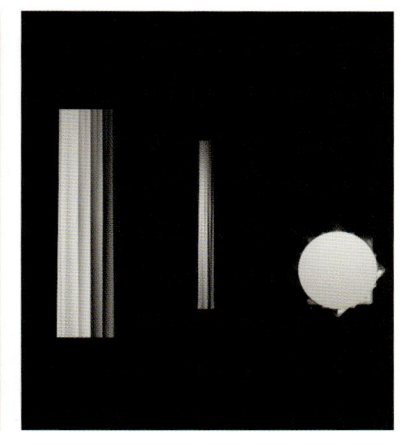

Eight-sided, square and rectangular column types showing generation through intersection of two counter-rotated helical 'barley twist' columns.

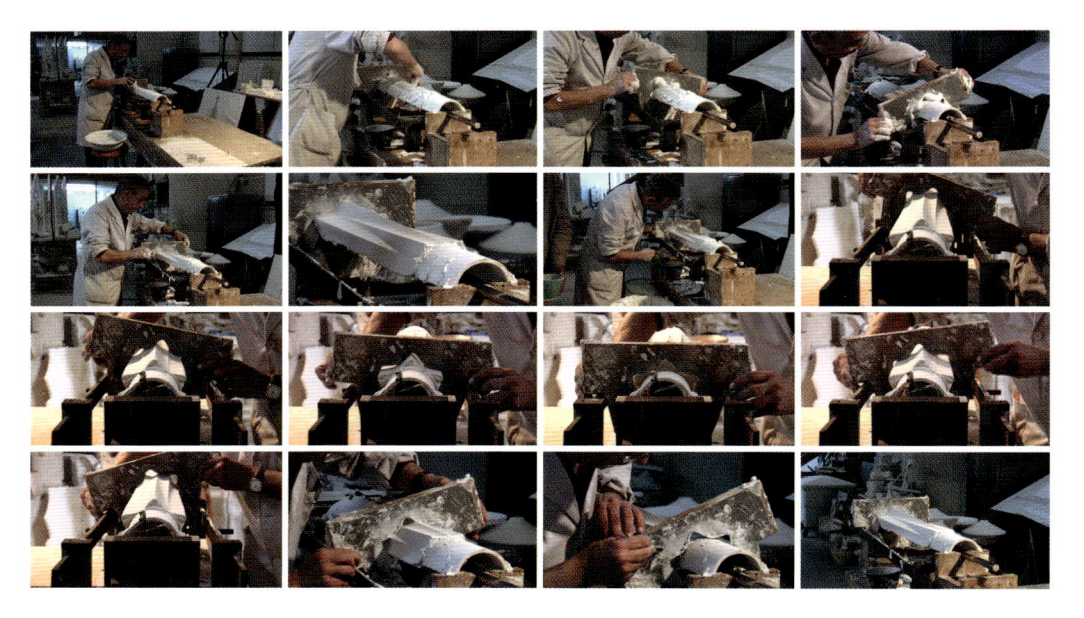

Whether we counter-rotate two profiles made from different-coloured Perspex revealing their evolving intersections against the light, or watch master craftspeople make the column from gypsum plaster using a device of their own invention, or watch video, or interact with a computer animation, or pore over drawings, each experience can be shown to be incomplete in itself, begging for the column to be studied *in situ*.

Series of stills showing the analogue technique for making the columns for Antoni Gaudí's Sagrada Família church, Barcelona, from gypsum plaster. The column takes approximately an hour to emerge from the counter-rotations of the base profile.

Paramorph: scripting and parametric design software

My adventures in the Sagrada Família church design studio have led to various probings of software for their potential to help unlock Gaudí's secrets. From 1991 I became aware of parametric design software for vehicle design through Dr Robert Aish, who worked then for Intergraph, based in Paris. Unfortunately, nothing remotely resembling this software existed in the architectural sector, and in 1992 I gained access to Computervision's CADDS5™, with its powerful parametric design engine. I was able to deploy it very successfully, and in a hybrid relationship with scripting overlays. It was a very useful medium for helping us drill down to viable design solutions with respect to Gaudí's posthumous challenges. What, I began to wonder, would be the creative spin-off from this pathway?

With the work at the Sagrada Família church, the parametric design software was being called upon to create through interpretation. I was interested in learning about creating through generation.

With 'parametricism' currently being elevated to a style and orthodoxy, I will pause briefly to explain what parametric software is, and how it differs from more typical 'explicit design' software from my perspective as 'early adopter'. With the latter, explicit design, the designer makes their model as they would in any traditional medium. Any change to the model requires erasure and remodelling whether it is with pad and pen or via CAD. With a parametric model every entity in the model (points, lines, etc) have links between their location in the software's database and their visualisation via the monitor. Parametric software allows the user to identify a line visually, for instance, and in doing so its length will be declared such that the user can interact directly with that information. All entities in the design are logically connected when they are related, so in changing the length of a line, the ramifications of this change update the rest of the model. I suspect this is what architects thought they would be working with when they first heard about CAD, but it is only in recent years that it has begun to be accessible for those who wish to experiment with it.

In our postgraduate research studio at RMIT University's SIAL today, we now dub the parametric model the 'flexible model', because we are able parametrically to adjust its dimensions and, if there is a viable solution, a new

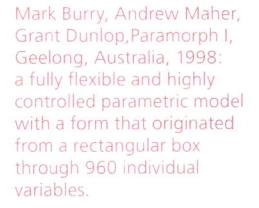

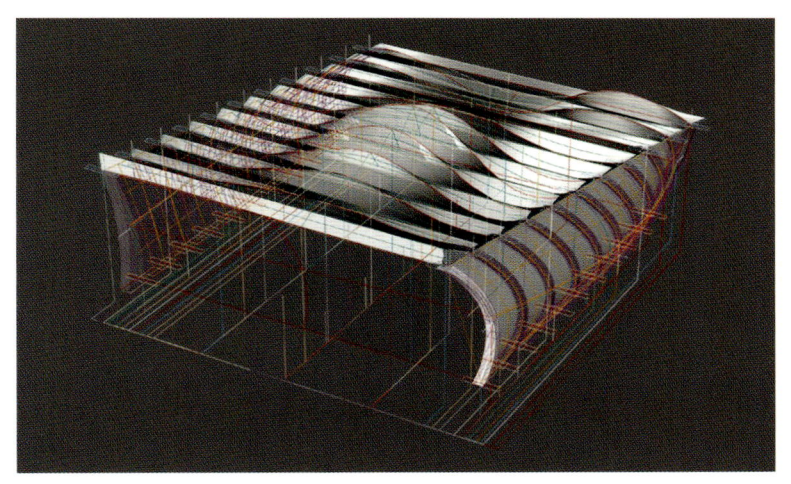

Mark Burry, Andrew Maher, Grant Dunlop, Paramorph I, Geelong, Australia, 1998: a fully flexible and highly controlled parametric model with a form that originated from a rectangular box through 960 individual variables.

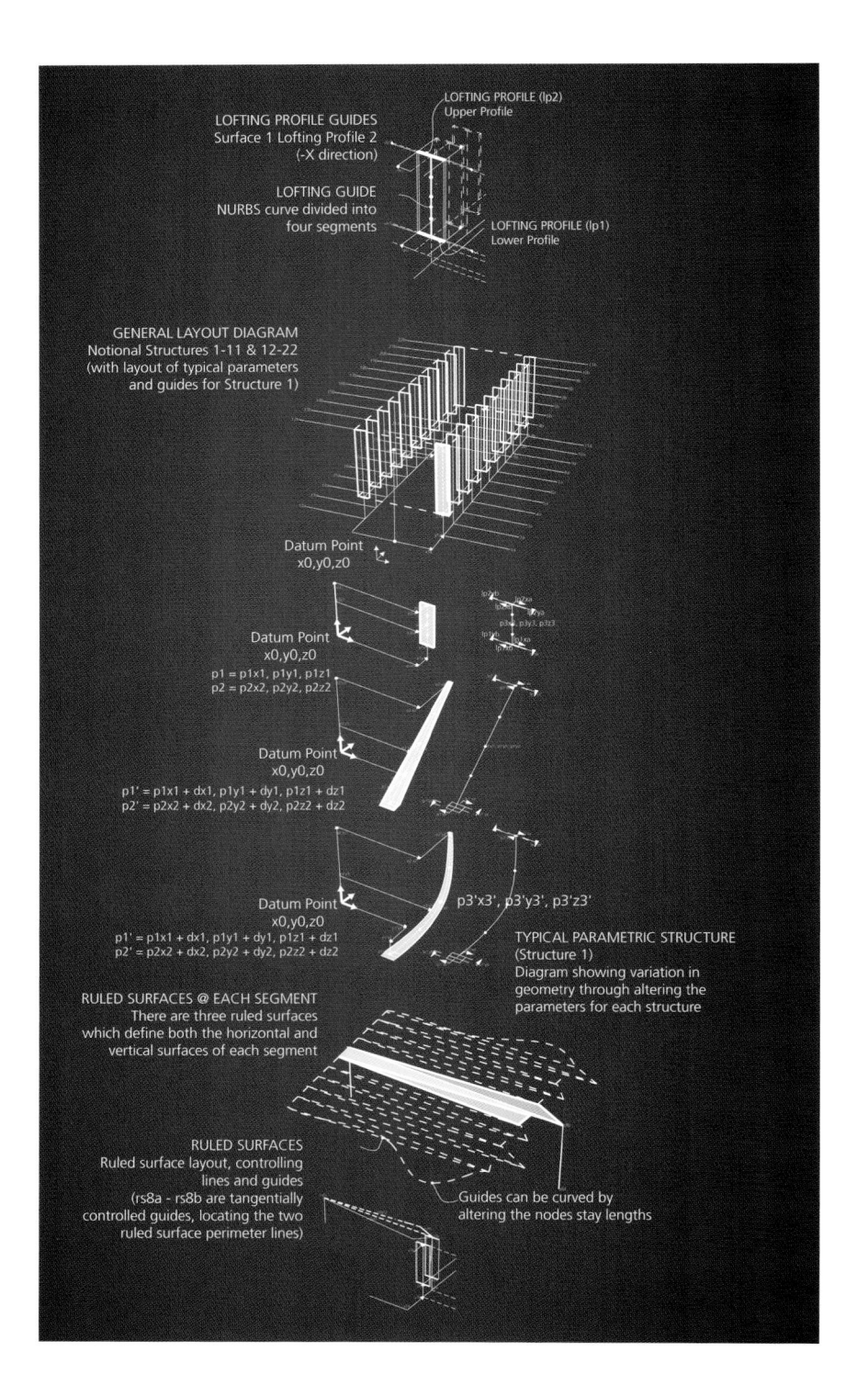

LOFTING PROFILE GUIDES
Surface 1 Lofting Profile 2
(-X direction)

LOFTING PROFILE (lp2)
Upper Profile

LOFTING GUIDE
NURBS curve divided into
four segments

LOFTING PROFILE (lp1)
Lower Profile

GENERAL LAYOUT DIAGRAM
Notional Structures 1-11 & 12-22
(with layout of typical parameters
and guides for Structure 1)

Datum Point
x0,y0,z0

Datum Point
x0,y0,z0

$p1 = p1x1, p1y1, p1z1$
$p2 = p2x2, p2y2, p2z2$

Datum Point
x0,y0,z0

$p1' = p1x1 + dx1, p1y1 + dy1, p1z1 + dz1$
$p2' = p2x2 + dx2, p2y2 + dy2, p2z2 + dz2$

Datum Point
x0,y0,z0

$p1' = p1x1 + dx1, p1y1 + dy1, p1z1 + dz1$
$p2' = p2x2 + dx2, p2y2 + dy2, p2z2 + dz2$

$p3'x3', p3'y3', p3'z3'$

TYPICAL PARAMETRIC STRUCTURE
(Structure 1)
Diagram showing variation in
geometry through altering the
parameters for each structure

RULED SURFACES @ EACH SEGMENT
There are three ruled surfaces
which define both the horizontal and
vertical surfaces of each segment

RULED SURFACES
Ruled surface layout, controlling
lines and guides
(rs8a - rs8b are tangentially
controlled guides, locating the two
ruled surface perimeter lines)

Guides can be curved by
altering the nodes stay lengths

Mark Burry, Andrew Maher, Grant Dunlop, Paramorph I, Geelong, Australia 1998: diagram showing the key variables for Paramorph I.

Mark Burry, Andrew Maher, Grant Dunlop, Paramorph I: 14 relaxation variants of Paramorph I, Geelong, Australia, 1998. The relaxations can be taken forwards and backwards passing the design intention 'test of repeatability'.

version is born; a version of the original. To maintain the biomimetic line of thought, the flexible starting model can be taken as the genotype, and the resulting versions as phenotypes. In those days (1997), each model variant had perforce the same topology, but changing topography, as the original. In search of a name to describe each variant we came up with *paramorph* at our postgraduate research studio at Deakin University where we were based at the time, and we still use the term today.[8]

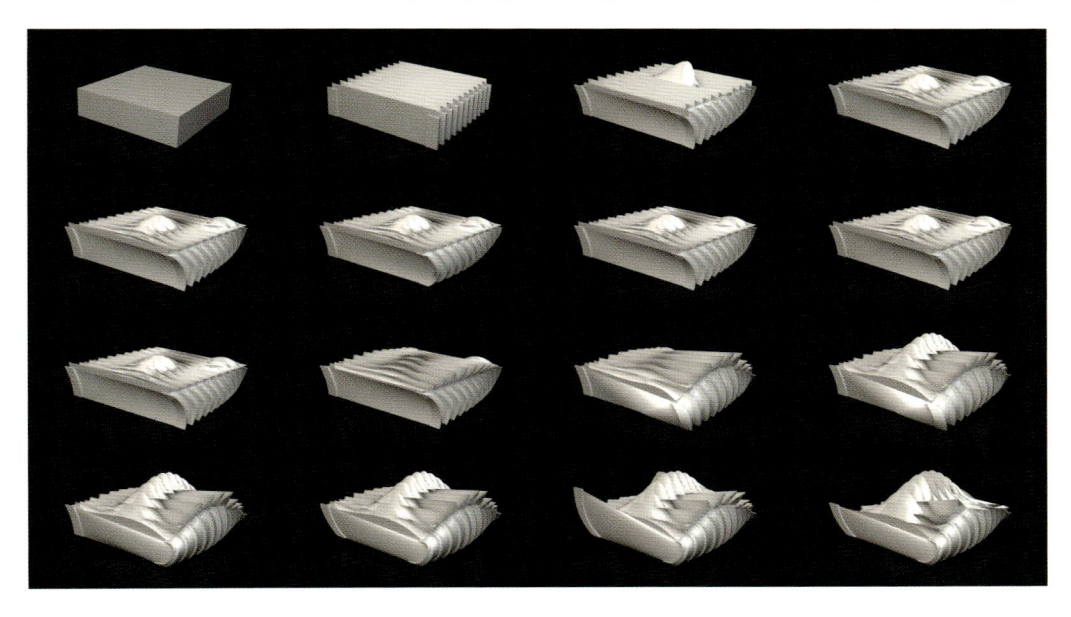

In that studio we devised *Paramorph I*, a 'dumb box' starter for a paramorph-based thought experiment, through which all 960 parametrically linked dimensions could be relaxed into all sorts of configurations at a time when such reconfiguration would have taken weeks by any other means, not just the matter of minutes our flexible model could be reconfigured in. Some very interesting implications for the use of creative parametric design software emerged from this experiment: without a scripting overlay, parametric design can be quite tedious in practice. For engineers wanting to change the size and position of a slot in a bracket, for example, being able to click on the respective parameters shown on screen as dimensions, constants or values, and change them is very appealing for its interactivity. To reform our dumb box, it was possible that we might require changing all 960 parameters and, naturally, scripting the changes came much more readily than clicking individually on all these parametric dimensions on screen, one by one. Apart from any other consideration, calculations would be useful such as bending the plan to a given curve.

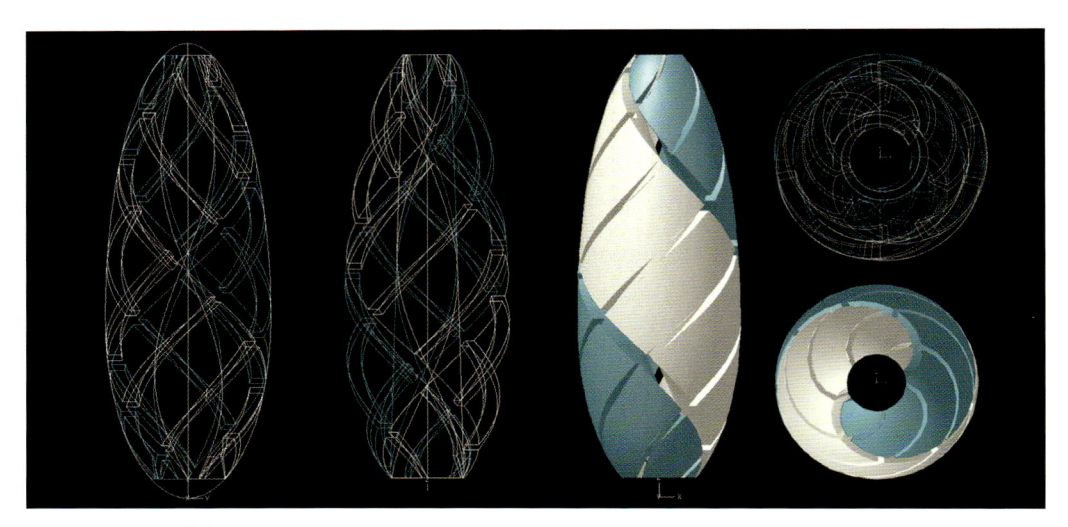

From that point on, my interest in parametric design software has been contingent on how well each package allows the user to use a scripting overlay, as this seems an essential ingredient to ensure a proper insinuation of designer intent into its use. Some packages manage this better than others. This position was tested when I contributed to the early-stage design of the Swiss Re London headquarters tower in 1998. Foster +Partners had been physically modelling their concept for the tower building with its circular plan and highly original elongated egg-shaped sectional profile. Each iteration was appearing as elaborate table-high physical models, taking many weeks to prepare. I was asked to test whether a parametric model would perform the same role in searching for the optimal shape. I believe that it was a demonstration of this facility of being able to adjust the egg profile through a scripted formula that encouraged the practice to focus more on digitally based design research. Foster + Partners' Specialist Modelling Group (SMG) has been at the vanguard of intelligently scripted enquiry ever since, and they remain among the most skilled advocates of the coupled analogue and digital architectural design dialogue within mainstream practice.

Intriguingly, Gaudí used an approach akin to the paramorph as part of his strategy to explain the projects to his future unknown successors.

Mark Burry, Foster + Partners, Swiss Re, London, 1997–2004: parametric design study to inform the early design process (2008) – a test of concept for a parametric approach to software use.

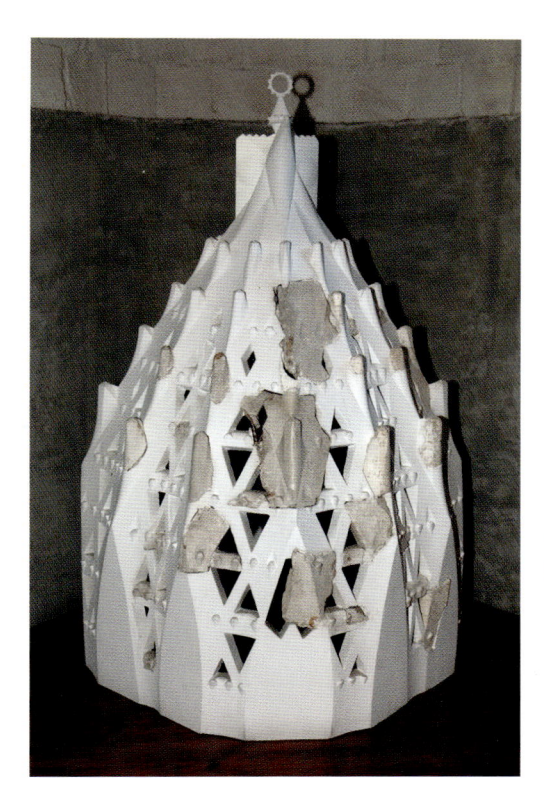

The drawings (destroyed but surviving as published prints at least) show his schema for the remainder of the building and are clear expressions of his general intentions. As such they would not be enough to provide sufficient detail in order to proceed with the same level of confidence were it not for their vital complement: a model of a prototypical cupola. Scaled at 1:25, and with the geometry inscribed medievally on a polished slab of limestone, this model is parametrically variable in shape and size to inform all the towers and cupolas that remain to be built.

Aegis Hyposurface: surface perturbation algorithms

My collaboration with dECOi Architects also began around this time, when I met Paris-based Mark Goulthorpe (currently based at MIT) at the 1997 biennial architecture student conference hosted by my school of architecture at Deakin University in Geelong. Possibly the most demanding project of the many on which I collaborated with him was his response to an invited competition from the Birmingham Hippodrome Theatre in the UK in 1999. The competition commissioners called for an art piece to adorn a large wall that soared out from the building above the passers-by below, and Mark's response was to propose that the wall itself become the subject, rather than simply the substrate to support a sculpture. Whatever was proposed, the intervention was required to respond in some way to the theatre's interior activities. I joined the project at this point: the challenges of making the wall respond to sensors placed inside the building. Whereas an artwork with lights going on and off would minimally answer the brief, making the wall fibrillate madly in response to wild applause, or shiver in ecstasy each time the cash register rang seemed far more appropriate, inspiring a journey that still resonates over a decade later.

What is a surface disturbance?

Antoni Gaudí, Sagrada Família church, Barcelona, 1882–ongoing: Gaudí's 1:25 scale model for the sacristies first appearing in a photograph in 1923. This cupola is the paramorph from which all the central towers were to be derived.

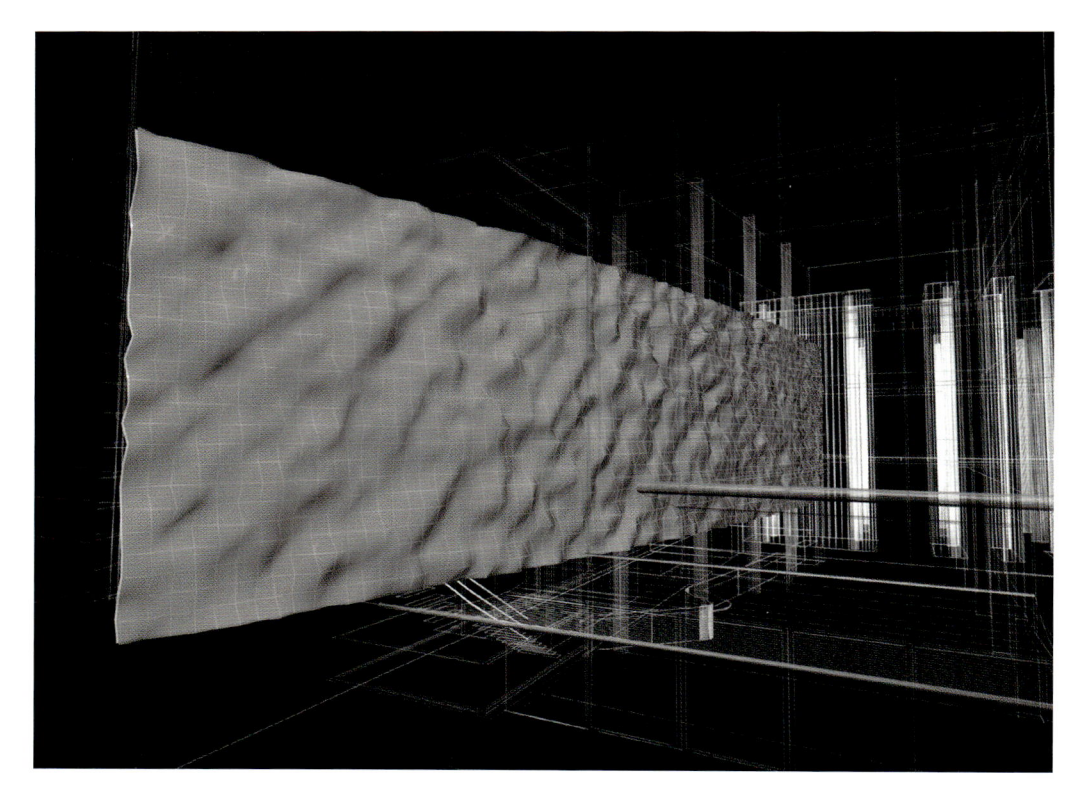

To make a convincing case for the concept, a multimedia presentation with a series of animations at its centre was composed, and the team Goulthorp assembled around the project pointed to a different kind of architectural practice ever since. Firstly, there were the mathematician professors from UCL in London, Keith Ball and Alex Scott, who offered the perturbation algorithms that are the base function for the necessary surface displacements – the fourth dimension parameter that would make the wall come to life on cue. I was party to some extraordinary architect–mathematician dialogues where each tried to explain in plain English what they meant from the confines of their own discipline language. It turns out that there are very few types of perturbation in the front line of opportunity: circular waves as formed when a stone lands in a pond, standing waves as we see at the beach, sprites as vector-based waves such as a boat leaves in its wake, and planar tilting and folding. The individual formulae were passed on to Peter Wood, a programmer and engineer based

dECOi Architects, Aegis Hyposurface™: extract from the competition-winning entry for an exterior art project to be located outside the Birmingham Hippodrome Theatre UK, Hanover, 2000.

in Wellington, New Zealand who made a series of deformation routines to be used with AutoCAD™ as AutoLISP code snippets.

My role was to assemble the snippets as a single script that would generate sufficient frames to make compelling animations of the wall in action. This I have likened to digital choreography, and it led to a fascinating set of discoveries. Principal among these was learning about the nature of disturbance, for to get a narrative to unfold I had to get each effect to propagate interactions with each other, effectively to create disturbances.

dECOi Architects, Aegis Hyposurface™: looking at and behind the skin of Aegis Hyposurface™, on display and functioning at the CeBIT IT fair, Hanover, 2001.

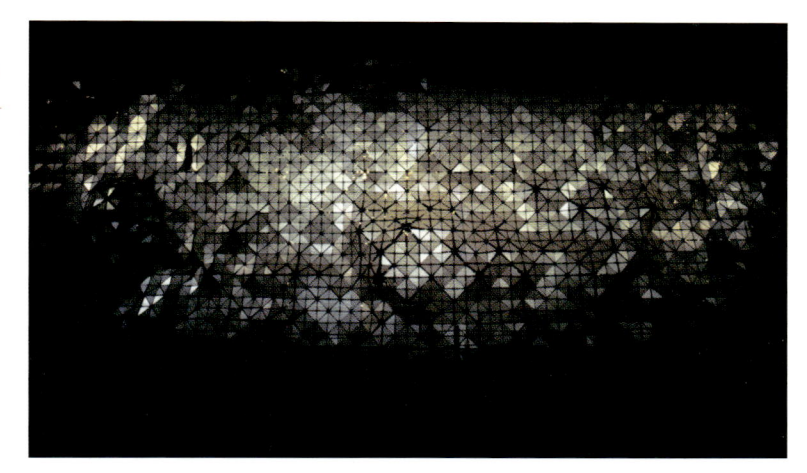

The only time the placid surface arced up was when effects with completely different parameters were invoked, ran into each other and argued, sometimes strenuously, sometimes with subtlety.

At its most simple, this type of outcome could be foreseen as each effect was individually propagated, but not the vigour of the interaction between the engagements. The inspirational leap came when I discovered that if each effect was given an independent trajectory, away from one another, belief became temporarily suspended. What would otherwise not have seemed especially unfamiliar – watching a fast-flowing river, for instance – became otherworldly as the various effects failed to move in concert with an underlying current, but were, in fact, doing quite the opposite. I remember tinkering with the various scripts for many hours tuning the effects to a desired result, aware that without scripting and animation none of what I describe would have been possible.

dECOi won the competition, but Aegis Hyposurface™, as it was christened, never made it to its original destination. Various prototypes have appeared

dECOi Architects, Aegis Hyposurface™: looking at the skin of Aegis Hyposurface™, on display at the CeBIT IT Fair, Hanover, 2001.

in the intervening years, the first of which went on public display at CeBIT in Hanover, 2001. It measured 10 metres wide by 3.5 metres high, and responded in real time to light, movement and sound sensors. Over the years Goulthorpe has found more sound collaborators, the mathematicians have contributed ever more intriguing algorithms, the interface engineers greater degrees of freedom and control, and so the project lives on.

Digital landscapes and tectonics

My design research into surface disturbance reached its peak at the same time as the more widely held architectural interest in form was at its most intense. What had become my fascination with displacement, disturbance and disruption extended into the philosophical implications digital craft was beginning to have on all that had immediately preceded it, not least the Modern Movement, vestiges of which were still being referenced by the practice giants of yore. There was a sense of being in an emerging dilemma as it was difficult to discern the extent to which digital capability was setting the agenda, with the tail potentially wagging the dog.

More senior practices resolutely stuck to traditional ways of working with their tried and tested sensibilities. Others, such as Gehry Partners, led through

Mille-feuille, Melbourne, 2002: interwoven layers of virtual pastry.

3 metals, Melbourne, 2002: digital perplications showing three metals interweaving in a manner virtually impossible to achieve physically.

their design with digital capability being coaxed along only as part of the journey. Foster + Partners responded subtly to the emerging opportunities, and relatively young practices such as Greg Lynn FORM and dECOi made digital design thinking into sets of guiding principles. I was curious about the situation as an academic heavily committed to the effort to complete the Sagrada Família church. It seemed to me that almost a century earlier Gaudí had set up many of the 'new' problems that digerati were now engaging with, as if they were exclusively of our time; meanwhile students were producing wild and wonderful cyberspace constructions that were difficult to locate critically.

The 'art of the accident' came back into vogue, but it was hard not to perceive at least part of that as a post-rationalist response to intriguing studio outcomes rather than being a genuine philosophically argued belief. For me, the essential digital design ingredient was to capture design intentionality, as I have mentioned in an earlier chapter. Scripting not only forces the scripter who commences with a blank sheet to come clean (as opposed to the adopter of the script who launches someone else's code to see what happens), it also forces a design to be logically deconstructed in order to be encoded. There may well be accidental effects along the way, some even useful, but the essential value of scripting appeared as the ability to pass the test of repeatability, which is why I personally have difficulty with chucking in a random function in order to spice up the mix. In darker moments I try to image Gaudí, for instance, resorting to the random function, but then surprisingly, he was a reactionary.

I like working parametrically to a point, because of the way the designer can move backwards and forwards. For this to happen with random intervention taking place, multiple versions need to be retained just in case the design goes irrecoverably wayward en route. Scripting offers the same authority over the design too as it can be run and rerun until a result emerges that satisfies whatever criteria are being applied or, through its use, modifications to the script are suggested in operation that can be enacted subsequently. The

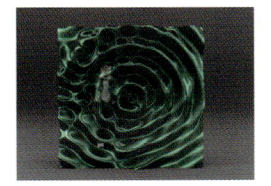

3 satin sheets, Melbourne, 2002: three sheets interwoven in a way that would not be practical in the physical world.

trouble, it struck me, was the facility with which we can now dabble in the surreal, hyperreal, and unreal arenas. While painters and trick photographers could simulate within this arena previously, they could never do so with the same facility as the digital dexterity now afforded. The same surface algorithms that had initiated the effects being sought with the hyposurface discussed above I found could be used for many other purposes. Digital terrains could be experimented with, landscapes of the subconscious could be evoked as Deleuzian perplications (by this I mean that meaningful surfaces could be simulated, hyperreal in their representation but utterly impossible to make out of materials).[9] Materials could be represented with photographic realism as being visually credible but impossible artifice in the physical world.

Columns of the Passion Facade

Gaudí drew his design for the Passion Facade for the Sagrada Família church as early as 1917, nine years before he died. The Passion Facade is the end of the west transept, one of the two arms of the church plan that extends away from the centre of the church (the crossing), and at right angles to the main body of the building, the nave. When I say 'drew', this is a euphemism, as it was in fact a multimedia production of its day including ink, charcoal, pencil

Antoni Gaudi, Sagrada Família church, Barcelona, 1882–ongoing: photograph of scale drawing by Gaudí for the Passion Facade, worked on several times between 1911 and 1917 (original drawing does not survive).

and gouache according to the accounts of his colleagues. The drawing does not survive but a fine detail photographic plate does. This has become the sole source of information on Gaudí's specific design intent, although there are highly detailed ways of working with particular geometries, some of which I explore in the next two chapters.

The construction of the facade proceeds today as I write, but the realisation of its design post-Gaudí has occurred in three phases: several decades of prior study by colleagues based on site, scripted sketches as a means to develop the design rationale, and a mathematically driven fully parametricised design model. In this chapter, the story of the middle phase of 'scripted sketching' is explained in some detail.

The benefits of knowing Gaudí's complete oeuvre in fine detail, and his working practice equally well for the last twelve years of his life, have led to an excellent apprenticeship in the amalgamation of analogue and digital design practice over my three decades of involvement. Post digitally I still start with a hand sketch with pencil on paper, even though my attitude to scripting is also resolutely in the sketching domain. Opportunities for design sketching using proprietary parametric design software are improving rapidly, but in 2001 when our design research studio began the design studies for this part of the building, such facility was not immediately apparent, and the relative facility then of the hand sketch prevailed.

In terms of finding a fourth dimension of displacement as per the nave columns described above, our starting material, the photograph of the original drawing, appeared not to offer too many clues. At best, through the powerful chiaroscuro effects that Gaudí wrought on his drawing, there was at least a 2 ½ D story to be extracted, as he had used shadow with good effect. The facade faces west and is designed to be viewed at its most compelling during sunset, and his drawing gives a strong hint of how the effect of the low setting sun angles were to be exploited. The facade as a whole had been thought through quite extensively by former colleagues, not least because the transept to which it is attached was completed in 1978 along with the lower half of the façade, the portico formed from six soaring inclined columns. Our challenge has been the upper half, the narthex, and my account here deals only with the development of the column prototype.

Valiant efforts had been made to form the columns previously, with a quest to combine two of the three second-order surfaces that Gaudí used to complete his design, the hyperbolic paraboloid and the hyperboloid of revolution, both of which are described in detail in the next chapter. The hyperboloid of revolution is a surface that we are familiar seeing in the form of power station cooling towers. Hyperbolic paraboloids are the doubly curved surfaces of horses' saddles and abundant in nature, for instance the webs between our fingers when we stretch them out. The characteristic that they have in common is that they can be described by

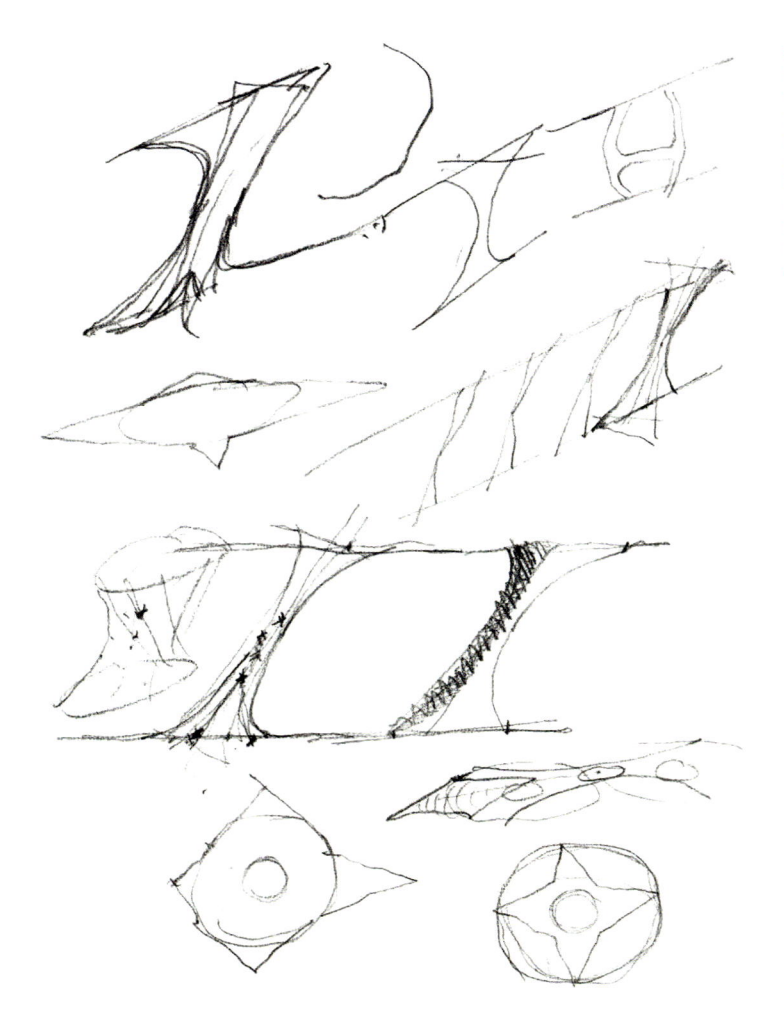

Mark Burry, 2001 sketch for the Passion Facade narthex of Antoni Gaudí's Sagrada Família church, Barcelona, interpreting possible combinations of hyperbolic paraboloids and a hyperboloid of revolution as column shaft, towards a solution very difficult to achieve without scripting.

a straight line moving through space following two vectors that are not coplanar. Working manually with gypsum plaster over several decades, the various versions of the columns seemed to have become ever more convoluted in an effort to match the apparent asymmetry between the 18 constituent columns that form the narthex. It seemed a good moment to attempt to simplify the arrangement.

The principal question here was focused on the art–sculpture–architecture interface: were these columns in the sculptor's court (Joan Subirach's), or the architect's? As principal architectonic components, this was not a particularly difficult question to answer. For the work to fall into the domain of the architect, however, certain of Gaudí's late working practices provided the guiding principle on how to proceed. This entailed treating the column (along with the rest of the narthex other than the associated sculpture) as an organicist system, which naturally brought scripting to the fore. The hypothetical question we asked was: 'Working within Gaudí's established procedures, what could he have done using the computer that would not otherwise have been possible?' An answer was very simple in concept and physical outcome, but very complex in between. Here is a brief account of that simplexified complexity.

The columns are an amalgam of a tall svelte hyperboloid of revolution with four hyperbolic paraboloids each at the top and bottom. Two of the straight lines that form the boundaries of each of the eight hyperbolic paraboloids (directrices) can coincide with selected straight lines on the surfaces of the hyperboloid of revolution (generatrices). There are an infinite number of possibilities if we parametrically vary the characteristics of both geometries,

Mark Burry, 2004 schema for the Passion Facade narthex of Antoni Gaudí's Sagrada Família church, Barcelona, with which to brief mathematicians and programmers to facilitate computational design.

Schematic model for the Passion Facade narthex of Antoni Gaudí's Sagrada Família church, Barcelona, showing the intention for all intersecting surfaces to be straight lines.

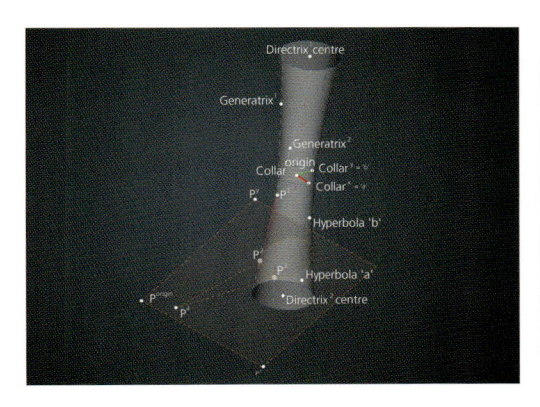

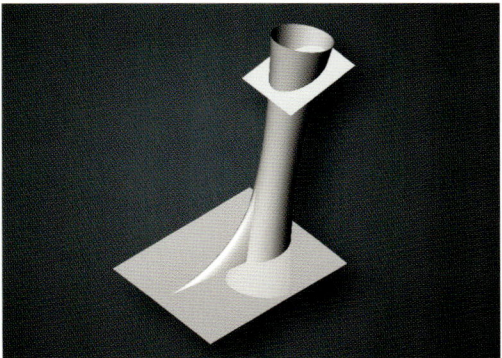

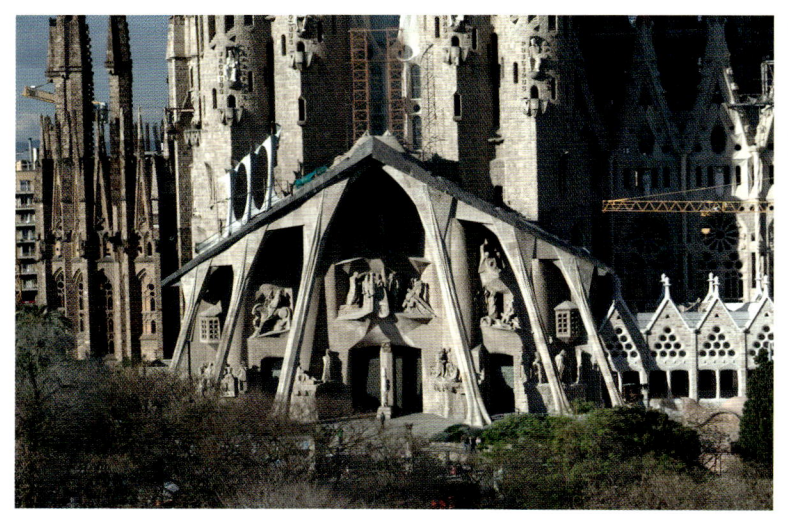

Antoni Gaudí, Sagrada Família church, Barcelona, 1882–ongoing: Passion Facade narthex – 1:1 prototypes to test design against Gaudí's original drawing.

but only one answer for any given hyperboloid and any given hyperbolic paraboloid. For the designer, the challenge is to find the optimal values for all the parameters concerned such that the geometry of the combined set of nine surfaces per column matches Gaudí's drawing. In the end we engaged a mathematician who first defined the various simultaneous equations that needed to be satisfied before we could seek programming assistance. The result was a Rhino 3D™ plug-in, which since 2001 has allowed us to model 3D circular and elliptical hyperboloids of revolution at whim completely through graphical or direct data input. Having inputted the desired hyperboloid of revolution, we can then define the best-fit hyperbolic paraboloid by nominating two points at the base from which two generatrices are identified or, if we know the position of the uppermost point for the intersection of the two geometries, the plug-in will identify the two points where the generatrices intersect with the base.

What I have described above is fundamentally a design operation afforded only through scripting. Answers could have been found using traditional media in conjunction with a calculator, but not only would this have taken an inordinately long time, evidence from previous iterations undertaken on that basis had not yielded convincing material. The column design emerging from the process I have outlined was then tested *in situ,* as three neighbouring prototypes in order to gauge their effect.

In the lifetime of this part of the project, the stone cutting technology and the expertise of the stonemason have meant that the 9-metre-high slender columns have moved on from considering their fabrication from five stone components to only three. The stereotomy challenge here (that is, the art of cutting three-dimensional solids such as stone into practical shapes) means that in moving to just three elements, the main shaft of the column is now made up from a single piece of granite 6 metres in length. The stonemason, Jordi Barbany, considers this to be an operation impossible to undertake by hand for a piece of this length and slenderness. Furthermore, we now

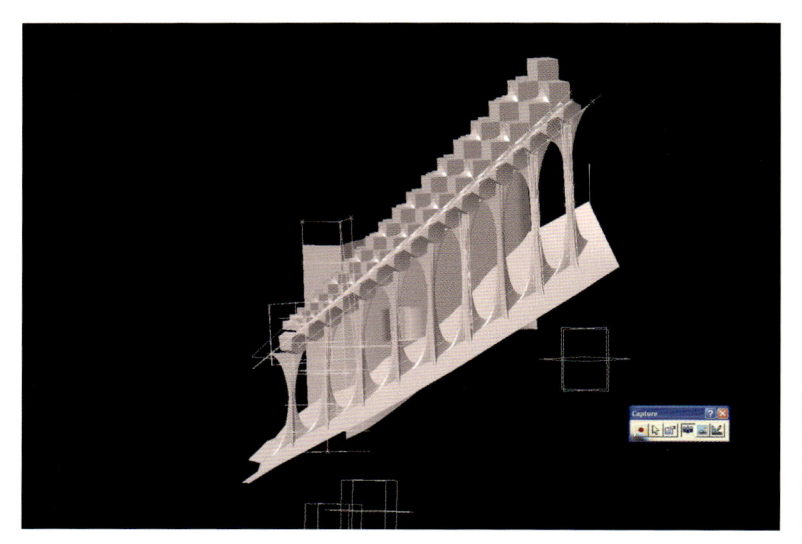

Jane Burry, parametric model for the Passion Facade narthex of Antoni Gaudí's Sagrada Familia church, Barcelona with scripted interrelationships between ruled surfaces.

parametrically design the blocks of granite from which the columns are made, which are cut to order from the quarry face, not blasted. This reduces the risk of fissuring, cuts back on the amount of stone being extracted, and minimises transportation costs.

1:25 rapid prototype of typical column and pediment intersection for Antoni Gaudí's Sagrada Familia church, Barcelona, showing parametric Plasticine modelling intervention.

Jane Burry, parametric model of the Passion Facade narthex to Antoni Gaudí's Sagrada Familia church, Barcelona, ready for construction.

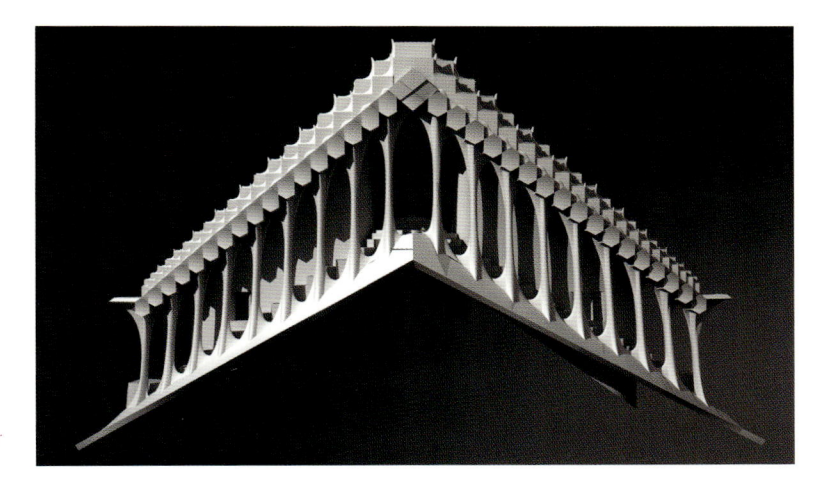

The whole narthex has emerged as a parametric model built by Jane Burry, mathematically conceptualised such that every single component is inextricably linked dimensionally to its neighbours. If anything has to change, the effect causes a ripple across the whole facade. The columns all have an individually unique angle of lean both towards the centre of the composition seen from the front, as well as increasingly towards the centre of the building at the periphery of the facade. In plan the column feet splay outwards increasingly towards the ends of the colonnade, guided by a parabola. Can the model update itself in this way when a single-dimensional parameter is altered? Sadly, that is an answer reserved for another time and another context as it is beyond the scope of scripting at this point in time. We are always able to conceptualise beyond the limits of available computer power, but well within the potentiality of coding itself, it seems.

Displacement as dimension

In this chapter I have positioned scripting as a fundamental tool with which to explore dimensionality in architecture: spatially, and as a series of levels that have mathematical and philosophical implications. I have addressed both the mathematical fallacy and practical utility of considering the fourth dimension, critical within my practice described here, as a time element and instead more aptly, as suggested in this chapter, as displacement. It may appear as sophistry of the pedant, but for scripting to arrive closer to its full potential,

The first of the colonnade columns for the Passion Facade narthex to Antoni Gaudí's Sagrada Familia church, Barcelona, being sculpted by a CNC disk cutter.

architects might want to engage more closely with mathematicians if not mathematics.

Looking at scripting in several dimensions, for even the addition of time or displacement as a fourth dimension allows its entry on its own terms as a singularly creative design adjunct, opportunities for envisaging possibilities are born from designs that would be very hard to achieve using analogue processes. This chapter is the precursor to the following description and discussion of five chronologically arranged projects that have used scripting at a fundamental design level. Each project demonstrates scripted outcomes from the past two decades, ending with a final project that is work in progress. The chapters can be read in any order: their chronological sequence is simply to show how the sands have shifted during this time as a means to reassert that scripting itself, in many people's opinion, is still in its infancy.

Exciting opportunities surely await the bold.

References

1 'Dimension' Def. 3. *Oxford English Dictionary*, 1989, 2nd edn, CD-ROM.
2 See chapter by Sawako Kaijima and Michalatos Panagiotis in T Sakamoto, A Ferre, M Kubo (eds), *From Control to Design: Parametric/ Algorithmic Architecture*, Actar (Barcelona), 2008, p 130.
3 See definition of 'Euclidian space' in Encyclopædia Britannica Online: 'Euclidean space is a geometrical construct whereby the axioms and postulations of Euclid (3rd century BC Greek mathematician referred to as the 'Father of Geometry') apply. It is a space with any finite number of dimensions for which all points can be designated by a positional dimension, or a coordinate for each dimension. In two dimensions or more a formula can be used to calculate the distance between any two points. For over 2,000 years it has remained the essential point of departure for mathematicians to study non-Euclidean space such as that emerging from elliptic geometry and hyperbolic geometry. Cartesian space refers more accurately to a coordinate system, a convention of three planes intersecting at right angles so forming the three coordinate axes with positive and negative values, all three axes meeting as a point referred to as the 'origin'. http://www.britannica.com/EBchecked/topic/194913/Euclidean-space
4 Proposition 9 : Theo van Doesburg, *Towards a Plastic Architecture*, 1924, in Ulrich Conrads, *Programs and Manifestoes on 20th-century Architecture*, MIT Press (Cambridge, MA), 1970, p 79.
5 Cybernetics is control theory applied to complex systems. The term is associated with situations where what is actually happening to a system sampled at regular intervals is compared to the standard of what ought to be happening, with a controller adjusting the system's behaviour to meet expectation.
6 Explained in detail in MC Burry, 'Beyond the algorithm: seeking differentiated structures through alternative computational and haptic design processes', in Michael Hensel and Achim Menges (eds), *Morpho-Ecologies: Towards Heterogeneous Space in Architectural Design*, AA Publications (London), February 2007, pp 334– 47. See also M Burry 'Re-natured Hybrid', *Thresholds Journal #26: Denatured*, MIT Press, Spring 2003, pp 38–42.
7 J Bergós, *Gaudi, The Man and His Work*, trans. Gerardo Denis, Lunwerg Editores (Barcelona), 1999, p 30.
8 'Paramorph (from mineralogy)' Def. 3. *Oxford English Dictionary*, 2nd edn, 1989, CD-ROM. A pseudomorph formed by a change of physical characters without a change in chemical composition.
'Pseudomorph' Def. 3. *Oxford English Dictionary*, 2nd edn, 1989, CD-ROM.
A false or deceptive form; spec. in mineralogy a crystal or other body consisting of one mineral but having the form proper to another, in consequence of having been formed by substitution, or by chemical or physical alteration.
9 John Rajchman, 'Perplications: On the space and time of Rebstockpark' in Judy Geib and Sabu Kohso (eds), *Unfolding Frankfurt*, Ernst & Sohn (Berlin), 1991, pp 18–77.

6

Scripted productivity: Gaudí's rose windows

In the previous chapter I briefly introduced the Paramorph, which now reappears here in more detail in the context of productivity. We saw in Chapter 4 a potential dialectic emerge between alternate philosophies of scripting to save time, that is productivity in the sense of automation towards labour-saving, versus scripting to be more productive in that time through assisting creative processes. The former could be regarded as being financially driven, while the latter is a quality issue. In Chapter 3 I described how it was the need to be more efficient at drawing Gaudí's curves that first pointed me to scripting. Here I am dealing only with the latter: using scripting to do more design in the design-allotted time.

This chapter looks at the generic design object and at the ability of scripting to pursue greater variety and subtlety than would be possible using traditional media. It uses an historical project as a means to show that the idea might transcend the technical knowhow, by considering an example of creative play from a world figure who died long before digital design had even been thought of.

I am going to condense Gaudí's clerestory window for the Sagrada Família church as the case study for both this chapter and the next. The clerestory window runs along the length of the central nave illuminating the central aisle over 35 metres below. This is an important architectural element of Gaudí's final design for the nave of the church. When he died he had only

Antoni Gaudí, Sagrada Família chuch, Barcelona, 1882–ongoing: central nave clerestory – photograph of 1:10 model made by Gaudí in the years shortly before his death in 1926. Exterior view.

seen the design at scales of 1:25 and 1:10. I had the task of unravelling the geometry of the window and of ultimately producing the documentation for actual construction. This work took me from being deeply embedded in traditional media through to developing into a total believer in scripting by the time the window was built. Scripting has been used in a number of ways, and this chapter will give the sense of the variety of coding that might be applied to this one project.

From 1914 until his death in 1926, Gaudí's architectural production entered a new and final phase, which although revealing links to all his preceding work, nevertheless exhibits qualities, depth and tension that place it in an entirely new domain. Debates around such taxonomic grouping vary in intensity and relevance. The construction of the Sagrada Família church represents a problematic enterprise, continuing as it has and will do, not only for the 43 years of Gaudí's long career (he qualified in 1878 and practised until his death), but also for more than three quarters of a century following his death, and continues today. Needless to say, the continuation of the works has produced problems that have challenged the most contemporary of resources – including information technology. There is no doubt that the work as Gaudí had planned it could have continued using the traditional techniques he so favoured, despite the difficulties he himself set up and was so conspicuously unable to surmount in the time available to him. While digital assistance is not a *sine qua non* of the project's viability today, there are nevertheless opportunities for reiterative and reflective design techniques that Gaudí might well have elected to adopt had they been available at the time. The techniques harnessed today

Mark Burry   127   Chapter 6 Scripted productivity: Gaudí's rose windows

take the work forward at a pace commensurate with opportunities offered by a codex of surface composition that Gaudí bequeathed his successors. A combination of digital representation of the design of the building and a range of automated material preparation techniques come together to allow construction to continue at a significantly accelerated pace. Interestingly, the new techniques sponsor a richer appreciation of Gaudí's mind's eye. In seeking to represent a distillation of Gaudí's three-dimensional thinking for constructional or intellectual understanding, we reveal further insights into his unique conceptual abilities. In this final period, we find Gaudí working with an architecture of *real absence*, and an architecture of *virtual presence*. This chapter deals with *real absence*.

Antoni Gaudí, Sagrada Familia chuch, Barcelona, 1882–ongoing: central nave clerestory – 1:10 model reconstructed from surviving fragments after its destruction during the 1936–9 Spanish Civil War.

An architecture of real absence

The work of Gaudí's final years consolidates a number of important aspects of his oeuvre present from the beginning of his career. There is a direct link to nature brought into his architecture through a reinterpretation of natural form in the materials with which he worked. Far from the level of motif or

obscure semiotic allusion, his reference to nature was in part a quest for some kind of divine truth, an organicist understanding of the substance of being, articulated in the forms with which he chose to enclose space. His uncharacteristic restraint within an already established Gothic Revival language somewhat masks the emergence of his 'originality', which he defined as 'returning to the source'.[1] The exaggerated call on the Gothic does not obscure Gaudí's own voice; it just makes it a little more difficult to discern the remarkable innovations from this last period. In these 12 years, Gaudí had retreated entirely from all secular work, focusing on the remaining design (almost the entire building) and bringing the completion of the Nativity Facade construction to a close. It is his studies for the rest of the building that draw our attention. He imbues these studies with an overriding order based on a particular surface geometry: ruled surfaces. Ruled surfaces are warped surfaces that can nevertheless be described by an array of straight lines lying across the surface in two directions, as discussed in the previous chapter.

His design for the nave, crossing and towers is broadly based on this geometry. This design work was not a casual exercise; hardly a version of the design that can be subsequently substituted by a substantial redesign. This was a 12-year-long, full-time design project and yielded his definitive proposal after two previous more orthodox Gothic Revival versions. Even if these models were mere paths towards something else unidentifiably intangible for the next iteration, what they reveal in terms of a design language and design process is quite astonishing. Their conceptual implications are contemporary in ways that few commentators have been able to assess.

The fractured models themselves require interpretation of an almost archaeological nature, and the very act of clearing the site and excavating the foundations continually yielded a wealth of model fragments that had survived their trashing during the Spanish Civil War, a decade after Gaudí's death. The surfaces themselves are not especially complicated – they share the common characteristic of being 'drawn' three-dimensionally with the arrays of straight lines referred to above.

We know that Gaudí was not an exemplary student. He appears to have struggled with his studies for a number of reasons, including financial, and we know that he was exposed to descriptive geometry as a significant part of those studies.[2] From the earliest projects, we see signs of his understanding of the role geometry plays in the exploration and description of form. We also see a practical expediency in its adoption. The *arcos falsos* in the Pabellones Güell (1884–7) and hyperbolic paraboloid corbelling in a now demolished garden structure at the Casa Vicens (1883–5) all herald a practical knowingness in the field of applied geometry. Later, glorious experiments at the Colònia Güell (design commenced 1898; construction of crypt and porch 1908–14) crypt bear testimony to a more concerted and contrived use of ruled surfaces. In the lead-up to the final period, ensconced within the

Antoni Gaudí, Sagrada Família chuch, Barcelona, 1882–ongoing: Gaudí's design process as a series of iterative assembly of half hyperboloids of revolution. A negative master for each hyperboloid is made for each of the positive copies from which a negative copy is derived. The negatives are cut to fit and the resulting windows assembled.

Sagrada Família church workshops, there is a rigour in their use that is at odds with his apparent abandon of convention in his earlier work.

Boolean operations at work

It seems that Gaudí's *modus operandi* during his final years became less predicated on day-to-day exchanges with the builders at the site of their

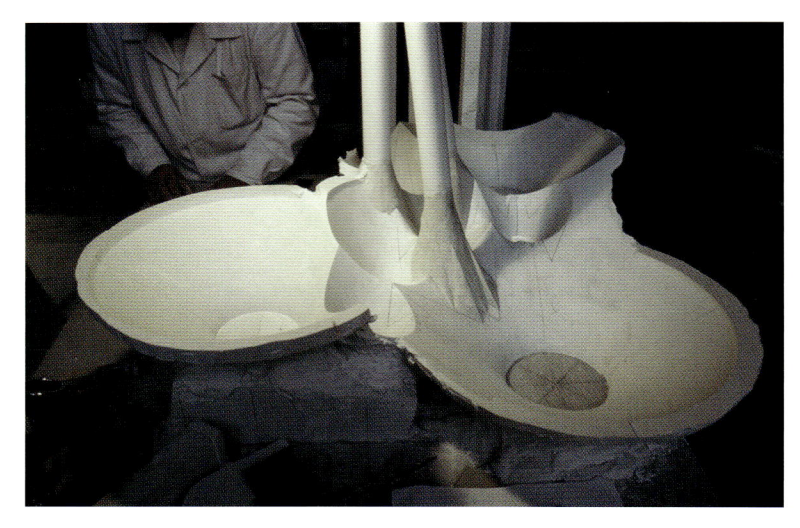

Antoni Gaudí, Sagrada Familia chuch, Barcelona, 1882–ongoing: provisional modelling is undertaken using Plasticine in order to 'tune' the parametric scripting.

labours, especially as he grew more infirm, and the theatre of operations kept moving to a higher level from the ground. His design had become more theoretical, perhaps, and less instinctive. Scaled at 1:10, the definitive versions of the central nave windows – clerestories – are large models in themselves, measuring 7.5 metres by 15 metres tall as built. First let us consider the way this piece would have been modelled by Gaudí in his time; the model makers today have had a continuous and uninterrupted link with the past through their apprenticeship lineage and can explain Gaudí's design approach. Gypsum plaster (plaster of Paris) has been the quintessential design medium from Gaudí's time until now and as a design medium its use has been consistently the same throughout. The sequence of operations undertaken by the model makers to prepare the primary forms for the window surfaces use *hyperboloids of revolution of one sheet*. We see first the negative, that is a model of what is not there, an *absence* as the *parti*. The section of the hyperboloid is a hyperbola that is made to swing around a pivot coaxing a mound of setting gypsum plaster to set as a circular hyperboloid. From this, a thin gypsum plaster shell is made. For each hyperboloid opening, the shells are placed in position and cut as close to their respective intersections as possible through approximation, and filled to form the whole window.

There is something quintessentially haptic in this operation. Apart from the hyperbola that can be derived graphically, just as effectively for

Antoni Gaudí, Sagrada Família church, Barcelona, 1882–ongoing: all such ruled surfaces have an infinite number of straight lines running across them. Straight lines on the surface can be selected in order to incorporate a layer of decoration that takes advantage of the selected straight lines extracted from the ruled-surface geometry.

these purposes as through calculation, the computation and geometry are comfortably distant from the physical modelling situation. Iterative experimentation might have proceeded thus: Gaudí sketches the curve by eye, and a technician then draws it accurately for use as a rotating template. The model makers, having made the thin shells based on the geometrically corrected curve, fit the shells together in the way described, and then refer the model to the master for critical feedback. If Gaudí was not able to be as active on the site of the actual building operations, we can see that this procedure might have been a useful substitute, and follows on from his experiments for Colònia Güell when he was known to visit site (where the hanging model was housed) on occasions several times a week. But this is to simplify matters, and even if Gaudí were to have kept the computation at arms' length, he would not have been so shy of the geometry. His predilection for the appropriateness of ruled surfaces would probably be more tuned to their occurrence in nature and their aesthetic qualities, not least through the play of light upon them. He surely recognised the practical advantages too, but with neither writing on this subject (nor, indeed, on any other), nor their use anywhere beyond the studio, any such assertions remain hypothetical. No doubt the building of the Colònia Güell crypt where he made extensive use of the hyperbolic paraboloids both structurally and in the formation of the porch vaults would have consolidated their usefulness at a pragmatic level. The combination there of the most efficacious structural minimalism represented in this use complements the extreme modesty of resources: window grilles made from discarded needles from the associated corduroy mills, and the recycling of clinkered brick make the crypt an exceptional statement of restraint in terms of material selection, especially in today's terms. Such work could not be further from the digital realm, whereas if we delve deeper into the articulation of hyperboloids for the yet to be designed proposal for the Sagrada Família church, interesting questions arise.

Let us take the hyperboloid of revolution of one sheet itself: this is richer in its variety and constraints than the hyperbolic paraboloid. In combination, they seem almost to offer a degree of personality. Each has nine variables that influence their situation with respect to their neighbours with which they conjoin: three coordinates of location, three axes of rotation, and three constants that determine the width and height of the opening, and the degree of slope (asymptote). A slight alteration when just one variable changes, such as the width of the opening, has a startlingly exaggerated effect. The effects of these profound shifts in appearance are exaggerated still further when the forms interact as a composition.

This is where the rude simplicity of the Colònia Güell church contrasts strikingly with the Gothic sophistication of the Sagrada Família church; Gaudí was clearly motivated to take up from where the medieval masons had left off. In doing so, using the formality of the ruled surfaces, he set himself up with problems that he had not yet had to resolve at the time of his accidental death – he was fatally struck by a tram while making his way back from church. The making of the circular hyperboloid of revolution of one sheet is a slightly disingenuous example to offer up as proof of concept, as the making of its elliptical equivalent is quite an extravagant feat in comparison. Towards the end of this period, the hyperboloids of revolution for the windows were predominantly elliptical.

Hyperbolic paraboloid.

A change to only one of the nine variables can bring such extravagance in its wake, an effect that is greatly increased when a second variable is also changed, such as the axis of rotation for one of the hyperboloids of revolution about the *x* axis. The elliptical forms show a greater richness: whereas the circular forms require little more than the derivation of their constituent sectional hyperbolas, the elliptical forms require an elaboration

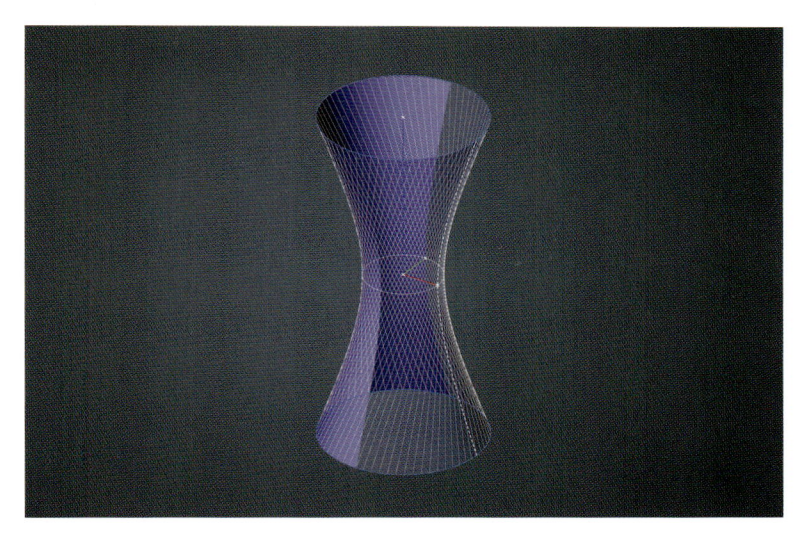

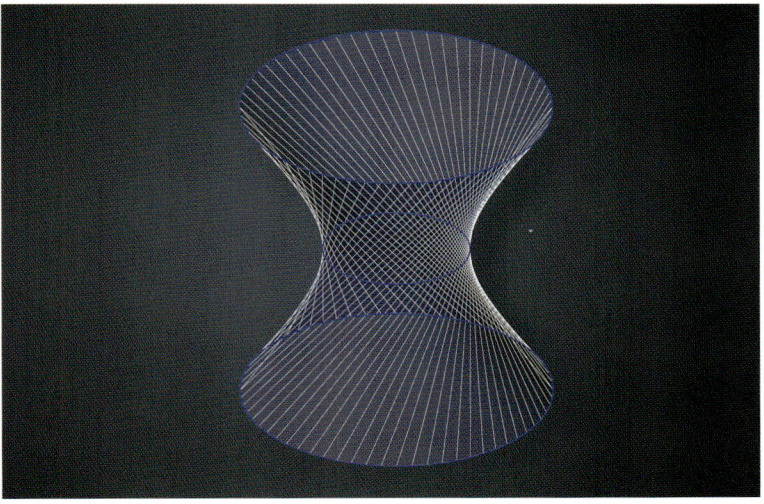

Hyperboloid of revolution of one sheet.

Parametric variations of a hyperboloid of revolution between two opposite end states of two cones and a cylinder.

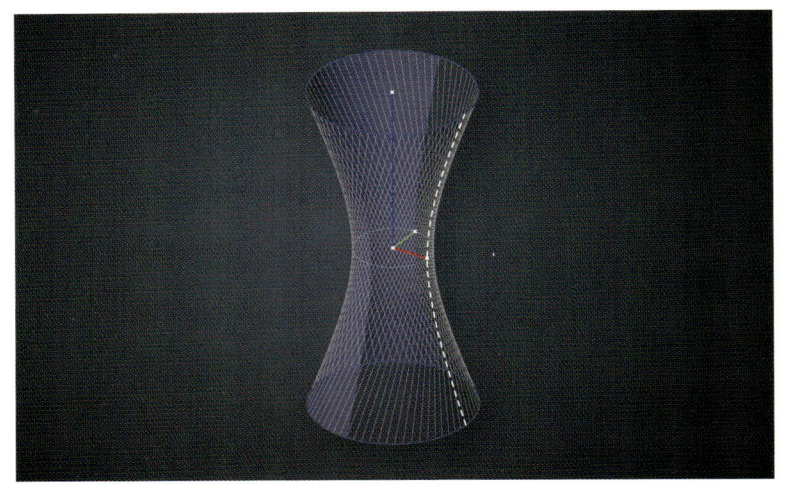

There are nine parametric variables for a hyperboloid of revolution in terms of its relationship to its neighbours: three Cartesian geometry coordinates, three axes of rotation, two constants 'a' and 'b' (red and green lines) and the slope (asymptote) 'c', that governs the degree of curvature with the hyperbola shown in yellow.

in the order of many days compared with the preparation of the circular. The elliptical hyperboloids cannot be made from rotating a single curve around the centre, and instead have to be 'constructed' by wholly different means.

Regardless of the extra efforts required at the level of construction, Gaudí himself would have appreciated the extra degrees of difficulty the subtraction of rotated elliptical forms would represent in comparison with the circular and axially right-angled orientations. Given that the order of difference between elliptical and circular hyperboloids is a factor of many times the amount of work, how much opportunity did he have in commissioning repeat work, when each repetition tied a group of model makers to many weeks of work preparing a single element? Here the difference between Gaudí's way of working and its digital equivalent is at its most paradoxical. Digital manipulation and subtraction by computer are the same for elliptical as for circular forms, and equally when these are rotated rather than orthogonally oriented, whereas Gaudí had to be intuitively almost certain of a positive outcome before making the commitment compared with his digital designer successors. Furthermore, as he was dealing with *an architecture of real absence*, he had to conceive of what was *not* in order to be sure of what was left, an approach to plasticity and form sculpting that probably has no precedent. All the more remarkable for what this represents for someone without access to today's design productivity tools.

Scripting Gaudí

My previous studies for resolving Gaudí's geometries had been as a series of three graphical projections to find the intersection curves between adjacent surfaces, as a means to accelerate the iterative modelling process by using the drawings (topographical maps in essence) to zero in on the 'triple points' core to this interpretive investigation. The challenge was to work out the values of all nine parameters for each hyperbolic surface. Surfaces intersect with 3D curves, and these 3D curves themselves intersect forming the triple points. In terms of hierarchy of information, the triple points are the richest source. The task was to ensure that all triple points in the interpreted model matched those measured from Gaudí's original. The graphical method was a more rapid means to predict the outcome using Gaudí's modelling method. It was a game, like squeezing a balloon. With considerable effort, I would get all the triple points in one area to relax through computation into their required positions, but in doing so the triple points higher up the modelled facade would fly out of position, and vice versa. In the main, the original models were very accurate, but at instances of inconvenient geometry, a certain amount of fudging had been undertaken: one could see evidence of the use of a rasp. This is the reason

Mountain scape showing the same lines of intersection between adjacent surfaces (ridges) with the triple points (peaks) formed where ridges intersect. Geometrically Gaudí was using surfaces in the same way as natural terrain relief is formed.

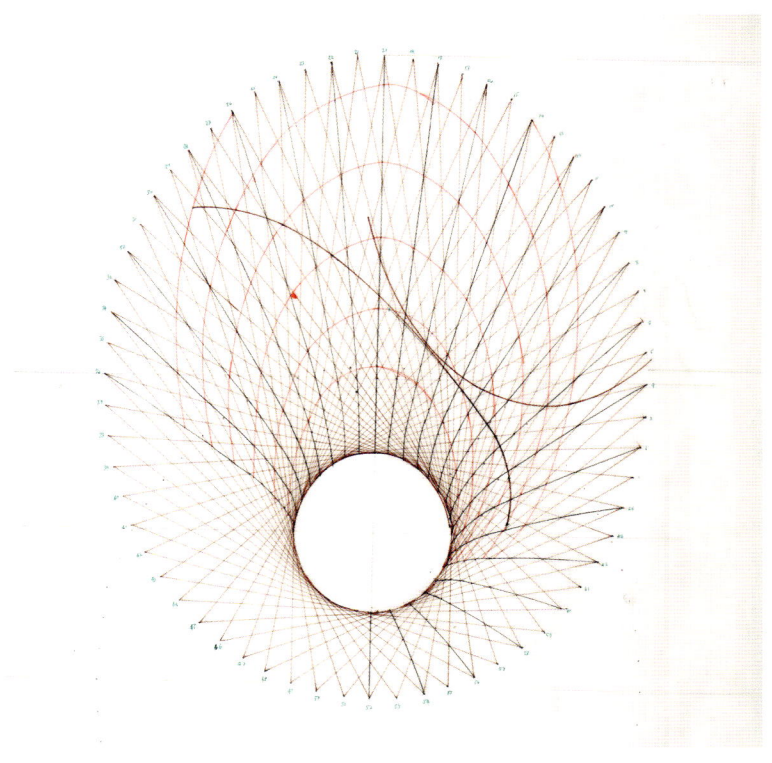

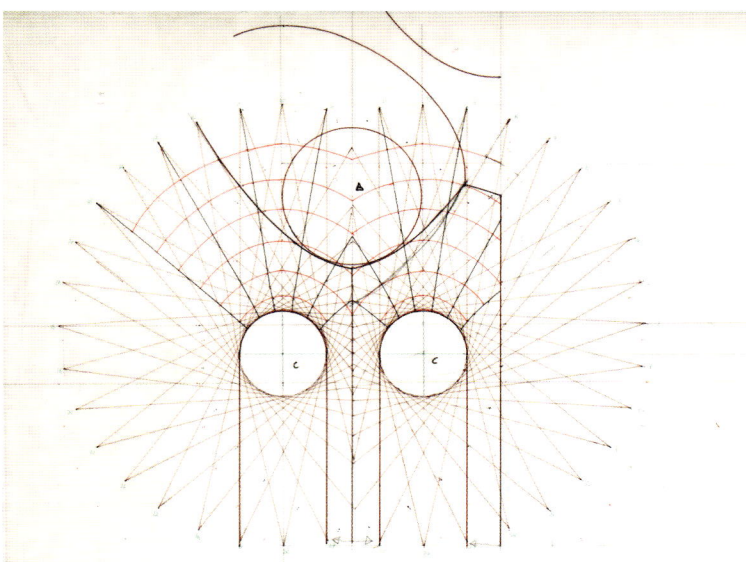

Pre-digital-era graphical approach to mapping the surface curvature to an inclined hyperboloid of revolution of one sheet (1980).

Tracing the intersections between adjacent surfaces in Antoni Gaudí's Sagrada Familia church, Barcelona by projective geometry (1980).

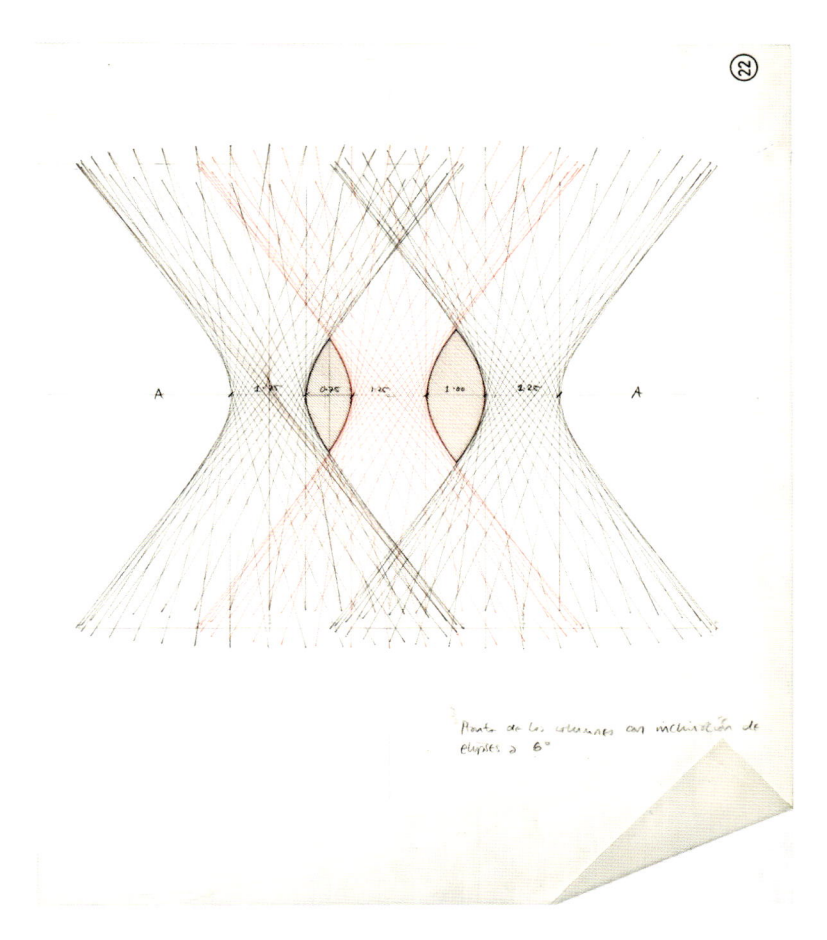

Horizontal section across a window design for Antoni Gaudí's Sagrada Família church, Barcelona (1980).

why the restored plaster models could not be simply scaled up and built, requiring instead exacting research, measurement and interpretation.

The first use of scripting was the need to draw hyperbolas, as outlined in Chapter 3. The model makers made copies of the geometries taken from Gaudí's models. They would cut these along the axes and I would trace the curves, measure them and try to generate a matching hyperbola. In many cases the geometry is so subtle I would have to make up to a hundred, all in 2D, varying the angle as well as starting and finishing points. As the 3D form was derived from these 2D curves, precision was a prerequisite for this method to have any chance of success. Given that most of the forms used were elliptical,

140

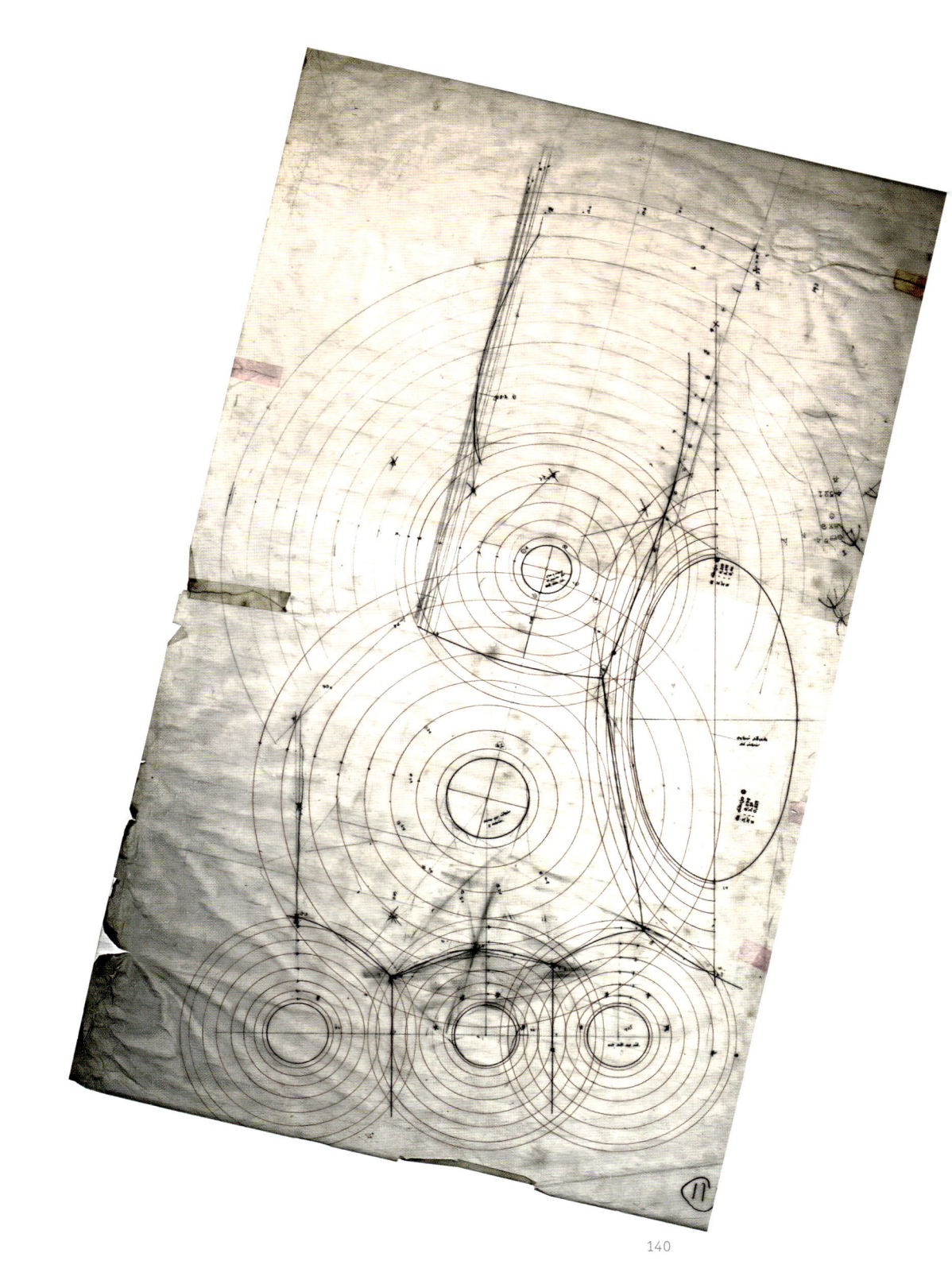

Mapping the exterior surfaces to the lateral nave window as an elevation (1979). The drawing was a projection, and has been rotated to correspond with the vertical axis of the central ellipse.

the horizontal and vertical axes had to be derived in this way, from which the hyperboloid of revolution matching these curves was derived in its turn.

Even with scripting assistance in drawing the curves, the process was too hit and miss. My colleagues in Barcelona faced the same problem for the roof vaults, albeit with circular forms. They wrote a simple programme using Basic. From the data input (points on the surface), it would calculate a range of options that fitted the points. This would commence with a very loose fit to ensure that there was a result, and sometimes we were startled by an overwhelming number of possible solutions for each surface. 'Near enough' could not work, because it would not guarantee that its intersection with its neighbours would align properly; still less the associated triple points. This sometimes entailed an excruciating process in drilling down to the best fit; the time taken for the algorithm to lurch through so many parameters meant that it could take several days to confirm that there was even a result. The ideal situation was to zero in on a single result – the best fit, and patience was required.

At Victoria University of Wellington, where I was working at that time (1993), I explained our waiting game to a computer scientist and engineer, Peter Wood, who seemed astonished that we did not use genetic algorithms to hone in on the best fit. My role was to measure every point possible on the surfaces, lines of intersection and around the collar of the hyperboloid of revolution. These were grouped for each surface and ordered around importance. Tier one (for importance) were the triple points and the four cardinal points on the collar axes. Next came the points on the intersection lines and, finally, least accurate and therefore least reliable, points on the surface.

In these years before Windows 95, PC users were accustomed to only the most basic of visual display interfaces, so it was a surprise when Peter conjured up a tool he christened 'Xhyper' for use on a UNIX workstation, with a visual interface no different to what we have now 17 years later, but utterly alien at that time. Xhyper would read in a data file for each group of compiled points and generate, within seconds, the fit that best matched the data for all nine parameters. This meant that with nothing other than a set of ordered points, the nine spatial, rotational and mathematical constants governing a hyperboloid of revolution would be presented in a dialogue box. At the press of a button, a script file would automatically be generated that would produce the hyperboloid in 3D in the parametric modelling software that we used at that time: Computervision's CADDS5™.

In all cases we needed to constrain certain parameters. The '*x*' dimension, for instance, which positioned the centre of the hyperboloid relative to a neutral wall plane was always zero. With Xhyper, once the algorithm

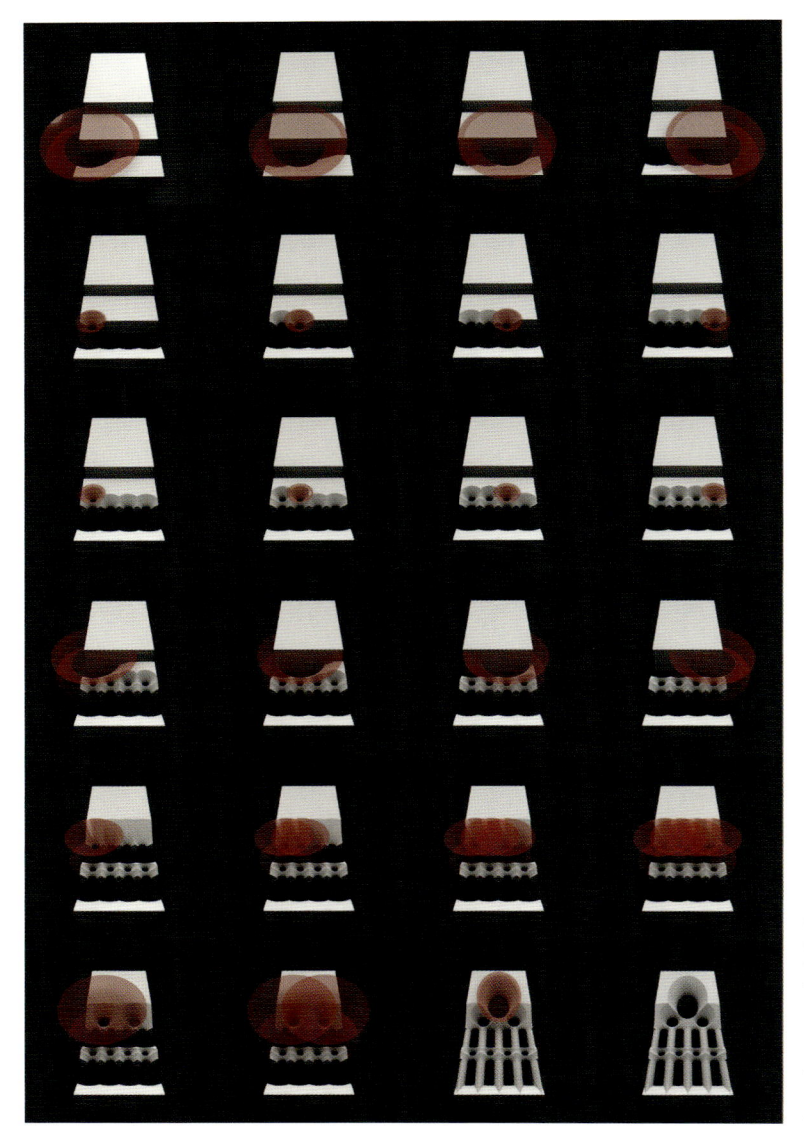

Sequence of Boolean subtractions as 'digital sculpting' for the Rosassa, the rose window between the towers of the Passion Facade of Antoni Gaudí's Sagrada Familia church, Barcelona. Each of the brown objects is a hyperboloid of revolution (2000).

'Xhyper', a genetic algorithm optimiser used to refine possible values for the hyperboloid of revolution parameters in order to zero in on the best fit to Gaudí's original models for the Sagrada Familia church, Barcelona. One window is the tool for finding the best-fit solution, the other is the 'automatic script generator' for building the resulting hyperboloids (1994).

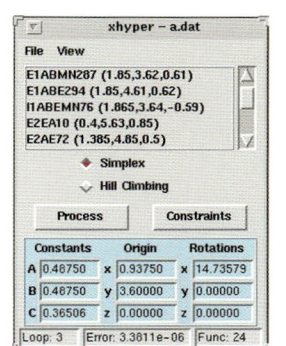

had run, whatever value had come up could then be constrained via the dialogue box and the process re-run. In some cases we had many unknowns with little data, and in other cases few unknowns (many constrained parameters) but abundant data. Xhyper had two best-fit algorithms to choose from: *Simplex* and *Hillclimbing*; the user selected either and went forward on the basis of the results.

I presumed that with the precision and focus of Xhyper, our work was done: all that was required was to complete the script to compile the individual scripts coming from each surface analysis operation described above. It all worked just as I describe, a compiling script would run and in just over an hour the entire window geometry would appear as a 3D parametric model, complete with dimensioning and labelling. The problem is that the effect of just a single adjustment of a hyperboloid of revolution by less than half a degree on any of its axes would have a visually disproportionate effect and a potentially disastrous result. In the end, 96 different compiled scripts were run over many weeks, the constraints being tweaked by eye in order to home in on a geometrically near-precise version of Gaudí's original. The wonder of it is Gaudí's intuitive ability to 'see' all this conceptually, and communicate the requisite moves to his model makers.

Even with our concurrent uptake of parametric design for the project with its hands-on flexibility, Xhyper was an invaluable analytical tool that was harnessed to work in conjunction. Compared with our initial scripting approach we did not find that the visual interfaces, that had made parametric design software so attractive as it matured as a software option, fully compensated for the ability to work with code.

By changing the variables governing the geometry of the extracted hyperboloids of revolution, the brown-coloured surface can be relaxed sufficiently to match Gaudí's original model for the Sagrada Família church, Barcelona, digitised and shown here in grey (1993).

Appreciating the design role of the variable

In his final twelve years, Gaudí eschewed his previous freeform approach to composition and in its place adopted this system of applied geometry. The system was composed of a tight set comprised of three surfaces known as second order or 'ruled surfaces': the hyperbolic paraboloid, the hyperboloid of revolution of one sheet and the helicoid.

As a set of only three geometrical surfaces, this appears as a highly restrictive precondition, especially for an architect with a predilection for freeform sculpting. Used in a particular way, however, an extraordinarily rich outcome results, but this comes from applying an inverse logic when considering composition as an additive process. Just as a sculptor thinks about what must be taken away from a block of marble to reveal the sculpture concealed within, so too Gaudí operated with these three surfaces. He was less interested in using them deliberately to compose an assembly than he was in employing them as a study of the consequences of their conceptual removal from an imaginary mass of material. In this case Gaudí was sculpting geometrically rather than 'physically' as a sculptor would work with hammer and chisel. Put another way, he was conceiving of the outcome of the geometries' use just as materially as would a sculptor working reductively with stone, but Gaudí was pursuing this outcome by manipulating the geometry of 'what is not there'. Mathematically he was assisted by Boolean operations, and his compositional strategy is essentially one of subtractions of

Computer-generated 'solid model' for Antoni Gaudí's Sagrada Família church, Barcelona. The images show a succession of iterations of sculpted surfaces (shown in orange) resulting from the sequenced Boolean subtraction of hyperboloids of revolution (shown as semi-transparent solids to aid clarity) (1993).

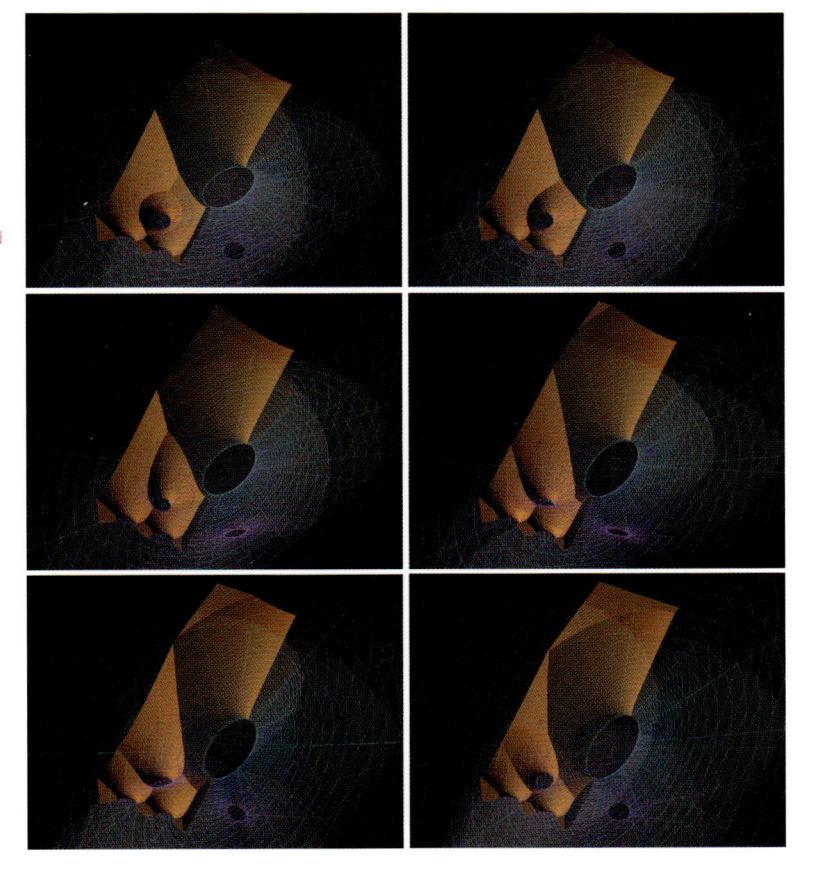

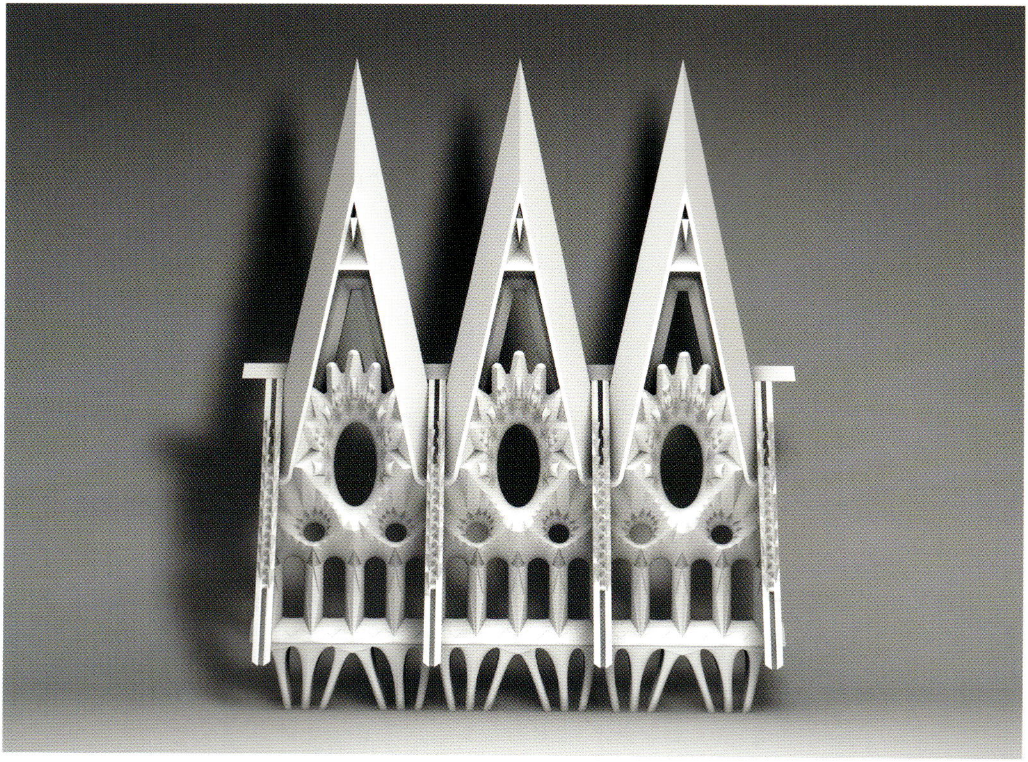

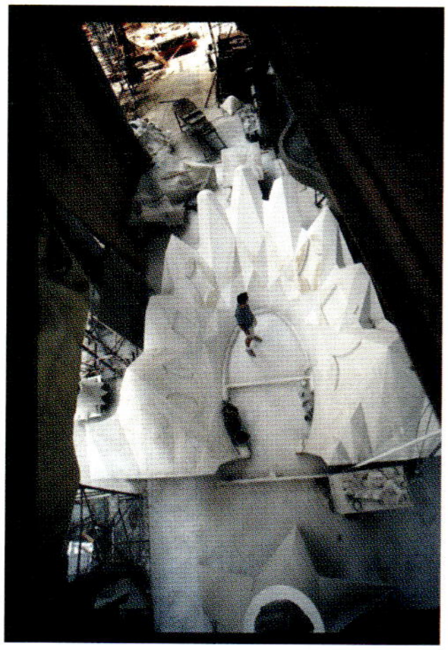

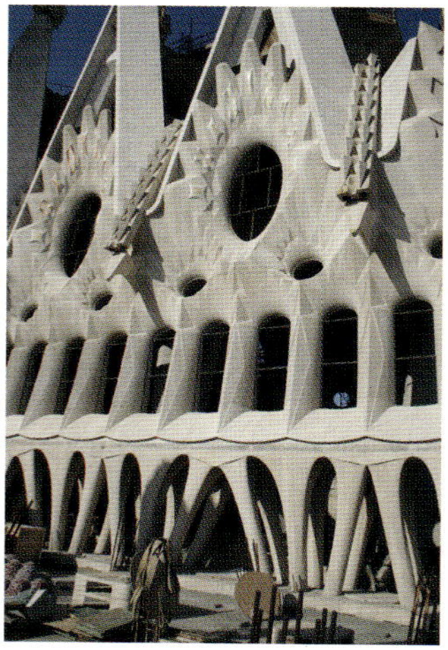

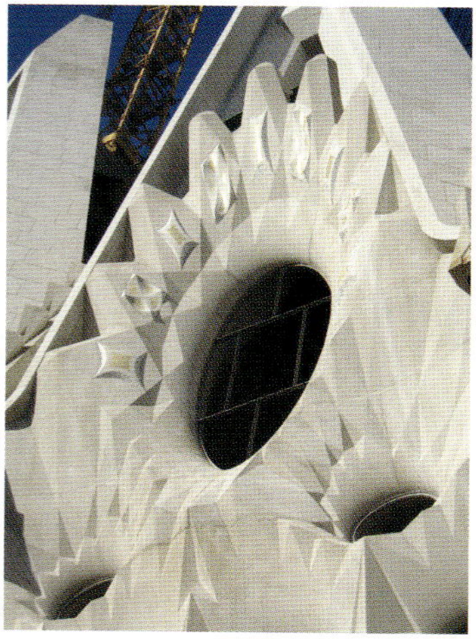

Central nave clerestory of Antoni Gaudí's Sagrada Família church, Barcelona: three bays of the digital model's exterior (1995).

Making the 1:1 mould master for the central nave clerestory of Antoni Gaudí's Sagrada Família church, Barcelona is simply a matter of scaling up Gaudí's design approach (1997). This process is largely taken up using CNC routers and polystyrene.

Antoni Gaudí, Sagrada Família church, Barcelona, 1882–ongoing: central nave clerestory: as built (1999).

Passion Facade rose window for Antoni Gaudí's Sagrada Família church, Barcelona: parametrically varied solids for Boolean subtraction. The mathematics for each surface parameter is controlled by a spreadsheet which, in turn, generated a script to perform the sculpting (2000).

Passion Facade rose window of Antoni Gaudí's Sagrada Família church, Barcelona: the decorative engraving on the right-hand completed digital model could only be partially scripted, but all the information for its building was extracted using scripts (2000).

solids from one and another. Boolean operations, named after the mathematician George Boole (1815–64), have three logics relevant here. The first is the union of two solids. The second is the intersection of two solids as in the example of the Sagrada Família church nave columns discussed in the previous chapter. The third is the subtraction of one solid from another, which is the Boolean operation Gaudí was using here.

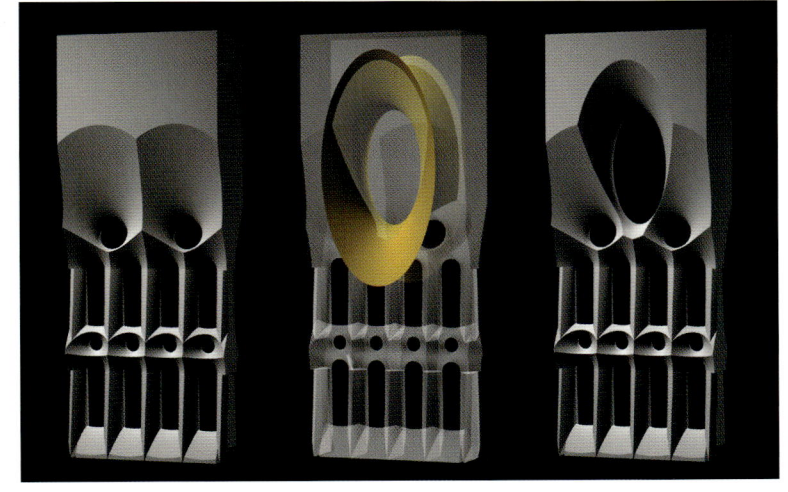

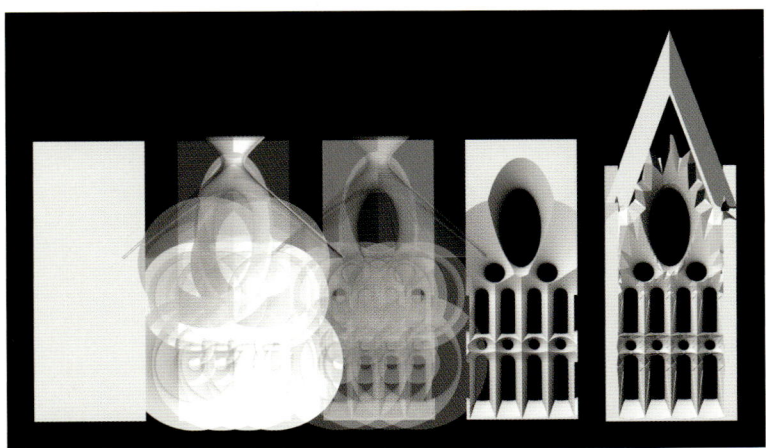

How is it that a theoretically simple (albeit visually complex) approach using just three types of surface could yield such richness of surface, solid and void? The answer lies with the nine variables that individually govern each surface and their relationships between adjacent interacting surfaces. Collectively, an array of different neighbouring and interacting surfaces, each with nine parametric possibilities for making profound or subtle differences in their interrelationships, means an infinite range of outcomes is open to the designer. Post-Gaudí, this presents us with a classic 'stopping problem' conundrum: at what point do we stop fiddling with the parameters?

Scripting is a powerful adjunct to this process, as much use for any application of this compositional strategy outside Gaudí's arena as for studying Gaudí's work itself. The ability to script alternative outcomes for comparison between one another is an invaluable aid to the contemporary digital design process. It is not just the fact that scripting can be shown to assist in the production of individual instances of the design objects ('paramorphs') for side-by-side comparison; more valuable still is the possibility for the designer to create sufficient instances for an animated sequence. As considered in the previous chapter, working in 4D is an essential adjunct for the emerging generation of designers interested in *performative* architecture. Being able to simulate how a design performs to the client will become as essential an element in the architect's communication toolbox as any other. This aspect is investigated in more detail in Chapter 10.

Looking back on this adventure, completed 15 years ago, combining scripting with any software with parametric potential remains today a potent design cocktail. The dilemma that I have not fully resolved is that of how much time to devote to making loose-fit of bespoke software such as Xhyper for any given project, as against taking advantage of fully featured and expensive industrial-strength parametric design software. Each has its limitations. I believe that we are on the cusp of a new era, where architects have the ability to build their own tools from open-source libraries as also discussed in Chapter 10, making this perhaps less of a dilemma. Such is the pace of change, this account of Gaudí's Boolean architecture of real absence will perhaps soon be one more of historical interest than actual relevance.

Antoni Gaudí, Sagrada Familia church, Barcelona, 1882–ongoing: Passion Facade rose window – exterior and interior views as built (2001).

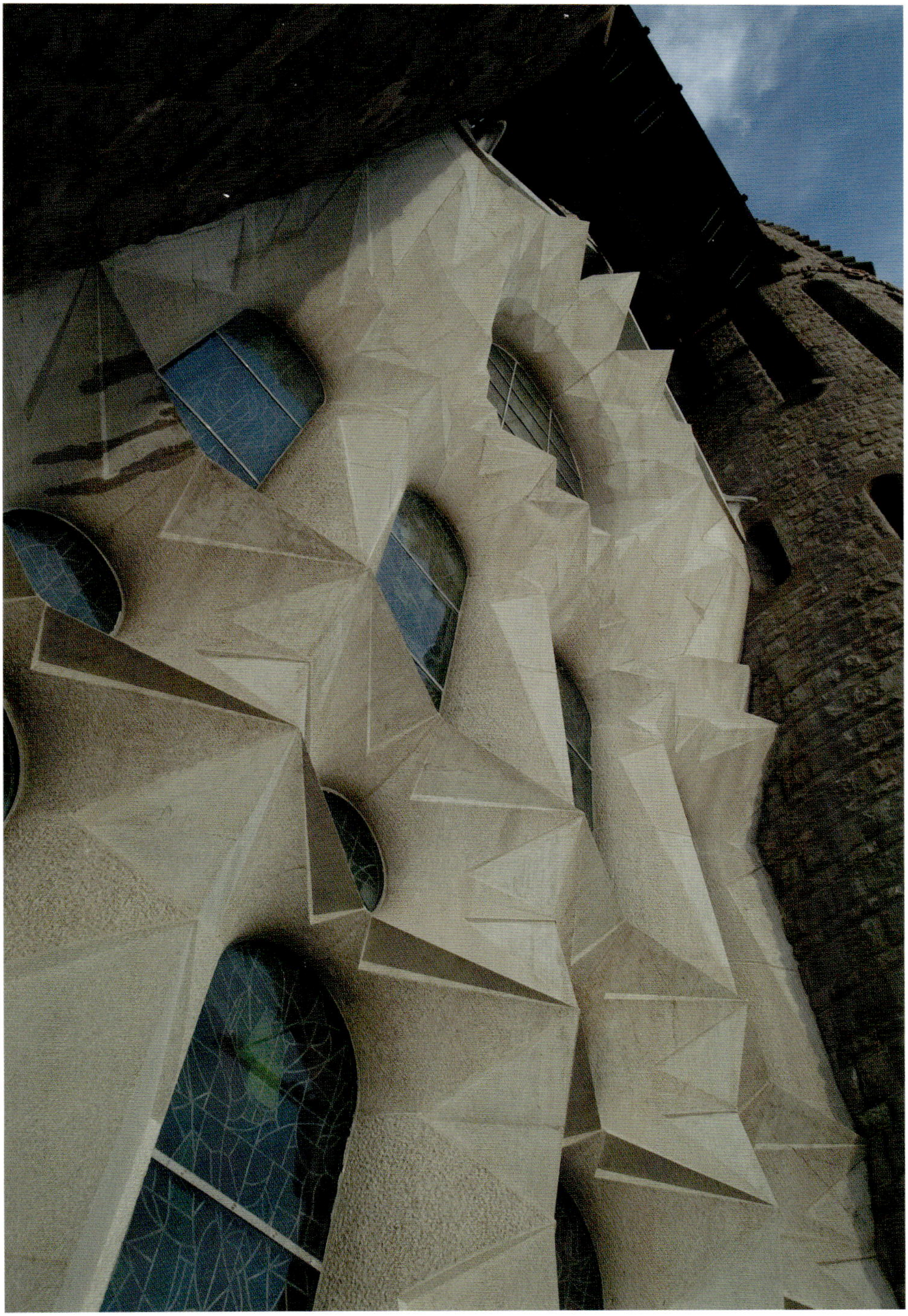

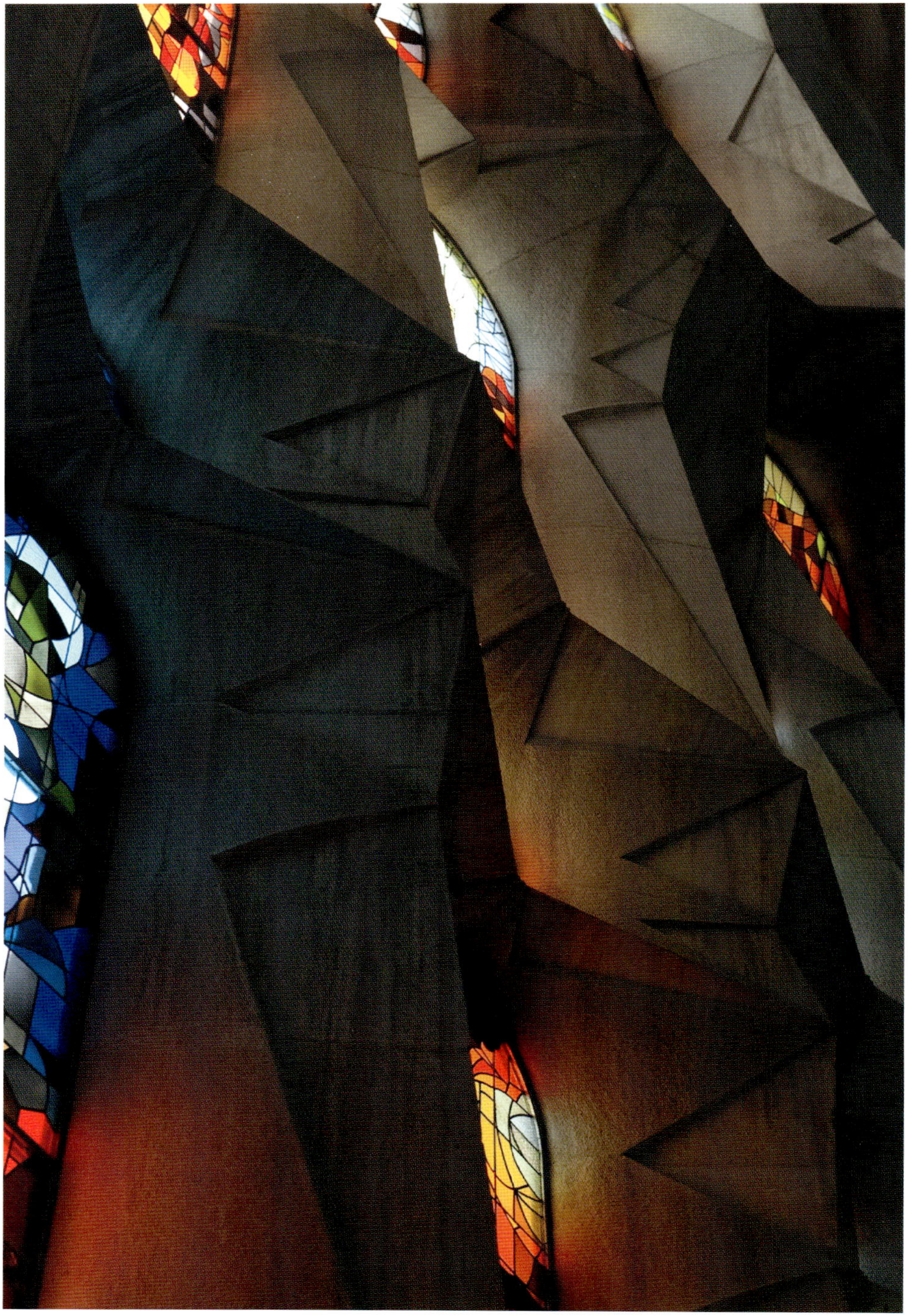

References

1 I Puig i Boada, *El Pensament de Gaudí,* Publicacions del Collegi d'Arquitectes de Catalunya (Barcelona), 1981, p 99 (quoting Joan Bergós).
2 Looking at the coursework from the period at the school where Gaudí studied (Barcelona University) we see that descriptive geometry was a significant course component and that Gaudí would have been undertaking exercises in solids description and what were effectively 'Boolean operations'. See: CFA Leroy, *Traité de Géométrie Descriptive,* Mallet-Bachelier (Paris), 1844.

7
Composition and form

In this chapter we will continue to look at Gaudí's nave clerestory window for the Sagrada Família church. At one level Chapter 6 described an operational approach to scripting. By taking known functions from within the software (Boolean operations, for example), a script automates the sequential activation of these functions to creative effect. At another level for the same project, scripting was used to develop a stand-alone program operating both independently as well as in conjunction with proprietary software. In this chapter we will consider the case where the design composition itself is hard-coded into the script. This requires an unusual set of moves for the architect who might otherwise rely on intuition, the sketch, and emergence. Through a study of Gaudí's sculptured motifs for the clerestory window, a number of further paradoxes and apparent contradictions will be presented. Firstly, even while being explicit about a compositional strategy through scripting, operationally the strategy may yet afford opportunities for intuitive input, sketching and emergence along the way. Secondly, compositional scripting is looked at for its potential inadvertently or deliberately to spawn the monster (*teratoid*), however much the designer might be endeavouring to engineer beauty.

An architecture of polymorphism and morphogenesis

A tavern waiter, about six feet tall, was discovered by Gaudí and became the

Roman soldier for the Massacre of the Innocents on the Doorway of Hope. As it is related by Juan Matamala, 'When we asked him to pose, we found that he had six perfectly formed toes on each foot. I still see them. When he was obliged to put a pair of Roman sandals on him, my father wanted to hide one toe on each foot, but Gaudí interfered, exclaiming: "No, no! On the contrary! It is absolutely necessary to have them the way they are. It is an anomaly, just as it is an anomaly to kill children!"' [1]

The freak invokes both interest and horror through a simultaneous expansion and contraction of our understanding of normality, a 'narcissistic delight at the shape of our own externality'.[2] Architects have been less inclined than philosophers to delve into teratology as a means to externalise inner disquiet, preferring, it would seem, to seek other preoccupations to sponsor the folding and pleating accompanying much of post-digital building form making. Antoni Gaudí is an exception, and no doubt a product of his Gothic Revival times: his attitude to the abnormal is as apparent in the creatures he employs as gargoyles fleeing earthwards down the face of the building as it is in his more abstract design decisions. This chapter focuses on the *virtual presence* in which his later treatment of surfaces is read as the boundaries to form; qualities that hover between the beautiful and the deformed. This is

Antoni Gaudí, Sagrada Família church, Barcelona, 1882–ongoing: statue of one of Herod's soldiers complete with the six toes of the model commissioned for the task. Gaudí insisted that the sculptor, Joan Matamala, accurately depict life's abnormalities.

the complement to the previous chapter, which considered *real absence* as part of his compositional strategy.

Ideas of monstrosity inhabit the domains of the natural and the supernatural more than those of the unnatural.[3] In Western tradition, the Gothic masons made literal use of the supernatural in their sculpted relief and figures, many of which use the monstrous to represent the reprehensible. The nature of the carved stone surfaces projected by Gaudí includes a literal use of figurative biblical reference for the Sagrada Família church, and is entirely consistent with his medievalist intentions for this great unfinished work. His more abstract work on the project demonstrates that he had an early understanding of our own post-modern abstraction: a belief that the organic life of architecture goes beyond the surfaces that appear to lock us down through their immutability. However frozen worked inorganic or dead material such as stone and timber might be, it is sufficient for other more volatile and more unstable worlds to be invoked by reference to rather than any inclusion of actual literal liveliness. Such impressions can be gleaned from the grain of inert substances through their worked surfaces; by implication if not by fact. Deeper than superficial readings lie more profound allegories that are ours for the unravelling when we let our gaze linger. In this respect, Gaudí's final project leaves more of a tale than might at first appear.

The Sagrada Família was established in mid-19th-century Barcelona to give a more pronounced voice to the Holy Family ('Sagrada Família') during times of profound change, increasing social dysfunction and undermining of the strength of the family unit. The building promotes Joseph the father as patriarchal leader of the family, and follows the Gothic model rigorously in both scope and layered meaning. Gaudí, however, went much further with his allegorical references in the small proportion of the whole actually built in his day, something amply evidenced too in the surviving large-scale gypsum plaster models he bequeathed his successors. Beneath, and removed from the stone and gypsum surfaces, are sufficient clues that he was well advanced in his thinking about the elusive intangibility of free-form; an 'intangibility' that, paradoxically, risks being conceptually lost when any free-form architectural composition is physically manifested as a building. Prior to his accidental death in 1926, he demonstrated a complexity and richness that foreshadow contemporary post-computer interest in less compliant form making; ideas that extend well beyond the merely superficial to the hypersuperficial. During these later years he introduced ideas of metamorphosis, morphogenesis and polymorphism into this work. The emblems that surround the elliptical clerestory window are examples of morphogenesis, and can be linked to an architectural teratology and the notion of 'evocative surface'.

D'Arcy Wentworth Thompson's description and analysis of growth and form[4] were introduced to the world arena at the same time that Gaudí completed his detailed design for the nave of the church. We have no evidence of any direct influence for Gaudí. While there may be much in common between Thompson's science and Gaudí's interpretation, Gaudí's work itself contains ingredients that step outside Thompson's analysis of growth, to include deeper and darker considerations of mutation and monstrosity. Although deviant in one respect, such deviancy is entirely consistent with the Gothic moral mysticism that Gaudí had consistently applied to the church during the 43 years during which he developed his design. In going beyond the superficial, to less stable and more transient realms that have to be visited more by the imagination than the eye, we can observe Gaudí both separating and drawing together ideas of kinship and excess as fundamental aspects of our human condition that needed, respectively, reinforcement and reduction.

At a practical level, the relevance of Gaudí employing second-order geometry for the entire composition of the nave[5] was alluded to by Collins,[6] but not unravelled fully until the 1990s.[7] A characteristic of second-order geometry is the way non-coplanar straight lines can variously describe warped surfaces, with an attendant practicality that is otherwise masked by an apparently free-form composition. Their principal practical advantage is the way each of these surfaces can be rationally fragmented into individual components which, when combined, will form a seamless whole. If we take

Hyperbolic paraboloid: as a ruled surface it is a relatively easy task to guide the sculptors' chisels.

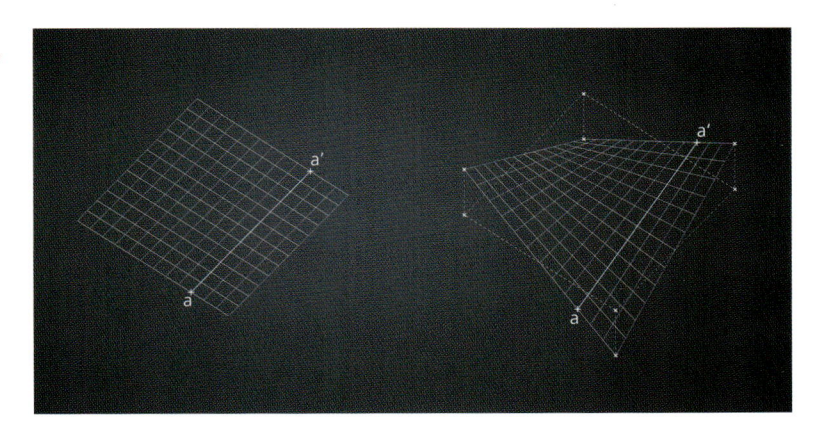

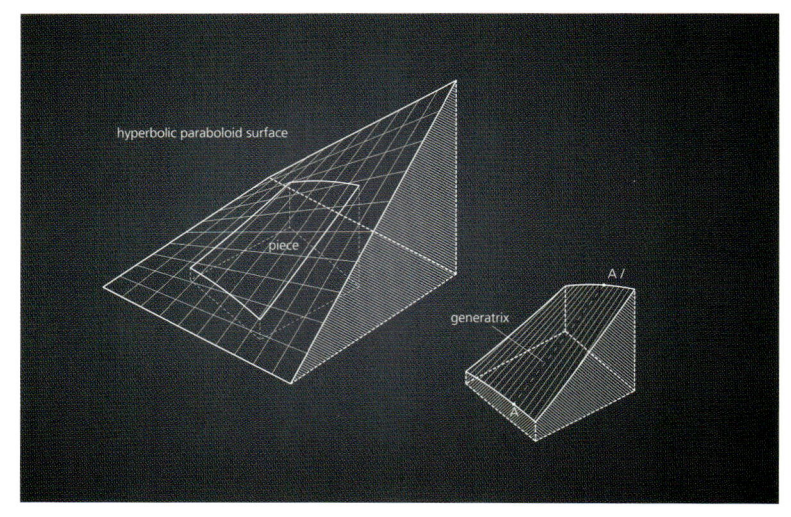

Diagram to show how an individual stone with a ruled surface can be carved independently of its neighbours with confidence so that it will match its neighbours with precision.

Gaudí's apartment building La Pedrera (c 1906 to c 1912) as an example of the opposite position, free-form rather than ruled surfaces (note the semantic distinction between free and ruled), we can see an important paradigmatic shift in Gaudí's surface modulation. La Pedrera required the masonry to be modelled in gypsum plaster at 1:1 in the basement on site, and for each piece to be carved at ground level, lifted to a position next to its neighbours, scribed, then lowered back to the ground for further refinement (a number of times). In contrast, ruled surfaces offer entirely different possibilities. Constituent elements can be carved once and carved well in isolation and without reference to their companions as the mason has to do little more than carve a series of straight lines between corresponding points marked on templates shared by adjacent pieces.

Gaudí had many reasons for this choice of ruled surfaces other than as an aid to building description. At an aesthetic level, he is alleged to have selected them to modify the play of light within the church – he describes light as 'gliding' along these surfaces, and providing enhanced acoustic attenuation; these are noted as being his primary concerns.[8] But it is also reasonable to propose that the nine parameters determining the spatial characteristics of each surface give a fluency of assembly that few other three-dimensional compositional strategies can offer. A sphere has only four variables – three Cartesian co-ordinates of location and a radius. A cylinder has seven. We can assess these ruled-surface figures as having the characteristics and nuances of a family group in ways that the sphere and cylinder do not, a broader range of qualities, some subtle, some extreme, some good, some not so good. The family grouping is crucial in order to appreciate the sophistication with which Gaudí operated. A sphere enjoys no relationship to a cylinder other than both forms being grouped as 'primitives' or 'Phileban objects'. One sphere differs from another only in size. In contrast, the hyperboloid can be anything between a cylinder and two opposed cones, with the aperture varying between a circle (let's say an ellipse with coincident foci for consistency) to a barely discernible slit. Beyond the unitary, each surface can relate to other family members with an astonishingly subtle bonding,

Antoni Gaudí, Sagrada Família church, Barcelona, 1882–ongoing: emblems surrounding the clerestory window. Starting from the left-hand side, the first, third and fifth (central) alpha emblems are the same topology as are the second and fourth beta emblems. They are all paramorphs.

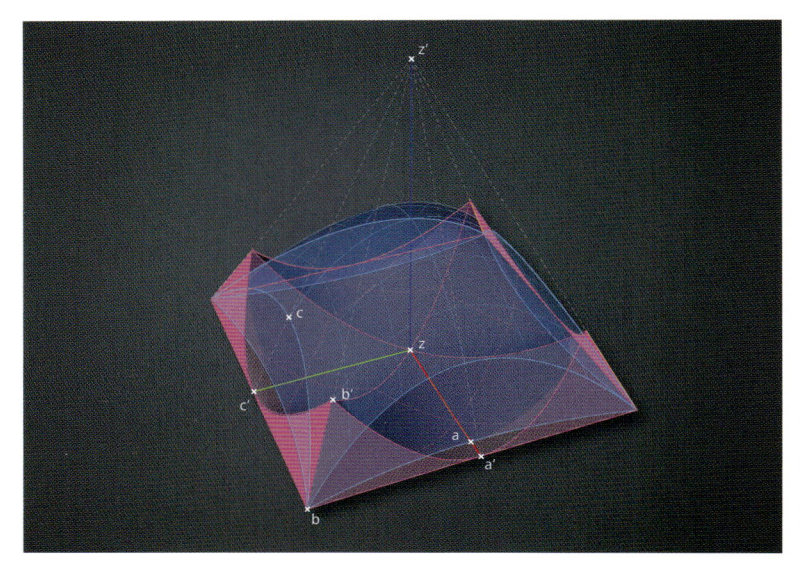

Diagram showing the relationship between the alpha and beta forms, and how the shifts between a and a' etc are all related to the invisible geometry of the pyramid.

revealed only by the mathematics of the resultant fourth-order curves of intersection between contiguous surfaces. Even the decorative faceting is derived from the hyperbolic geometry as combinations of triangular planes bounded by selected intersecting generatrices, the lines (straight by definition) that form the surfaces.

There is a kinship between these geometrical forms that goes further than the variables that tie each to the same species. The production of the applied decoration to the exterior and interior of the clerestory window appears at first glance to be arbitrarily related to the geometry, but it is actually a consequence of the composition. Equally, the emblems or motifs around the exterior of the clerestory rose window seem to be arbitrary but are neither whimsical nor entirely free from geometrical constraint. Each emblem might seem to be uniquely fashioned. In fact, they are based on a single genotype or species with two genders; lets say an alpha and a beta. In order, from the centre of each side, there are five separate motifs, including the largest that sits directly above the elliptical opening. The elliptical hyperboloid shows both life and force by exerting some kind of gravitational pull on the emblems that individually occupy quadrilaterals[9] formed from intersecting straight lines that rule the surface. They can be identified more specifically as alpha-1, beta-1, alpha-2 etc. Not only are alpha-2 and alpha-3 genetic variants or phenotypes of alpha-1, alpha and beta are morphogenetic variants of each other.

As a group they share kinship. The kinship is an invisible pyramid that is *virtually present*. The pyramid is the armature upon which all the geometry for the alpha and beta emblems is supported algorithmically. The proof is in the simple coding of an algorithm used to transform one to the other. I find it fascinating that Gaudí conceived all this but it is only by unpicking the invisible rationale that the extent of his underlying order or codex for the design is revealed. If even the smallest decorative elements are subject to such rigour, there can be no room for any arbitrary input. This is the extent of the scripting, relatively trivial, but it packs in an extraordinary amount of genetic narrative all the same.

'Organic' architecture might be one of our more problematic descriptors if not actually a misnomer. Buildings in their static condition are anything but organic, free-form no longer free, but fixed following its translation to built building. Too often, organic means that the built free-form may do little more than bear characteristics attributable to natural form. One can speculate on the degree of frustration Gaudí might have experienced in freezing life as immutable building fabric for the Nativity Facade; certainly the stiffness of the sculpture (but not its setting) is in contrast with other work of his mid career. Our consideration of the relationship between alpha and beta is more easily explained through a fourth dimension: displacement interpreted as movement. By morphing between the alpha and the beta forms sticking with the parental DNA, it is possible to show a selection of frames animating

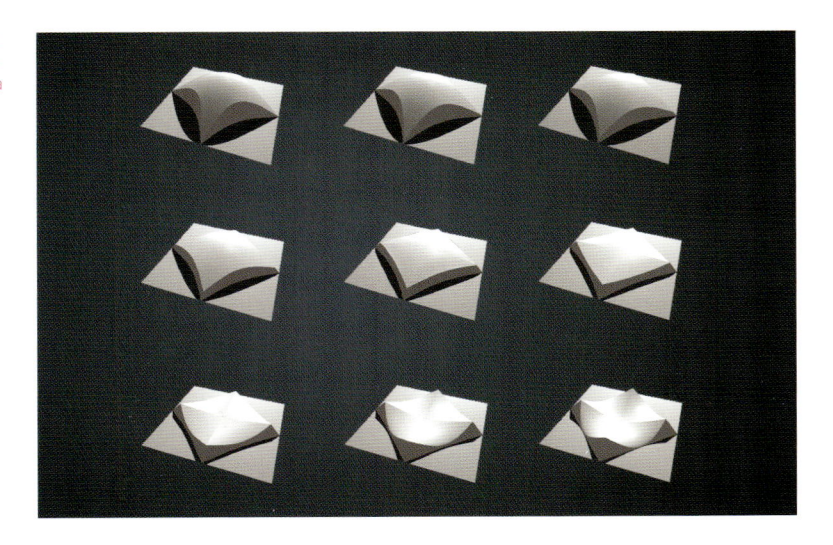

Progression of nine generic emblems scripted to morph from alpha (top left) to beta (bottom right) (1998).

the transition between these two opposites. At mid-morph we can see the neutering of the hermaphroditic dome boundary: an alpha-beta hybrid.

Our speculation on the organic nature of architectural composition can go further, deeper, into the hypersurface gene pool; the virtual rather than the real beyond that which Gaudí has delimited through his models. The legitimacy for such experimentation lies in the algorithm that generates the exact and simplest morphogenetic relationship. In the case of this

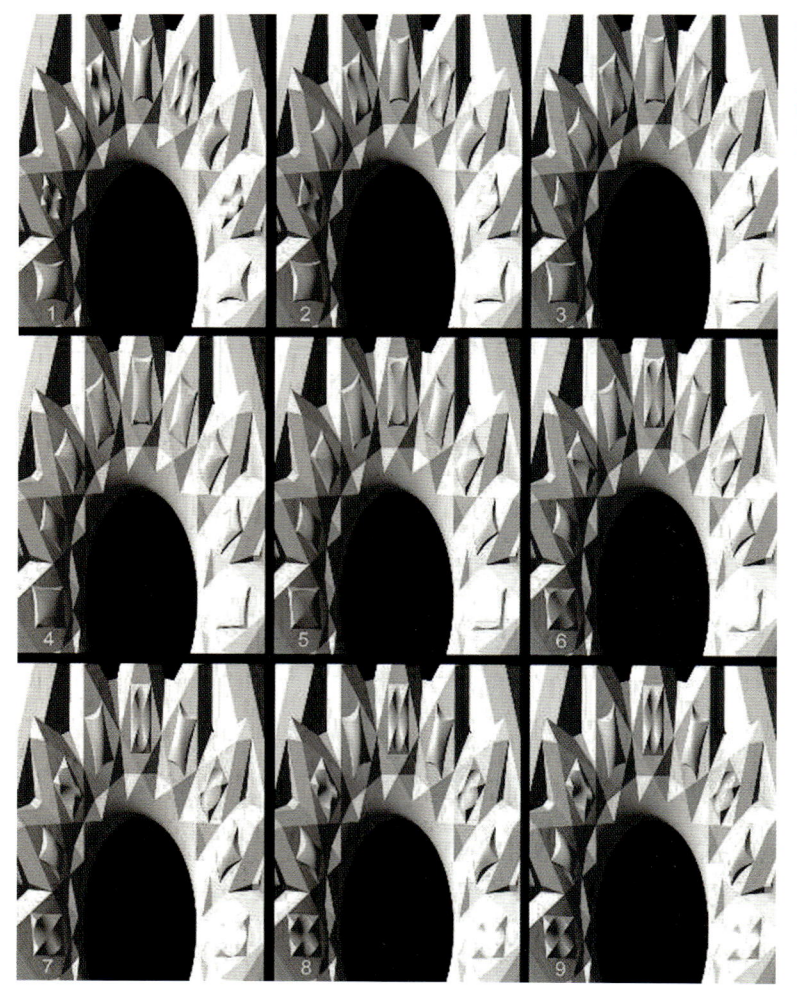

Antoni Gaudí, Sagrada Familia church, Barcelona, 1882–ongoing: central nave clerestory – emblems around the perimeter morphing in situ (top left to bottom right).

architecture, there are implications of being truly organic, attendant on our going further than the immediate and tightly controlled constraints that give alpha and beta such poise and stasis, a reduction that is simply a constraint borne from actual construction.[10]

What if we engineered a route from proto-alpha to retro-beta? By doing no more than altering two numerical parameters in the algorithm which produced the original perfect morph between alpha and beta, this growth extender and the age accelerator cause extraordinary and terrible consequences: a vigorous bolting growth spurt and a premature decrepitude going beyond the dignity of normal aging or, in this case, that which is constructed. The emblem is thus transformed into a teratoid: *'having the appearance or character of a monster or monstrous formation'*.[11]

Antoni Gaudí, Sagrada Família church, Barcelona, 1882–ongoing : cloister rosary door (Nativity Facade) – youth tempted into terrorism by being offered a grenade by a reptile with a humanoid non-uniformly scaled head adding to the sense of monstrosity (1896).

Chapters 6 and 7 have considered the family relationship between nave surfaces and the elements bounded by their geometry. My morphogenetic and progerial reading may seem to be taken beyond any conscious creative thinking by Gaudí. As a personal reading (as it should be) it can, however, be complemented by consideration of his more figurative sculpture dating from an earlier period. The cloister, for instance, has an entrance arch that springs from two sculpted scenes on opposite sides. Both tell stories of corruption – one depicts the plight of a young woman tempted into prostitution, the other of a youth to violence. In the former, a perverted version of a mermaid offers a bag of gold to the innocent. The companion scene shows a salamander with an exaggerated human head (as has the 'mermaid'), offering a grenade bristling with detonators to the anarchist recruit. Of particular interest to digerati is the extraordinary distortion of the human features to both creatures. It would almost seem that Gaudí deliberately stopped the morphogenetic hybridisation of the human element before the process had fully developed. This suspended animation is akin to a violent mid-term removal of a metamorphosing pupa from its chrysalis, an even more suggestive portrayal of the dance between good and evil, and the freakish and the sublime

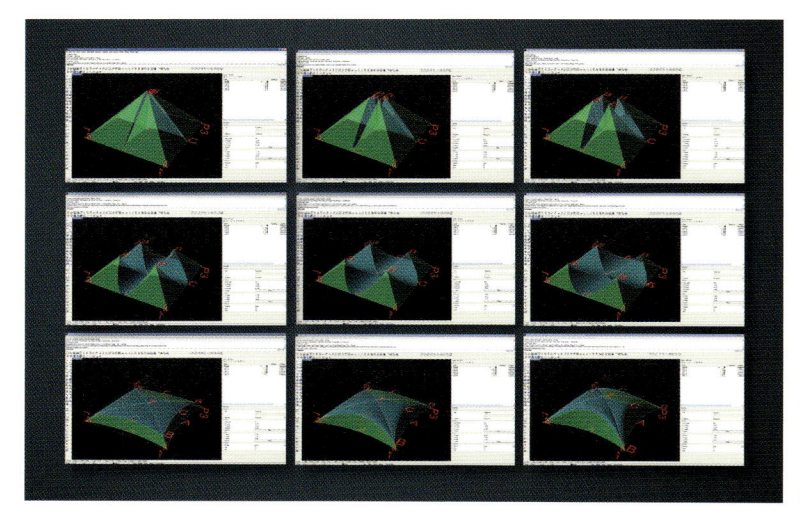

The emblems become teratoids (growths) when the script coaxes them beyond the alpha and beta states at each end of the cycle.

than that depicted by the gargoyles and sculpted relief of the Sagrada Família's Gothic antecedents. Corruption is better represented here through the power of the suggestion over the literal. In modern parlance, the head has been morphed or 'non-uniformly scaled' along a single axis.

Triforium 'columnetes'

The clerestory window is supported by a three-dimensional arcade forming a triforium and gallery. The elegant muscularity of the *columnetes* (little columns) belies a surprisingly simple regime: a composition of whole and bisected hyperbolic paraboloid surfaces. Looking at the overall composition,

Teratoids spanning way beyond the ideal states of the clerestory window emblems for Antoni Gaudí's Sagrada Família church, Barcelona.

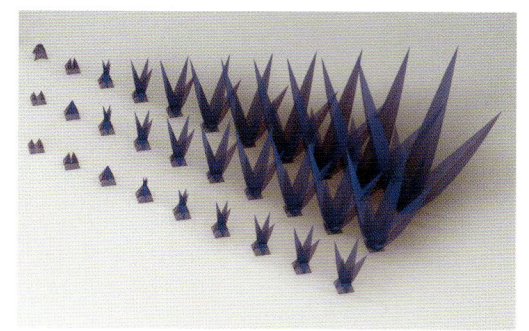

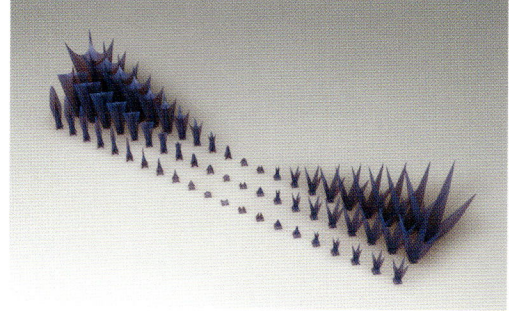

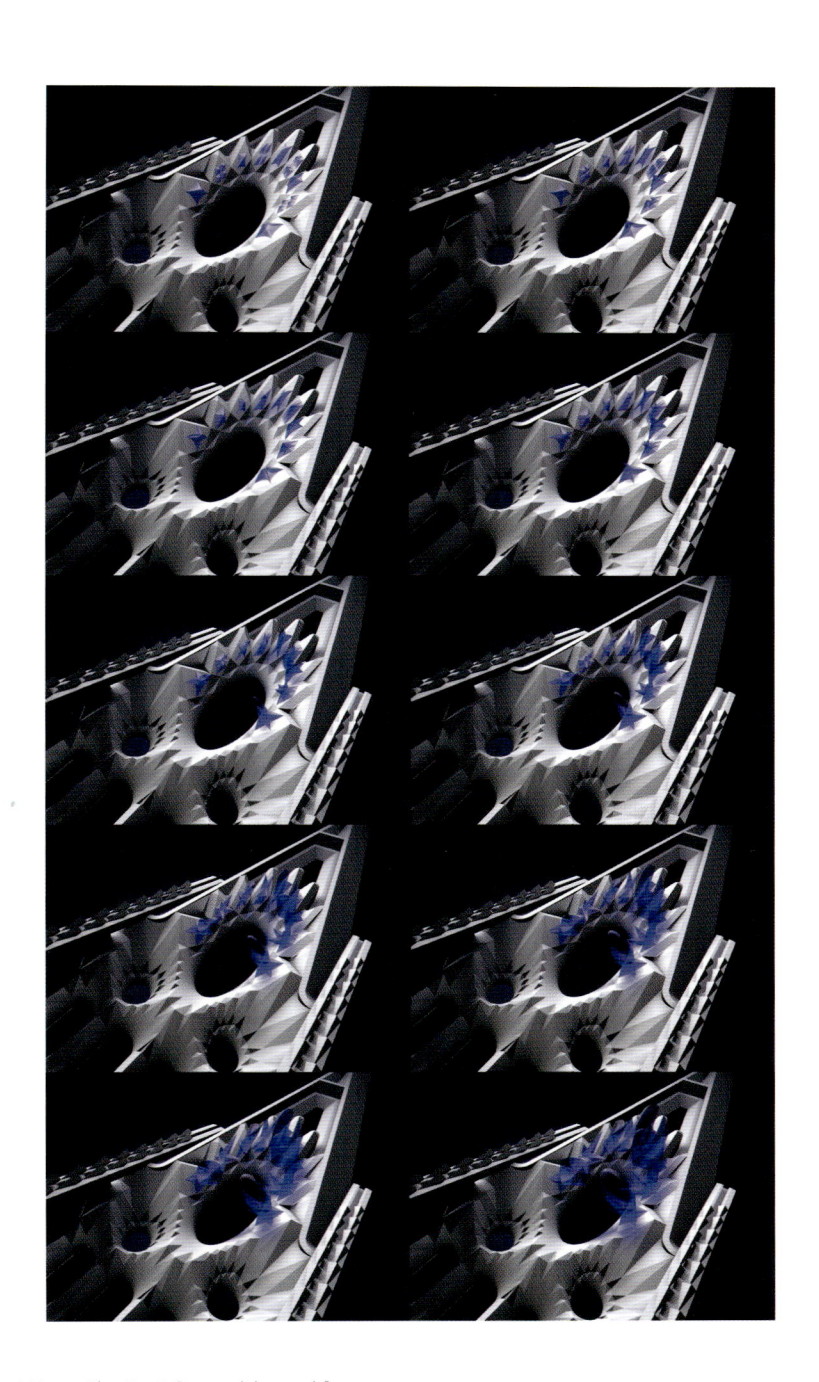

Antoni Gaudí, Sagrada Família church, Barcelona, 1882–ongoing: central nave clerestory – emblems blowing out simply through the script moving beyond Gaudí's stopping points. Scripting reveals the poise of Gaudí's emblems in their ideal rather than exaggerated states.

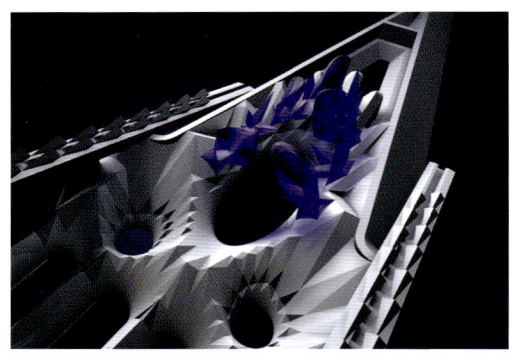

their geometrical derivation is not readily apparent, yet the use of the ruled surfaces in this way allows for a unique blending of adjacent forms into a seamless skin barely disguising the tautness of the work-formed structure.[12]

There are several interesting aspects to this composition. The first is the alignment of each group of six columns (three to the fore mask three symmetrically placed to the rear) such that extensions of all six axes reach down to a virtual point in space, which is the node of the main column below from which the extended surfaces virtually branch. They are 'dissolved' into the horizontal structural elements that support the triforium floor: this is another example of *virtual presence*. They are related to this virtual point by structural implication and visual connection, but are truncated by a neutral

Antoni Gaudí, Sagrada Família church, Barcelona, 1882–ongoing: central nave clerestory – exterior front and oblique view. The stone has liquified.

Antoni Gaudí, Sagrada Família church, Barcelona, 1882–ongoing: triforium – restored version of Gaudí's original 1:10 scaled model.

plane (the triforium floor) at a certain height above the virtual confluence of their axes. As in nearly all the columns for the building, these too tend towards a circular profile, in this case at the base where they meet the floor. How, then, is the geometry determined such that the hyperbolic exigencies are met yet, when bisected at triforium level, all four cut surfaces for each column combine to form an approximate circle?

As the lower portions are missing, turning to the original model for help does not offer any real evidence of the means by which Gaudí arrived at the solution. The models are a reasonably complex task for the makers, so reiterative experimentation would have been time-consuming. With the computer we have been able to script possible design criteria as a prelude to modelling the outcome. Using software that allows the designer to work with associative geometry, that is form defined relationships between geometry with the ability to change the values of the various parameters, the digital model can be reconfigured to be bolder or more svelte in a matter of seconds.

The implications of these digital gymnastics are an important difference between pre- and post-digital design. In the case of the composition for this set of columns, the philosophy behind the design may be clear, but the particularities are rather harder to organise in order to conform to this construct. By tweaking at the relevant parameters, the designer can find the appropriate set of hyperbolic paraboloids, which when bisected by a plane, yield profiles that are effectively quadrants. As a set, these yield the required circular profile at the point of ground contact.

Comparing a view down the length of the triforium that supports the nave clerestory window built in the late 1990s at the Sagrada Família Church with

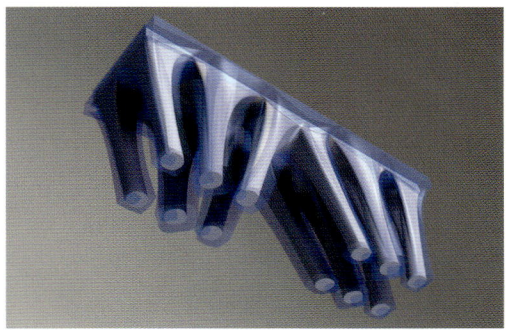

Antoni Gaudí, Sagrada Família church, Barcelona, 1882–ongoing: triforium – the invisible axes and extensions of the columns composed of hyperbolic paraboloids all converge at a virtual point in space coinciding with the node of the column end below.

Antoni Gaudí, Sagrada Família church, Barcelona, 1882–ongoing: triforium – this was the first example of scripted parametric design used for the Sagrada Família church – here, three variants are shown (1995).

△ Mark Burry   165   Chapter 7 Composition and form

the well-known gallery at Gaudí's Teresianas Convent (1889; one of Gaudí's earlier works), there is a strange progression from what is effectively a 2 ½ D sequence of flat parabolic arches at the convent to the 4D version at the Sagrada Família church, a magical space that he never lived to see.

There are some very subtle differences that point to a maturity emerging during these final years, and although Gaudí never experienced the triforium space personally, these differences offer further proof of his ability to conceive spatially captivating environments with unerring intuition. The similarities between both galleries are the use of the straight line to describe intentions. In the case of the Convent, the lines describe the parabolas that form the arch profiles. These parabolas double as an original aesthetic statement while assuming the most structurally efficient profile. In the case of the triforium, such two-dimensional flair is readily translated into four-dimensional mastery. The surfaces, all of which are hyperbolic paraboloids, as well as being structurally efficient are more builderly than if they were not made from ruled surfaces.

Antoni Gaudí, Col·legi de les Teresianes, Barcelona, 1890. The sequence of flat parabolic arches at the convent seems poised between two and three dimensions.

Antoni Gaudí, Temple Sagrada Família, Barcelona, Spain , 1882–ongoing: Triforium: as built (1998).

The nave roof

The nave roof provides further evidence of Gaudí's use of the virtually present as a point to anchor cohesion to a formal spatial construct. In an account of Gaudí's intentions published two years after his death, Josep Ràfols i Fontanals (1889–1965), an architect, artist and historian who had collaborated with Gaudí and wrote the first biography of him, observes that the nave roof is an assemblage of hyperbolic paraboloids, all meeting at a point.[13] In considering the 1:25 scaled gypsum plaster model, this observation is not readily substantiated by eye. If, however, we reduce the surfaces to their underlying geometry, we can see that with the right combination of parameters the hyperbolic skins relax into the original surfaces.

The role of the computer to find the curves of inflection relies on scripting a set of contiguous associative geometries. The first step was to make a digital model of the surviving and restored original and to use the wire frame outcome as a skeleton onto which a skin could be grafted. The digital model was made in 1996 and measured by a point digitiser, an articulated arm that has a digital probe with a sharpened point. Fourteen years later this already seems an archaic relic, but at the time it was regarded as an invaluable new digital tool. The resulting 3D wire frame model was imported into a parametric geometry design package and was used as reference for building a geometrically precise version. Using the digitised model as a base, a notional flexible model is built around it. This does not need to be accurate in terms of positions and line lengths, for example, but the flexible model needs to be the topological equivalent. Once built it is only a matter of scripting a sequence of likely range of values for the determining parameters, by which the virtual model was built up or relaxed, fattened or made more slim until it finally folded into the original. By building the model from hyperbolic paraboloids that meet at a virtual point that itself can be varied in height, in minutes the correct (in terms of matching the original) form was found that is also composed entirely of ruled surfaces and planes. Of course, today we would use a genetic algorithm within the script for an automated best-fit solution.

Quite what use Gaudí himself would have made of such versatile virtual design exploration potential is no more than idle speculation, as is the precise manner in which he achieved a complex study such as this, with the virtual apex not physically in evidence. At issue here is the reverse engineering of a stated design solution from Gaudí that requires rebuilding

168

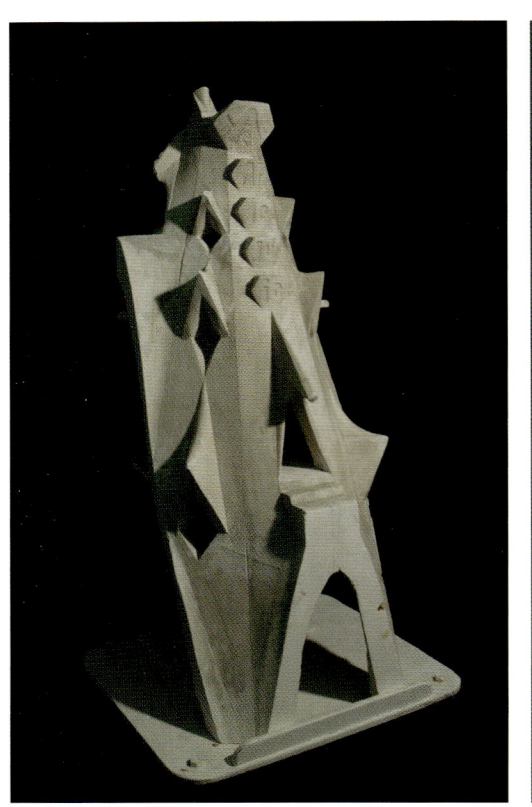

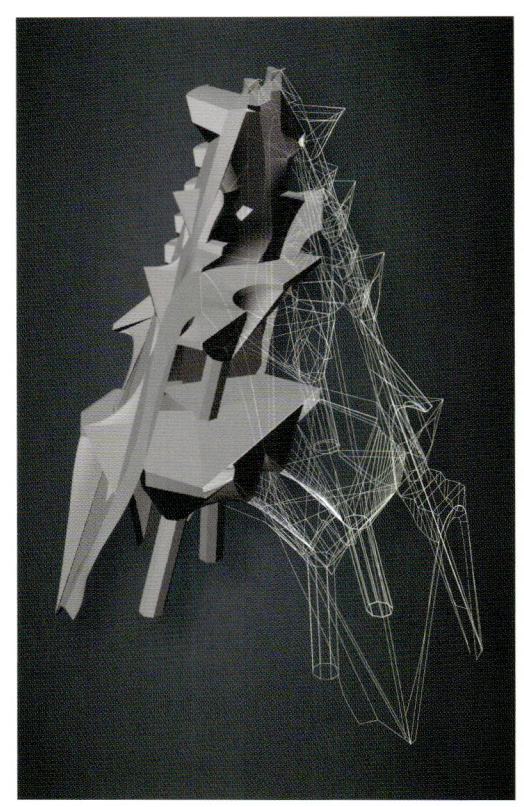

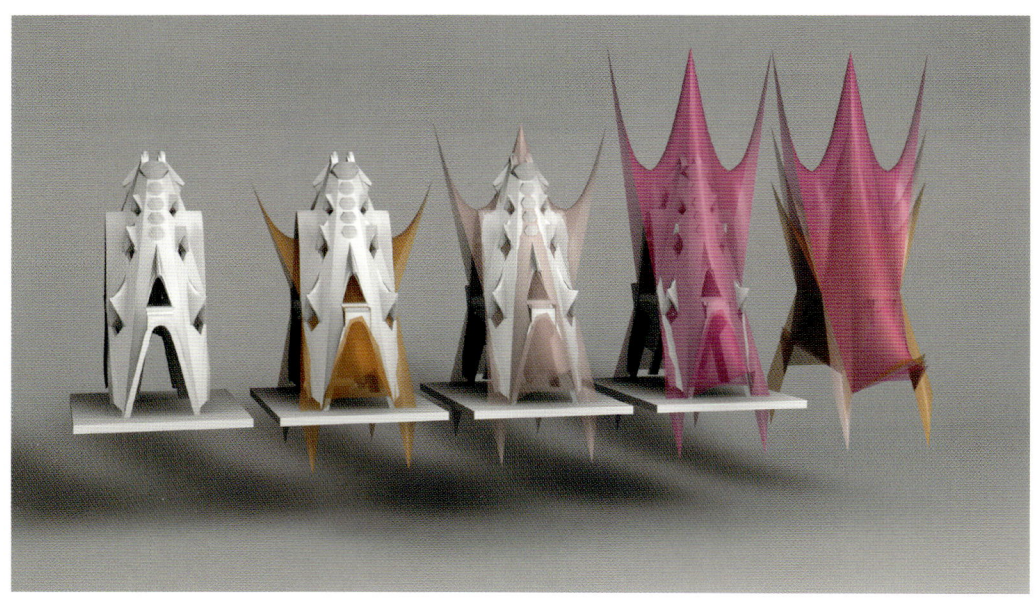

Antoni Gaudí, Sagrada Família church, Barcelona, 1882–ongoing: nave roof designed by Gaudí at 1:25, but not photographed until 1926.

Antoni Gaudí, Sagrada Família church, Barcelona, 1882–ongoing: 3D virtual model of nave roof digitised and surfaced with precision made ready for overlay of parametrically controlled ruled surfaces.

to provide information for the built artefact. The virtual point, so present in the act of making the digital model, is fascinatingly elusive once the form has taken hold.

Liquid stone

Whatever Gaudí's formal intentions, his surface composition for the nave was never realised in his time at any scale greater than 1:10, and never written about by him. He nevertheless conceived and exploited a compositional geometry with rare grace. The animation or life implicit within the geometry is necessarily suspended as carved material, a static representation of kinship, variety and perfection. Yet the same surfaces provide all the clues and threats of violation and corruption through their concealed revelation of such potential. Read in this way, they point through inference to humankind's striving for the ideal while keeping a careful eye on the monstrous, an ineffable benchmark of extremes. The implied perfection is only skin deep. Closer reading provides the stimulation to extrapolate new ways to release the music and hear different architectural cadences from those with which we are familiar.

Antoni Gaudí, Sagrada Família church, Barcelona, 1882–ongoing: seeking the right combination of values for the virtual cloak of hyperbolic paraboloids – the centre model has the closest match of the three variants shown.

The rewards that scripting brings to the study and implementation of Gaudí's design using the best of digital technology also support the communication of aspects of the design to interested parties with no special knowledge in the area. Such endeavours for an architect as enigmatic as Gaudí are perhaps means and ends that justify themselves. Much of the research findings reported in this and the previous chapter has only become comprehensible in terms of Gaudí's design plan through the efforts to complete the Sagrada Família church, and inevitably this work has been dragged into the digital arena. But it is inevitable also that the issue of whether it is appropriate to tar an architect such as Antoni Gaudí with the digital brush will rapidly become less of an issue as society becomes more accepting of the way this medium has infiltrated all aspects of our creative lives. Suffice to say, the formal geometrical gymnastics performed by Gaudí years before such electronic aids emerged, challenges the best of whatever we have on our digital workbenches today. Such architecture of what is not (real absence), and of what is only there by implication (virtual presence), and the attendant morphogenetic lyricism both transcends and humbles information technology *per se,* reminding us that some *a priori* values remain transcendent.

(This chapter is adapted from my 'Gaudí, Teratology and Kinship'[14] and 'Gaudí and Information Technology: an architecture of real absence and virtual presence')[15]

References

[1] R Descharnes, C Prévost, *Gaudí the Visionary*, Bracken Books (London), 1971, p 140.
[2] E Grosz, 'Freaks' in *Social Semiotics*, 1991, Vol 2, pp 22–36: 'Our fascination with the monstrous human is testimony to our own tenuous hold on the image of perfection; the freak confirms us as bounded, belonging, a "proper" social category …'
[3] M Dorrian, 'Monstrosity Today', *Artifice* 5, UCL The Bartlett (London), 1996, pp 48–59. Dorrian includes images by Serrano and Orlan in his piece, all of which are unnatural images or juxtapositions. They are not examples of natural or supernatural monstrosity.
[4] See D'A W Thompson, *On Growth and Form*, Cambridge University Press (Cambridge), 1917.
[5] See I Puig i Boada, *The Church of the Sagrada Família*, Ediciones de Nuevo Arte Thor (Barcelona), 1st edn 1929, rep 1988.
[6] GR Collins, 'Antonio Gaudi: Structure and Form' in *Perspecta 8: The Yale Architectural Journal*, 1963, pp 63–90.
[7] See MC Burry, *Architecture in Detail – Expiatory Church of the Sagrada Família, Antoni Gaudí*, Phaidon (London), 1993. Also, J Gomez, J Coll, JC Melero, MC Burry, *La Sagrada Família: de Gaudí al CAD* Edicions UPC, Universitat Politècnica de Catalunya (Barcelona), 1996.
[8] Before actual construction of Gaudí's second-order doubly ruled surfaces for the first time in the 1980s, which was when the practical advantages first became apparent, only the aesthetic qualities of the surfaces were commented on.
[9] Each of the quadrilaterals is a figure bounded on four sides by intersecting straight lines that rule the surface.
[10] The fluidity of purpose is extrapolated from the actual built fabric, beyond that frozen into stone.
[11] 'Teratoid' Def. 3. *Oxford English Dictionary*, 2nd edn, 1989, CD-ROM.
[12] Ruled surfaces appear abundantly in nature. When we attempt to spread our hands, the webs that separate our fingers from each other assume the hyperbolic paraboloid shape, a surface formed by the work the webs are subjected to in keeping the hand together.
[13] JF Rafols, *Gaudí*, Editorial Canosa (Barcelona), 1928, p 201.
[14] MC Burry, 'Gaudí, Teratology and Kinship', in *Hypersurfaces, AD*, Academy Editions (London), April 1998, pp 38–43.
[15] MC Burry, 'Gaudí and Information Technology: an architecture of real absence and virtual presence' in *Gaudí 2002. Miscellània*, Editorial Planeta (Barcelona), 2002, pp 200–15.

Simplifying complexity for fabrication 8

How can a complex 3D curve such as a non-uniform rational B-spline (NURBS) be resolved into a set of simple geometries that suits the fabrication industry working to its current capability, and without a loss of design quality? This chapter begins with a discussion of an approach taken to resolve this conundrum when the Melbourne-based sculpture/architecture practice of Cat Macleod and Michael Bellemo presented us (RMIT University – SIAL) with a model comprised of a loose tangle of wires to describe digitally in order to proceed to make it buildable. I begin by outlining the nature of the problem and show how we applied the resulting theory to a single NURBS curve as a precursor to making an essential contribution to this public art project. My account moves on to reflect on the case study sited in Melbourne – *Shoal Fly By*, a series of four sculptures up to 50 metres in length. Representing 'movement through water' and composed predominantly of a profusion of wildly intersecting NURBS curves, the construction represented a significant challenge to the

Cat Macleod and Michael Bellemo, *Shoal Fly By*, Melbourne, 2002. One of the completed sculptures as built.

△ Mark Burry 171 Chapter 8 Simplifying complexity for fabrication designers, engineers, fabricators and erectors. The chapter unpacks the workflow for the fabrication description and production and looks back over a strategy to convert the metallic spaghetti into affordable stainless-steel arc tubes cut into practical lengths.

Shoal Fly By

Shoal Fly By actually consists of four independent works, *Shoal*, *Fissure*, *Sailor* and *Net*, each comprised of a jumble of loosely woven metallic strands, the largest of which is approximately 40 metres in length. The site is the city of Melbourne's rehabilitated waterfront, which at the time was in the early stages of redevelopment from redundant port to the extensive Docklands precinct, located very close to the city's central business district.[1] The practice had won a competition for the project, and the sculptures, which are all quite linear in composition, were to be stretched along the wharf's edge aligned between the marina and the new sports stadium.

The first handcrafted 1:100 scale model that we were presented with in 2002 was for a sculpture designed as a filigree skein that *'floated over head out of the corner of the eye, not a monumental scene stealing thing but ghost-like slipping through the air'*.[2] The wire model was a little more than a foot in length and there had been no immediate practical challenge to the artists beavering away, bending here, tweaking there until their eyes were satisfied

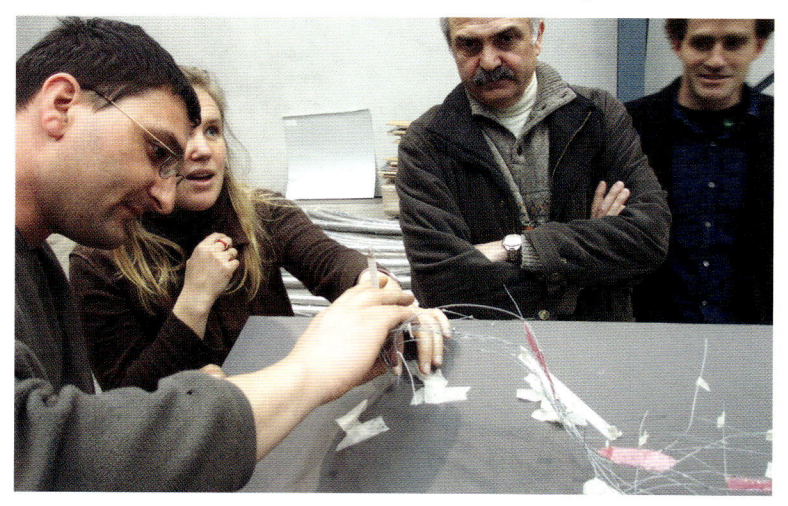

Cat Macleod and Michael Bellemo, *Shoal Fly By*, Melbourne, 2002. The artists' original scale model being prepared for digitising with a point scanner.

with the outcome. The real challenge lay in translating the intentions to a constructed piece one hundred times larger.

The conversation between the sculptors and the fabricators can be easily envisaged with all the mutual head scratching it necessarily invoked. Conceptually it all looks very straightforward: just grab pieces of pipe up to 40 metres in length and manipulate them in space until they all conform to the models' accurately detailed registration. Of course it was not only the need to be able to bend each tube precisely as modelled with every highly deliberate kink, wobble and faithfully recreated flutter borne out in the full-scale version; there was also the need to get the elements to pass each other in space with precision and fuse adequately with one another and so form a structurally competent object capable of supporting itself. The sculptors demanded a 'seamless yet not smooth' aesthetic.

We were confronted with four principal tasks:

1 capturing the data;

2 interpreting the data as a 3D digital version of the model;

3 seeking a methodology for interpreting the curves so that stainless-steel tubes could be described accurately such that a fabricator would be able to reconstruct them;

4 discovering a way to convey this information to the fabricator.

This, then, is the story of developing a specific methodology for dealing with complex 3D curves in order to fabricate a challenging art piece. It also provides a pathway to dealing with this same issue in a more generic situation. What follows is a detailed account of getting *Shoal Fly By* up and swimming, as it were, and extending the application of the methodology to fabricating tubular contorted structures as a general condition. Along the way we shall briefly touch on 'problem decomposition' as an essential part of successful algorithm generation, and there will also be a reminder that even when confronted by complex problems the solution does not necessarily require complete novelty.

Data capture

Compared with the hand-measured work for the Sagrada Família church described earlier (Chapters 6 and 7), in 2002 we had two digital measuring tools available to us. The first and in theory the more ideal was a point-and-click digitiser. With the highly accurate probe on the end of an arm we could pick an appropriate number of points along each of the wire strands and interpolate a polyline between the two ends through the intermediate points. The problem with this method was that apart from the difficulty of recalling which of the strands had been measured, the slightest movement of the wire when touched by the probe introduced an unacceptable degree of error from the artists' viewpoint. They had made it clear that even the most accidental-looking kink in a strand was anything but casual. The second measuring technique available to us was using our point-cloud scanner. In making a pass over the model, millions of data points were collected. At that time there were very few software assistants to make automatic sense of the mass of information collected in this way, but we were able to parse it through an intermediary software into Rhino 3D™. There we could identify the strands as clusters along which we could nominate sufficient key points with which to draw the appropriate polylines defining the centre line of each strand as closely as possible.

Interpreting the data as a 3D digital model

Using the mass of centre lines extracted from the point cloud, it was a relatively simple matter to make each polyline into a pipe of uniform diameter along each length. Once all the pipes had been re-created digitally, and the small slivers of mesh that adorned the cluster of pipes digitally added to the work, we were able to compare the resulting 3D digital model with the original handmade prototype. The sculptors, tube benders and fabricators were consulted at this very early stage in order that the team could settle on a working methodology that would make the artwork both constructible and affordable. Gathering the team together at the first opportunity for projects of this nature is essential lest anyone, especially the architect, proceeds on entirely false premises. And, of course, there was no wonder machine available to us from which a perfectly bent and kinked tube, tens of metres in length, would emerge from the description of the tube entered as a digital file.

Cat Macleod and Michael Bellemo, *Shoal Fly By*, Melbourne, 2002. Point clouds from digital scanning.

Cat Macleod and Michael Bellemo, *Shoal Fly By*, Melbourne, 2002. Tracing lines to follow the scanned wires that form the model.

Seeking a methodology for interpreting the curves' geometry

A sculpture of this size and complexity needed to be constructed in a yard close to its eventual site. In Melbourne there were only two tube-bending options for us to consider. One was a bending machine working to a constant radius and producing a spiral, which was not appropriate for our project. The other was a company able to bend any radius within a useful minimum and maximum radius, and to any sectoral length. It was at this point that two pieces of prior knowledge intervened. How could a NURBS curve be converted into smooth 2D assemblies of cotangent arcs, given that this was the only bending technology available to us? And could this be translated into 3D?

My first useful recollection of a possible precedent was the problem that bridge engineers and architects traditionally faced in seeking the appropriate stereotomy for oval 'flattened' arches. Typically the outside edges of the arch would need to be tangent to the vertical, and obviously the top of the arch would be horizontal. I happened to have worked with ellipses before.[3] I had one method of constructing them using a string loop and two drawing pins at the foci of the ellipse. This method was the most prosaic, hands-on and haptically intelligible, but not accurate. The second method was to construct the ellipse from two circles with different diameters but a shared centre.

French curves would do the rest. The third and more accurate was using a calculator and the equation for the ellipse with a centre at 0,0,0.

$$\frac{x^2}{a^2} + \frac{y^2}{b^2} = 1$$

With a > b > 0.

Again, the drawing of the ellipse would be a matter of joining sufficiently calculated points with a set of French curves.

A search of the literature revealed that, despite the fact that there were several approaches to finding a set of arcs to more or less combine to produce a smooth impression of the ellipse, it is difficult to find a method that has great precision. The essential theory is to combine arcs that are cotangent to each other where they should join. In this way a sequence of cotangent arcs with increasing radii can join to give the impression of the ellipse meeting the essential horizontal condition at the top of the arch, and finding the vertical at the sides. Depending on the number of arcs used, the resulting geometry would be described as a 'three-centred arch' or a 'five-centred arch'. This construction was contingent on the technology available at the time. It is far easier for the stone cutter to work with a set of compasses to describe the necessary components (arcs), there being no accurate device

Ferdinand Meldahl, elliptical arch, Grovsmedje (former naval forge), Copenhagen, 1861.

to draw ellipses. A true ellipse could not be described on individual pieces of stone by the mason regardless of the fact that a 1:1 template could be produced by the string-and-two-pins solution (the first option described above), especially when at that time there was no suitable stable sheet material to use as a template. This stereotomy problem was resolved during

Three methods to draw an ellipse.

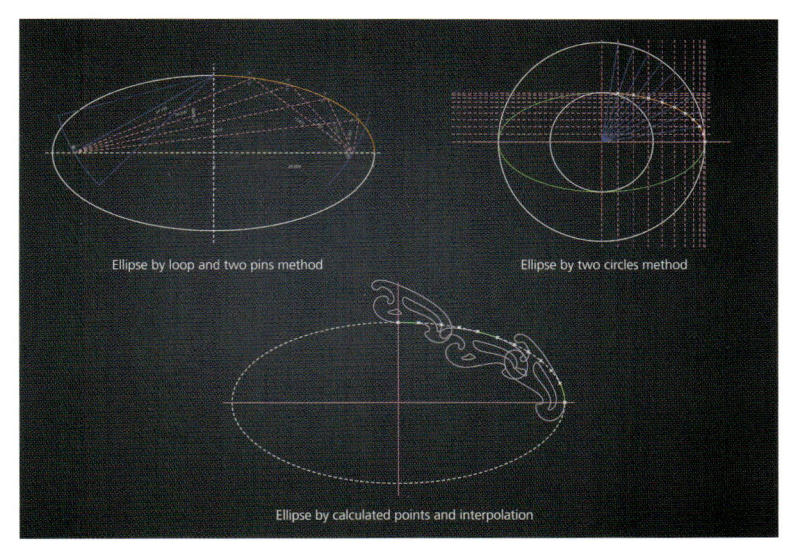

Ellipse by loop and two pins method

Ellipse by two circles method

Ellipse by calculated points and interpolation

The route to cotangentiality in 2D.

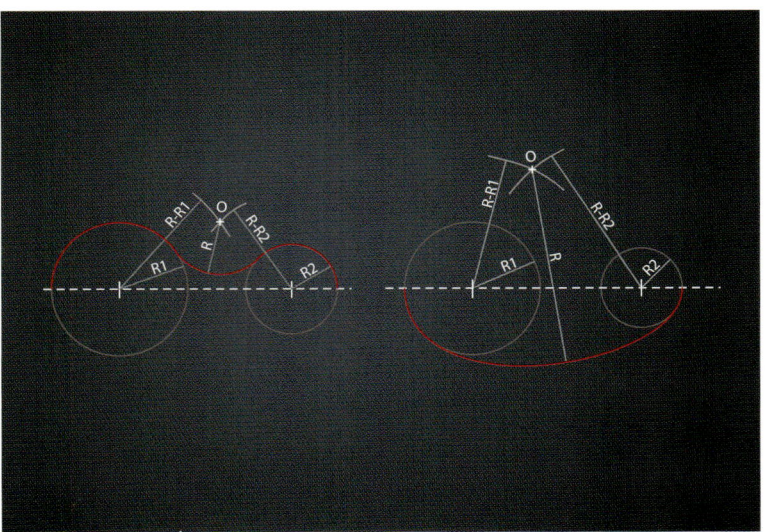

the years of the Enlightenment using descriptive geometry, an approach that characterises the situation we found ourselves in more than two centuries later: simplification of the compound curve to facilitate construction using best available technology.

If a set of cotangent arcs could combine to produce smooth approximations of a 2D NURBS curve, could the same principle be applied in 3D? That answer was easily furnished by considering a plumber at work, whose task is to ensure the silent flow of water either by bending selectively a length of pipe to smoothly follow each given route, or by using a selection of pipe elbows. For us the use of elbows was the necessary conceptual quantum leap to allow us to begin the description of the brief from which a suitable algorithm could emerge. It was a matter of testing it in our modelling software.

In 2002, we were using Rhino 3D™ version 1.1. Version 2, though out in beta, was not with us at the crucial time and so its very handy 'curve to arc' function was not available, obliging us to make our own customisation. First we had to test the viability of the approach as a proof of concept, by dividing the NURBS curve arbitrarily into a number of straight line segments. Each segment is used to generate notional subdivisions that, for each pair, define a plane. Each pair of line segments creates a fillet on that plane – a notional arc that by definition is cotangent with the residual straight lines on the plane and sized to remove as much of the straight lines as possible. The same operation is undertaken on the next pair of straight lines extracted from the original 3D curve. A best-fit fillet for the second pair of line segments (lines 2–3) is then constructed that most probably calls for a readjustment in the first fillet (lines 1–2) and *vice versa,* until each sequential fillet finally joins its neighbour. In this way, we have produced a series of cotangent arcs that roughly approximates with the original NURBS curve. Of course, approximating the result is rather woeful in terms of matching the actual curve, but it nevertheless served to first test the viability of the approach, as well as providing a graphic description of what was required to assist us through programming support. The essential point here is that before beginning to script, the problem has to be broken up into discrete packages and a logical process initiated.

Could we have worked up a script ourselves?

Pending the arrival of the Rhino 3D™ *curve to arc* tool, the description above shows just how imprecise a hand-built approach would be simply to reach an approximate outcome. It was clear that we needed sophisticated

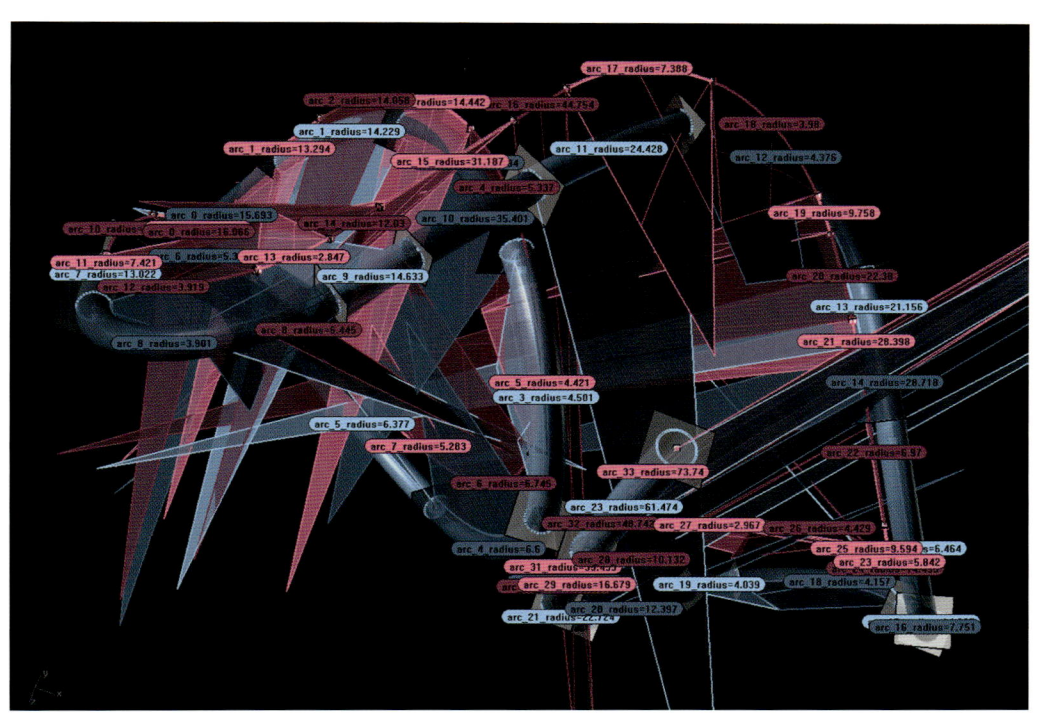

Scripting alternative solutions with visual feedback. The user can interact with the script as it runs, effectively decision-making on the fly.

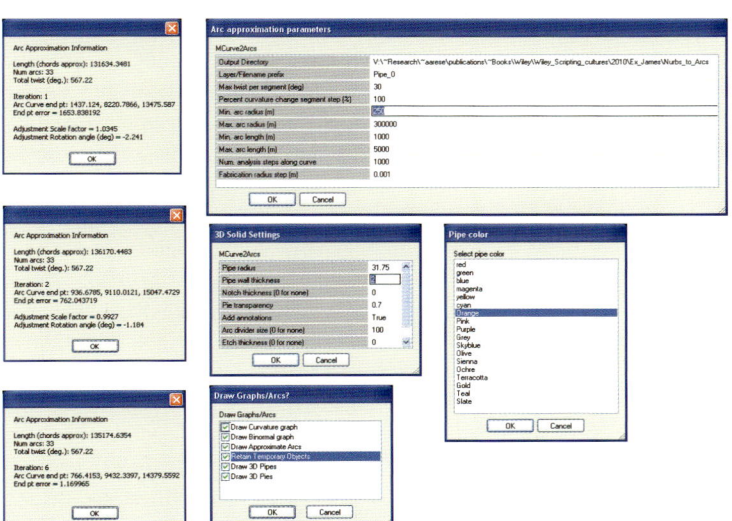

△ Mark Burry   179   Chapter 8 Simplifying complexity for fabrication

Pt			Mid			Pt			Right			Pt			Radius	Arc	Centre	Arc	Length	Arc	angle(deg)	Twist	angle(de	#NAME?	anti-clockwise
0	-2003.693,	-14775.895,				1472.278	-4024.549,	-14122.723,				2784.573	13601.082	-2513.098,	-2040.808	-3276.141	5000.076	21.06	0	Arc_1	nil
2784.573	-5436.055,	-13430.807,				3600.542	-6815.388,	-12581.877,				4317.243	16639.027	-2596.484,	426.942,	-5160.557	3543.935	12.2	-2.3	Arc_2	nil
4317.243	-7472.941,	-12118.342,				4625.912	-8123.747,	-11627.546,				4905.363	18321.431	-4421.046,	205.86,	-8582.979	1723.548	5.39	-11.45	Arc_3	nil
4905.363	-8701.168,	-11168.135,				5128.984	-9275.083,	-10692.456,				5326.048	18968.423	-6577.574,	-1322.264,	-10944.293	1542.162	4.66	-10.71	Arc_4	nil
5326.048	-10047.976,	-10027.938,				5547.993	-10817.664,	-9344.247,				5716.379	19098.817	-8973.648,	-3601.045,	-12404.88	2086.603	6.26	-10.88	Arc_5	nil
5716.379	-12673.585,	-7621.371,				5897.913	-14482.779,	-5846.155,				5752.551	19278.847	-9979.176,	-4603.399,	-12951.648	5081.354	15.1	-4.5	Arc_6	nil
5752.551	-15422.687,	-4888.243,				5530.129	-16336.225,	-3937.831,				5194.483	15884.602	-11827.025,	-5910.789,	-9908.336	2721.489	9.82	-5.54	Arc_7	nil
5194.483	-17413.202,	-2808.643,				4583.969	-18411.296,	-1768.772,				3729.483	10340.624	-14409.017,	-6210.215,	-4707.57	3354.898	18.59	-7.8	Arc_8	nil
3729.483	-18709.498,	-1454.897,				3400.709	-18987.531,	-1153.345,				3043.919	8062.812	-14272.895,	-4165.689,	-2761.847	1087.468	7.73	10.47	Arc_9	nil
3043.919	-19242.294,	-862.729,				2660.469	-19469.968,	-582.526,				2252.982	7865.556	-13588.006,	-3035.949,	-2356.473	1089.061	7.93	9.82	Arc_10	nil
			42448.898										43023.024								

mathematical support, for we were dealing with a *prima facie* optimisation problem; or rather, we were seeking an optimised solution. The narrative went something like: 'if we are going to use "n" arcs to make a particular strand, what is the optimum subdivision of each NURBS curve, such that the sequence of joined arcs (via fillets) would provide an acceptable fit with the original curve?' In terms of user operation, for each strand we needed to probe the subdivision interactively getting 'n' to be as small as possible, yet make the fit as close as possible to our sculptors' wire. The lower the value of 'n', the cheaper the fabrication costs. This implies a tool – one that would allow the sculptors, the tube benders, the fabricators and the cost consultants to work together when necessary, to ensure that for each piece the total number of constituent arcs would be less than a given number for 'n'. We collaborated closely with engineer Peter Wood based in Wellington, New Zealand, who made the project possible, assisting us as both mathematician and software engineer.

Clearly, with an exceptionally large number of arcs per strand, an almost perfect match could have been achieved, but at unreasonable cost. Nevertheless, working within the exacting budgetary constraints that the project demanded, a very good result still emerged. We were interacting with a bespoke Rhino 3D™ VB Script (effectively a plug-in) working with eight constraints. Principal among these were maximum and minimum arc radii, maximum and minimum sectoral lengths, maximum number of degrees of curve, maximum curvature change, total number of arcs and a maximum allowable deviation from the sculptors' NURBS curves. The sculptors wanted the result to be quite smooth on the one hand, with the joints absolutely invisible, yet the completed full-scale strands themselves had to have the odd little kink and quirk exactly as per the original 1:100 model. Kinks demanded rather more arcs, which required the smoother parts to use as few arcs as possible, to compensate and constrain the total number of arcs. The software extension afforded the opportunity to meet this stringency, and the sculptors were able to allow some flexion along the straighter sections between tight curves to help keep the number of sections down, with no discernable consequential visual impact. The provision of a clear user interface was an essential component to the script itself.

Extract from a typical spreadsheet generating results with each cycle providing the fabricators with all the information they need to bend and cut tube and register.

Thought experiment: resolving a complex curved tube into fabrication-friendly elements, 2002. The approach taken: defining a set of cotangent arcs that will form a seamless and uninterrupted curve when assembled together. The script provides registration marks at each tube ending to assist assembly.

Conveying information to the fabricator

The largest sculpture was built from 420 arcs and required 3,800 items of information documented as a set of spreadsheets. The primary data source was therefore a spreadsheet and not a set of drawings. The script was adapted to produce three spreadsheets for each strand, each with columns of data that suited the fabricators' workflow. Intrinsically the data comprised an arc radius and sector length, an order and a position. The digital model created served only for cross-reference – drawings were of no

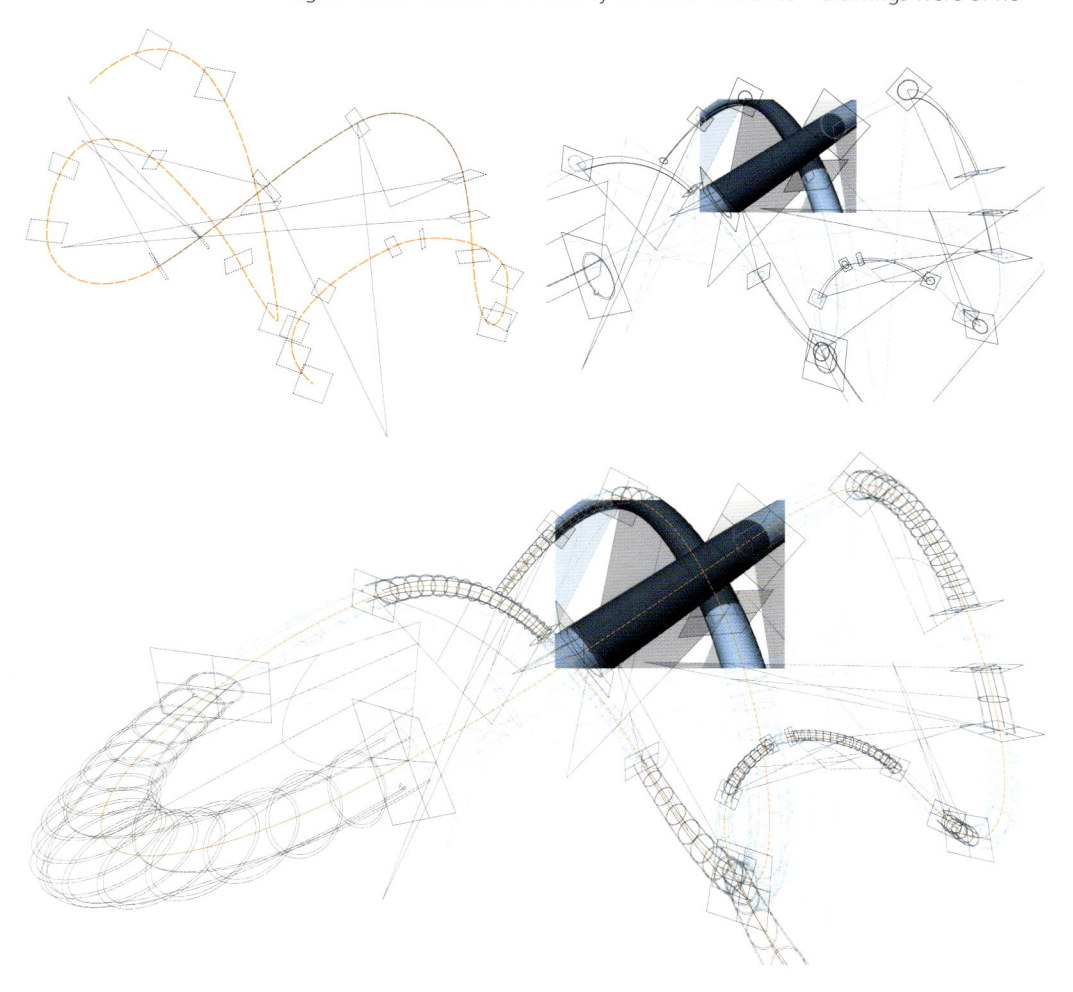

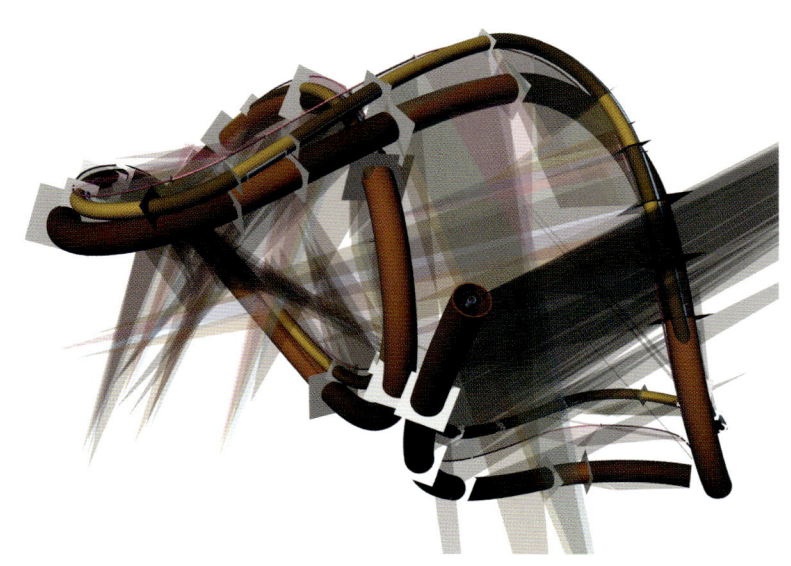

Squares mark cutting planes, triangular 'shards' show the radius, arc centre and segment. The script allows complete choice in number of arcs per strand length, maximum and minimum curvature, and tube diameter and wall thickness. The tighter the match of the resulting set of arcs, the greater the number of components and smaller the diameter of tubes.

use at all. A spreadsheet provided the information that identified each arced pipe by reference number, along with the relative twist between adjoining elements, allowing them to be joined with each other accurately. Once cut, the arcs were brought to the large shed where they were joined firstly into the various strands and then the strands intertwined to form the piece. In this dry capacious space, the sculpture was first erected in its entirety, then cut up into sections small enough to be transported to site where, as components, they were reconstructed. The fabricators executed their work immaculately and it was impossible to see the joins once they had been ground back and polished. Although fragile looking, the lightweight structure is surprisingly strong and it is not unusual to find young human fry swimming among the fronds of metal mesh several metres above ground level.

Five different tube sizes all starting and finishing at the same point, all generated by direct user input as the script runs.

Looking back, we might have been slightly more canny, and the code that we used for the project could have included features

Experiment to test hypothesis.

Cat Macleod and Michael Bellemo, *Shoal Fly By*, Melbourne, 2002. Resolved virtually modelled version made fully from cotangent arcs.

that would have enhanced the project construction had they suggested themselves at the time. Principal among these would-be features is the ability to notch each arced tube end, such that two connecting pieces can be joined together using a sleeve, and twisted until the notches correspond. Additionally, it would have been helpful too had we been able to identify the lowermost point of the connection (z^{min}), for example, such that the fabricator would always be aware of the final orientation of the strands relative to the ground. Despite not including such refinements at that time, the project was built with the minimum of difficulty.

A bigger picture

At that point in the rapidly developing global digital fabrication repertoire, there was a predilection to solve practical problems using what I term the 'salami approach', which means working reductively from a series of sections. Then (2002) it had only been 10 years since architects had first been able to consider solid modelling complex geometries using software not actually intended for architectural use. Even if such form could be modelled in 3D, the designer quickly reached a zone that was described by Greg Lynn in 1997 as *'contractor space'*.[4] Lynn was referring to the inevitable descent back down to earth from conceptual flights of fancy through the need to meet contractors on terms they were able to deal with, tied in the main to their experience, which probably did not include building many 'blobs'. In contractor space, a highly simplified technique was usually called for, and the salami approach was the required digital dumb-down. Even if extravagant architecture could not be digitally unravelled as elements elegantly fit for purpose in the same

Cat Macleod and Michael Bellemo, *Shoal Fly By*, Melbourne, 2002. Fabrication sequence.

way as those compelling exemplars that nature offers for our consideration, at least we could digitally slice sections and work from that basis.

Let us take the ellipsoid as an example of how a highly complex doubly curved surface might be supported by an armature of cotangent tube arcs. There are two straightforward ways to decompose this using the

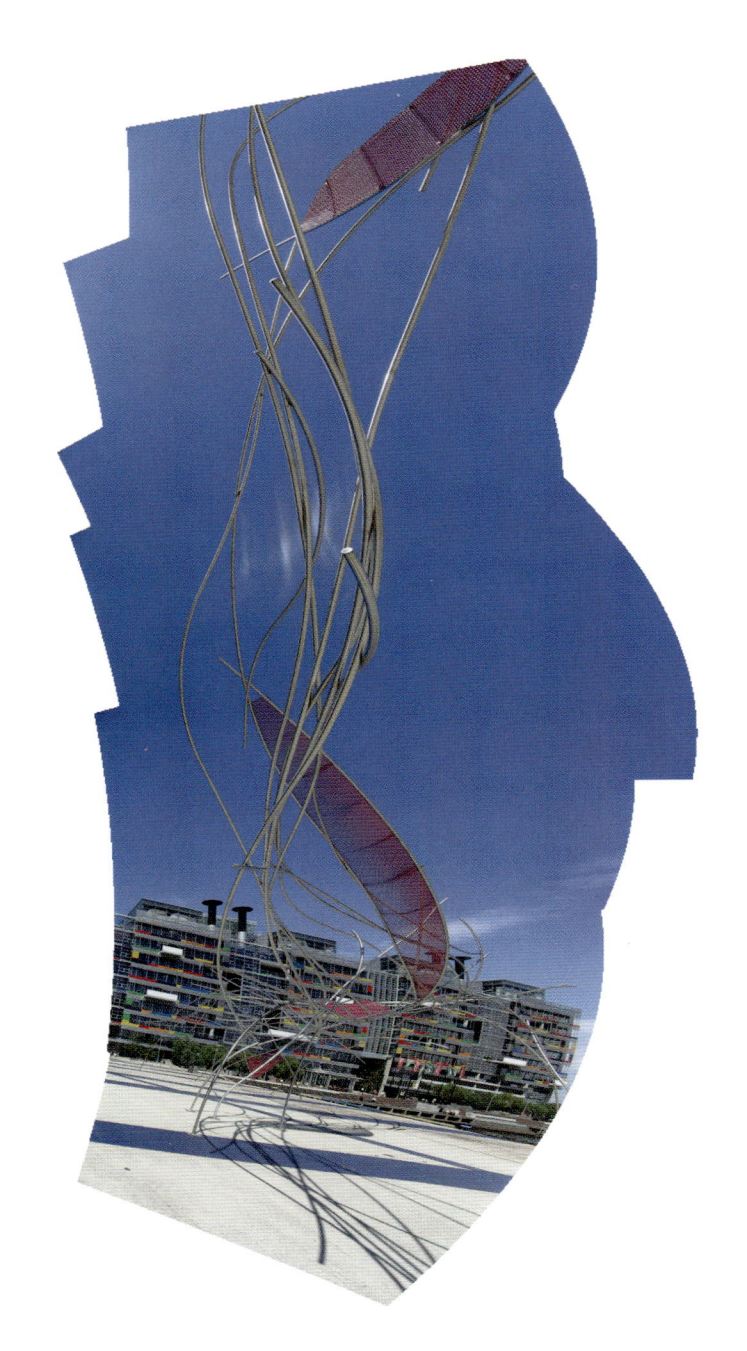

Cat Macleod and Michael Bellemo, *Shoal Fly By*, Melbourne, 2002. As built – over 40 metres long.

software available at that time. One is to simply slice the building up into structurally appropriate dimensions, and apply a ruled surface between each 2D structural portal – the salami approach. Slightly more sophisticated is the faceted approach. Here the structural system is Buckminster Fuller-style faceting obtained by reducing the geometry to a mesh, allowing for triangular planes to spangle the surface relatively economically. But to provide a surface that could truly echo the NURBS curves from which it was derived, there was no textbook method available to us. The *NURBS-to-arc* software we had come up with to resolve a particular problem, a sculpture, could clearly be extrapolated to challenges such as the hypothetical ellipsoid roof we are considering here. The opportunity to take contractor space into design space by applying the NURBS-to-arc methodology comprehensively is an accidental discovery. Using appropriate materials, the true NURBS curvature to the form could be exploited in full, and not reduced. This thought experiment is explored further in Chapter 10.

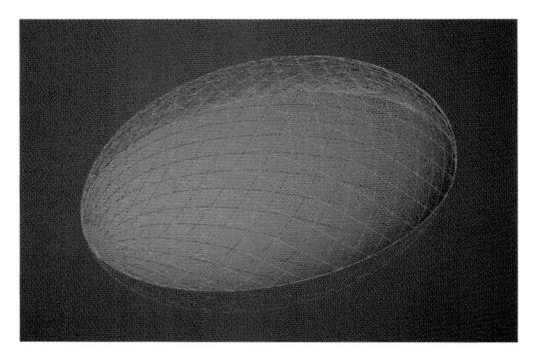

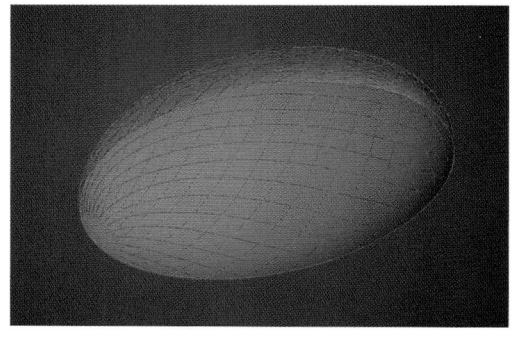

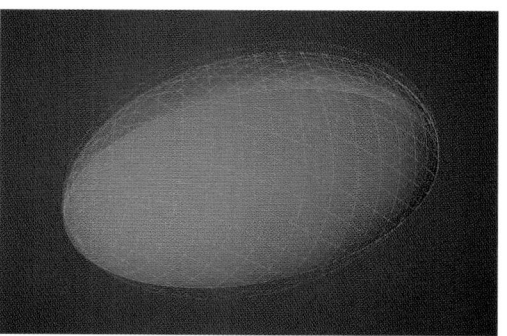

Reflecting on the project there were several lessons learned. The first was that there probably exists a precedent for every design mystery. By looking back over the problem of forming compound curves from cotangent planar arcs, familiarity with historical examples gave relatively ready access to a working methodology for deriving close-enough approximations to NURBS curves. Using the same approach to three-dimensionalise the 2D approach yielded dividends despite apparently working from within a *terra nullius* in this regard. A few years later in September 2004 at the Non Standard Architecture Symposium conference organised by Mark Goulthorpe at MIT, Kas Oosterhuis pointed out that he had successfully overcome a similar conundrum earlier when resolving the roof structure for the Salt Water Pavilion, the seaward end of the NOX and Oosterhuis Associates collaboration at Water Worlds at Neeltje Jans

Ellipsoid, 2010. Extracting suitable 3D curves from a meshed surface, and through planar projection. The ellipsoid was chosen because of the possibility of a non-uniform surface governed by different values for x, y, and z axes.

(Netherlands), completed in 1998. Had we realised this, perhaps we might have approached the problem differently – we do not know. Since then, in more recent years, we have seen many prestige projects move forwards, still adopting the salami approach; albeit with compound 2D cotangent arcs forming compound curves. Similarly many projects continue to be built with triangular faceting of surfaces, which may be cost-conscious solutions rather than aesthetically driven. The more contemporary Slavin House (Greg Lynn FORM, 2005–present) shows us that as well as defining a different 'contractor space' in the intervening decade, Lynn has also produced a project that celebrates the NURBS curve without an obvious and overly reductive simplification.

Ellipsoid, 2010. Finding the optimum set of cotangent arcs to make the ellipsoid.

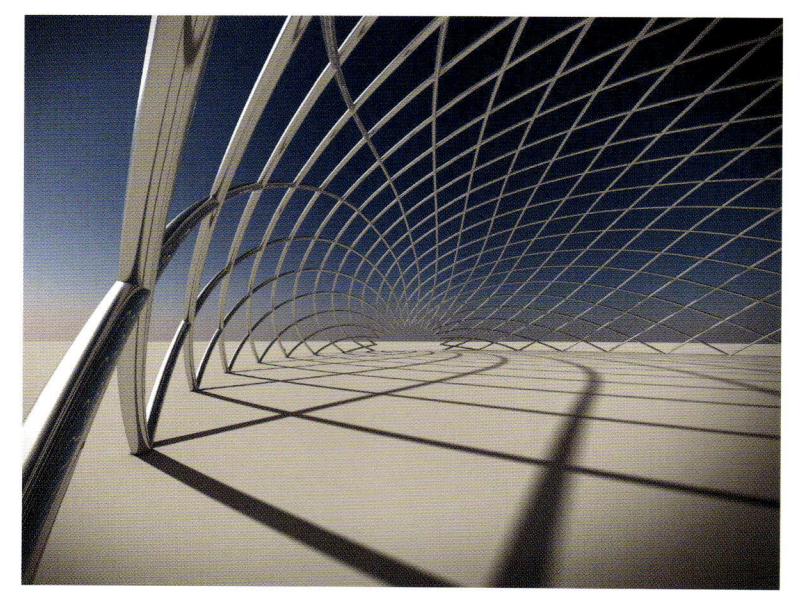

Ellipsoid, 2010. The NURBS-to-arc software capabilities extended to a hypothetical ellipsoid roof structure.

Ellipsoid, 2010. The NURBS-to-arc software capabilities extended to a hypothetical ellipsoid roof structure.

In the same year that we scripted our own software extension used to make our sculptors' work achievable, Rhino 3D™ 2.0 launched with a perfectly useful *curve to arc* tool with which to assist projects like *Shoal Fly By* to digital fruition. The principal lesson is therefore not how necessary or practical it is to seek to acquire useful intellectual property from others: clearly it is the best option. It would seem that the main benefit derived from this project for our team was the ability to get to grips with 'problem decomposition': the essential reduction of a problem into a series of tasks in order to formulate computational assistance. All scripting relies on packets of code that tackle these tasks in sequence or in parallel and, as in simultaneous equations, satisfy two or more conditions at once, for example. We cannot usefully look for precedents for coding if we have not formally resolved our approach to solution seeking in the way I have outlined in this chapter.

References

[1] In 2010, Melbourne Docklands has approximately 3,300 apartments built or under construction, 400,000 square metres of commercial Net Lettable Area (useable office space), 280 occupied retail tenancies (210 shops, 70 shopfront businesses). Completion of the precinct is scheduled for 2020.

[2] From Bellemo & Cat website: http://www.bellemocat.com/ Bellemo & Cat is a Melbourne-based architect/artist partnership.

[3] One of my first tasks in joining the research team at the Sagrada Família church as a young architect in 1979 had been to draw ellipse after ellipse for the studies I was making of Gaudí's lateral nave windows.

[4] Stated during his keynote speech at Morph 1997, the Australasian Architecture Student Biennial Conference hosted by the School of Architecture and Building, Deakin University, Geelong (6–11 July 1997).

9 Scripting narrative space: Our World and The Third Policeman

Thus far *Scripting Cultures* has presumed a coded analogy with the physical world. With our ability to augment design digitally using time as a function – whether as an animated simulation of performative architecture[1] or for an enriched iterative experimentation in ideas – we have reached a new level of architectural sophistication, one without precedent. As a virtual design companion scripting can assist the designer to escape reality constraints through immersion in cyberspace. With carefully thought through protocols the designer can interoperate as a collaborator within large virtual teams, potentially anonymous in terms of authorship but vital co-contributors all the same. Their individual input can be crucial and the whole team interdependent: remove any one of the worker bees from this hive and it no longer functions.

Building Our World

This chapter draws on one such hive, *Our World*, which serves two unrelated purposes. Firstly, Our World is an analogy for 'our world' – one of identifying and staying within particular domains, a condition of our propensity to place a boundary around what we regard as being 'in' to the exclusion of everything else. Our World is a metaphor, then, for the working environment of the curator, and considers their custodianship on behalf of the interests of others, looking after collections ranging from objects to concepts. Secondly, and quite inadvertently, Our World offers a visual insight into the spatial and temporal dilemmas explored with such mind-stretching élan by Flann O'Brien (1911–66) in his novel *The Third Policeman* published posthumously in 1967.[2] Making this scripted analogy for the work of the curator, and developing a visual proxy for a novel that never specifically called for one, evolved from putting a team of coders together to collaborate on a single script. Is it inevitable for creative outcomes to be constrained by working with one voice – the committee approach to design? Or, to put this question another way: if more than one coder in a team is a designer, will conformity to a common goal be confounded by the designers' resistance to being constrained by the logic of program code? The essential dilemma addressed here is whether creative scripting can only be the work of one person within the team. This was a question posed to senior architectural students at Australia's Deakin University in the mid-1990s – I wanted to investigate the implications of scripters working together to create one program. I therefore begin with an account of the generation of Our World, exploring the challenges that an apparently simple task can generate due to unexpected complexity emerging along the way, and the unintended riches that can still result as a consequence.

As a class (a world), we looked at the inevitability of coding conformity undertaken to ensure the inheritability of encoded characteristics, which could only be effective if each member (worker bee) of the class (hive) worked to agreed protocols. Daring to be different, the preternatural instinct of the designer is potentially compromised by any purposeful encoding cooperation designed to afford fluency in a multi-authored script or program. Designerly instinct combined with the celebration of the individual is potentially the destroyer of formal taxonomies that result from within populations of teamed-up scripters, whose number includes designers and not just coders. But the constraint of membership to a coding community does not necessarily mean an inevitable outcome, however rigorous the regime might be. Every member of the Our World hive community cooperates; they conform to mutually agreed protocols, but the results can nevertheless reach beyond their individual or collective human capability to embrace the full extent of variety that is created, especially when we step outside three dimensions. In other words, while the contents of our world may be computationally inevitable, they may not be capable of being humanly envisaged: the precision of the machine's cold logic might be enlivened by the excitement induced by surprise.

The conceptual framework behind Our World was based on working for an avid collector-curator. At their hypothetical behest we were to assist in forming a collection of hybrid objects each of which would be unique, but at the same time formally associated with each other: they would form a family of variants on a theme. We chose 'family' as part of our Our World metaphor, and we began our quest by considering a seed object at its centre, and a sequence of genetic shifts through which the seed would evolve into myriad variants. Essentially the class first worked together to develop a genetic code defining the evolutionary path. Using this core code each student then looked for related but different outcomes. From the genotype (the seed) there developed a controlled number of phenotypes (variants). Having first defined Our World as a coded construct, we then sought to populate it with ranges of objects. Our conclusion, far from being a tidy and coherent family, actually yielded examples of transgression and aberration at the margins. This outcome, while corrupting the cleanness of the original concept, enriched it at the same time through various manifestations of the unexpected, which segued neatly into a partnership with Flann O'Brien's masterpiece *The Third Policeman*.

From genotype to phenotype

The first example that the class laboured on involved taking the sphere as our genotype and morphing it into a cube. What I am about to describe will seem trivial, but the various commonly available software packages we tried revealed their innate peccadilloes as surprisingly unfriendly to the task. Surfacing routines work differently in different circumstances – a selection of a surfacing algorithm might work better in one situation, a sphere for instance, than in another, such as the cube. How should we proceed in this case – what is the genetic connection between a cube and a sphere that suggests an easily encoded transformation?

The essential shared quality for a sphere and a cube is that they are single closed volumes, but there the obvious similarities cease. The sphere is a single surface with any point on its surface being an equal distance from the centre. The cube is composed of six identical square surfaces bounded by twelve edges that connect at eight vertices. In encoding the transformation we therefore need to fraction the spherical surface up into six individual contiguous surfaces in such a way that topologically there are the same eight vertices and twelve edges as the cube. Even if there is a displacement by the

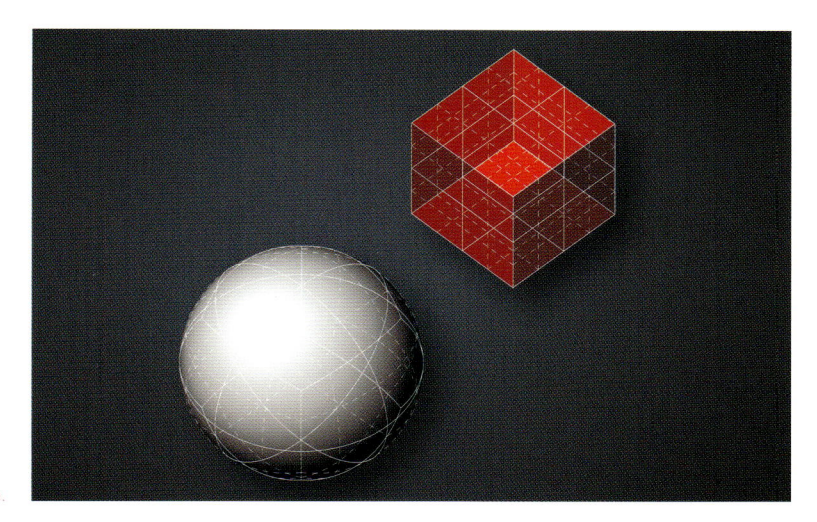

Seeking a link between the geometry of a sphere and a cube in order to be able to script a bi-directional morph.

dimension of a single atom from the perfection of the sphere's single surface towards the cube, the sphere's single surface *de facto* becomes defined as six facets, the eventual six faces of the cube. Computationally perforce this demands that we define the sphere as six contiguous surfaces in terms of code, as clearly six surfaces cannot simply appear from nowhere: we end up relying on the software's shading algorithms to hide this inopportune lack of negotiability when working with code. There is no ambiguity here: it either is or it is not. Conceptually we can nimbly dance between single and multi surfaces; computationally we cannot. I will delve into this condition a little more as I explain the production of Our World in greater detail.

The evolution of the sphere to a cube is undertaken as a series of iterations. We see the sphere losing its uniform perfection as a single surface through the cube's genetic code asserting itself already in the first of just ten iterations. The sphere inwardly implodes as if being gradually deflated while the vital geometrical armature for the cube framed by the eight vertices, there invisibly from the start, stubbornly refuses to budge, revealing itself only as the morph proceeds. Comparing the cube's surface with that of the sphere, these eight vertices are the only attributes that remain static in space. As the sphere deflates, what eventually becomes the cube's right-angled corners emerge as an intrinsic element of this plastic transformation. Simultaneously the edges become more confident as the sphere's bounding arcs straighten out into lines. The eight vertices (corners) of the cube are therefore defined from the eight points evenly distributed on the surface of

Iterative transformation of sphere to cube (10 steps).

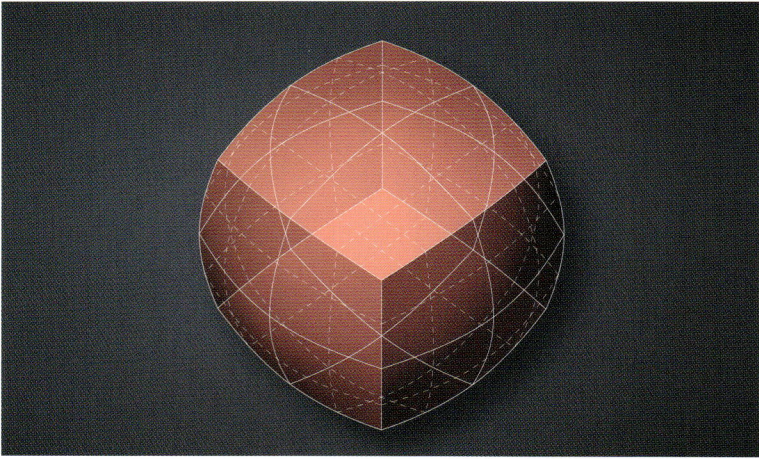

Cube–sphere mid-morph. The cube's vertices are on the sphere's surface while what are ultimately the cube's straight edges appear as arcs.

the sphere. The status of the cube's edges changes as they evolve from the sphere's arcs. On the sphere these arcs are invisible delineations between adjacent surfaces only in that they have far more tectonic status for the cube.

In this classroom exercise we need to consider the minimum number of declared geometrical entities to build the necessary encoded relationship between the two end states: the sphere and the cube. We look for the minimum to keep the code to the minimum as well as keeping the computational gymnastics as light as possible. We have agreed a common set of six surfaces, twelve bounding edges and eight vertices that are the points of intersection for each triplet of bounding edges – 'triple points'. In this case our code does not need to operate on the eight vertex points because they remain static. Now the arc, defined by three points on a plane, only needs its midpoint to migrate to a position in space where it is collinear with the two points that mark its ends to span as a straight line between the cube vertices; in other words, once all three points are in a straight line it becomes a cube edge, the midpoint is effectively redundant at this point. Any closed set of joined edges to the cube defines the boundaries to a planar square surface. These planes only apply when the cube is fully formed. As soon as the midpoint moves and transforms the cube edge into a curve, potentially we need to use a different surfacing definition. Any of a broad range are acceptable until the morphing solid becomes a sphere, when our choices are greatly reduced.

In summary, we are obliged to seek a surface that conforms equally well to being planar faces to the cube as to being divisions of the spherical surface. Also, within the code, we are challenged to find an algorithm for a curve that works equally well as an arc as it does as a straight line. Already we have complexities for what on the face of it seems a simple task. For instance, by definition an arc cannot be generated using three collinear points that lie on a straight line: if we are to use geometrically produced arcs, at a crucial point within the software's inbuilt tolerances the code must switch from defining

There are different degrees of success with combining surfaces in order to produce a smooth sphere with no apparent surface imperfections. A compromise has to be reached as some combinations of surface algorithms fare less well when extremely distorted.

ever flattening arcs trending towards the cube edges to being a straight line between two vertices. But as we are working with three points – two ends and a migrating midpoint – we can of course use a curve defined by three points. Most software will produce a straight line when the curve is defined by three collinear points, but when the curve spans across three points that lie on the circle that circumscribes the sphere, we find most software gives only an approximation of an arc. This means that some of the potential spherical surfaces will not be perfect. To attain the perfect result, then we need to input condition statements to allow the switch between one geometry-defining algorithm and the next, or define extra points with which to form the arc.

Enriching the collection with some hybrid vigour

From our commissioning curator's perspective, we have made a script to generate a collection of objects that span between a sphere and a cube. Were the curator to put these on display they can place them on a shelf. Because we are working computationally, we need to be more precise in our spatial definition, so the shelf becomes an axis: the x axis in this case. Our next step is to enrich our collection with a different transformation, again starting with the sphere as our genotype. What is the basis of the collection and from what is it being formed?

The sphere is one of six Phileban solids, and the cube is also one of five Platonic solids. The Phileban solids are the sphere, cube, cone, pyramid, cylinder and the prism. The Platonic solids are the tetrahedron, cube, octahedron, dodecahedron and icosahedron. Let us draw from one of these sets, for both are appropriate to the architect. The Phileban set of solids is perhaps more apt as we have had an illustrious Late Modernist, Alan Colquhoun (born 1921) extending Reyner Banham's (1922–88) take on these primary forms as the essential stuff of sculpture, as constituting an aesthetic core to the Modern Movement. Indeed, in assessing their relative import for Buckminster Fuller (1895–1983) and Le Corbusier (1887–1965), Colquhoun identifies bridging points of difference:

> *The difference between Fuller and Le Corbusier lies not in the ideal importance which they attach to mathematics but in the symbolic role it plays. In Fuller's domes the forms are identified by their lines of force, resembling those High Gothic structures where a framework alone defines the volumes which it*

encloses, and seeming to exemplify Fuller's philosophy of the forms of art being absorbed back into the technical process. In Le Corbusier, the plastic act is hypostatized. His forms are, as it were, congealed in space, as in a solid graph. In both, the Phileban solids play an essential part; in both, the aesthetic and the discipline are identified. [3]

So, while the Platonic solids offer another challenge altogether for a scripted journey from one to another, we will be guided by more contemporary aesthetics and work with the Phileban forms. Our next task then is to morph a sphere into a third sample from this group of six: arbitrarily we choose the cylinder. We need to consider how this sits within the sphere-to-cube geometrical construct and look further at what needs to change. From a single spherical surface we are going to three, and from no edges to two, but neither the sphere nor the cylinder has vertices and, in terms of difficulty, this challenge presents fewer complexities than morphing to a cube. Effectively we are flattening out the sphere's top and bottom to form circular disks whose diameter is the same as the sphere's. The circumference is extruded between the two disks thus forming a cylinder. Operationally the script needs more than two circles and a polar top and bottom point. Cannily we should consider adapting the sphere-to-cube script where possible, and in fact it turns out to be as good a surface fractioning as any other. The surface is initially defined as the same six contiguous and similar-shaped regions,

Seeking a link between the geometry of a sphere and a cylinder that is consistent for a bi-directional morph.

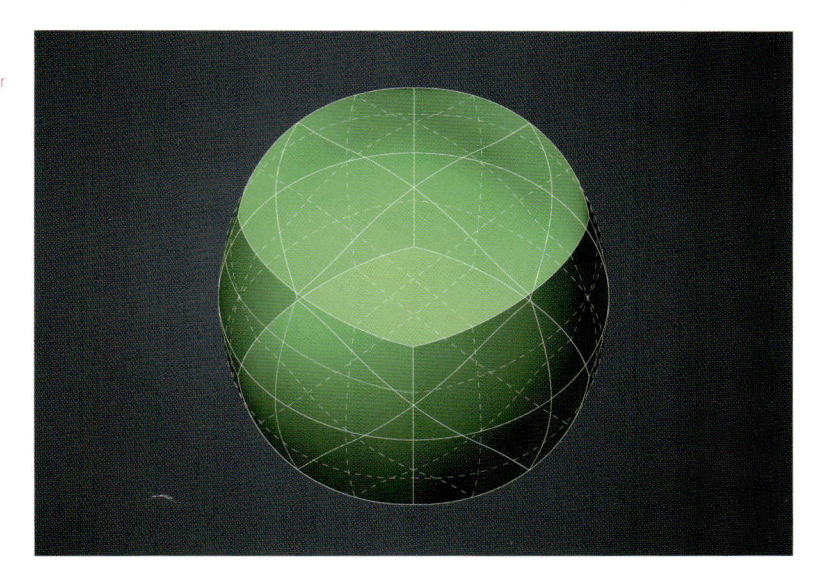

and the various edges are moved in space to effect the required gradual transformation. We have been able to adapt the code with the minimum of fuss. We are happier with the description of the edges as, for both the sphere and the cylinder, all curves are arcs.

Our curator does not need a second sphere as the original seed from the sphere-to-cube morph is in the collection, so a decision is made to lay out the new collection of the sphere-to-cylinder morph along the ground at right angles to the sphere-to-cube series so as to share the sphere. We see this as a *y* axis. These two 1-dimensional collections form two adjoining edges to a plane that is noticeably devoid of content. A map of the situation seemingly cries out for a 2-dimensional array of hybrids to populate the empty territory. In so doing we will have created Flatland.[4] To succeed in this new ambition there needs to be an algorithm that operates in common on the genotypic sphere such that it can produce the different DNA for the cube and the cylinder by subtle shifts in code but working from a shared construct. Zipping along the *x* axis the code only applies the *cube DNA*, and along the *y* axis only *cylinder DNA*. Anywhere else on Flatland each variant phenotype has a mixture of DNA. This means at the furthest corner marked x^{max}, y^{max} the hybrid has the full genetic offering from both the cube and cylinder DNA. A rich array results, with no two members of the collection being the same. The phenotype at $x^{max}/2$, $y^{max}/2$ is the emasculated hermaphrodite, being exactly half a cubed sphere and half a cylindrical sphere.

Iterative transformation of sphere to cylinder (10 steps).

In order to satisfy the curator we have had to grapple with two new complexities. Firstly, we have had to find a common approach to computing the geometry that works for both hybridisations and, secondly, we have had to address sequencing. Just as conceptually we have no real difficulty in bending a straight line in our mind's eye, but computationally some extra thought is required, so too do we need to unpack the mental

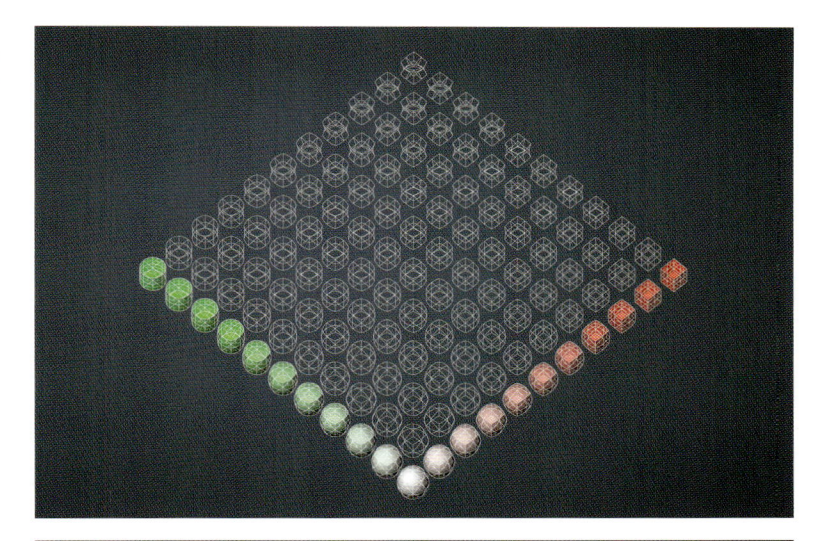

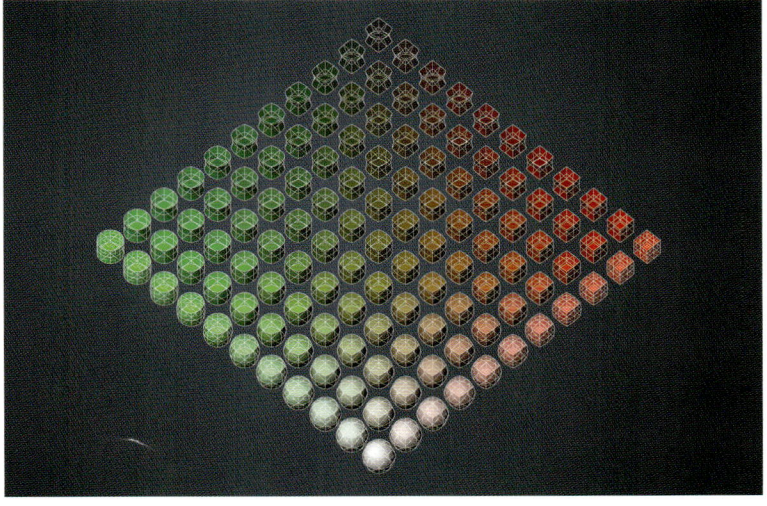

1-dimensional series perpendicular to each other suggesting the opportunity for a 2-dimensional array.

Flatland, with variants of sphere-to-cube, sphere-to-cylinder and mixture of both hybridisations.

Mark Burry   199   Chapter 9 Scripting narrative space: Our World and The Third Policeman

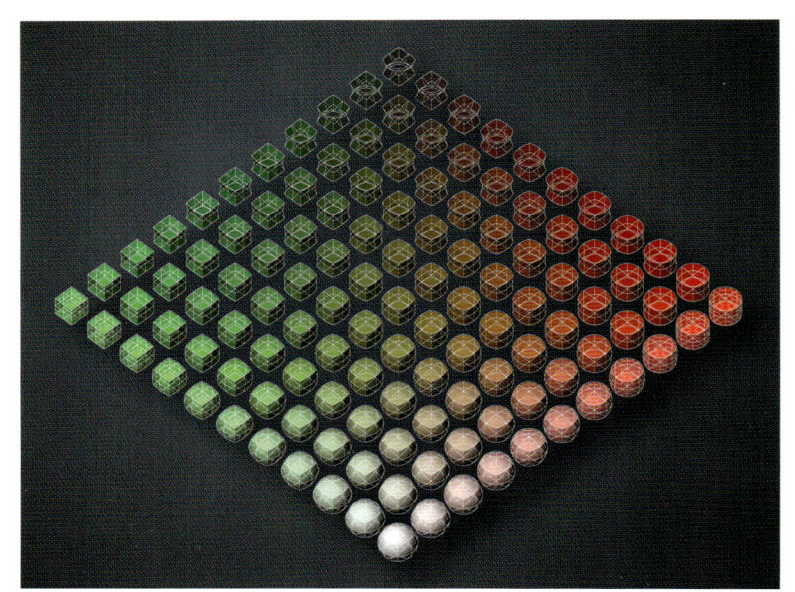

Flatland, with variants of sphere-to-cylinder (x axis), sphere-to-cube (y axis), and mixture of both hybridisations.

tidiness of 'half cube, half cylinder' for the purposes of computational comprehension. We know what we mean by 'half cube, half cylinder' just as we know by mixing three primary colours we produce brown. Holding pots of all three colours in one hand, we pour them into a bowl simultaneously while stirring with the other. Patently this is not possible computationally as its binary nature demands sequencing, and this implies privileging the order of one hybridisation sequence over the other: we either start with the sphere morphing to a cube up to a certain value, then we apply the sphere-to-cylinder morph and again morph to a given value. This means at x^{max}, y^{max} we have settled on the *cylinderised* cube with no vestige of the sphere, whereas at $x^{max}/2$, $y^{max}/2$ we have said first the sphere will be *cubified*, then it will be *cylinderised*. This has presumed the convention of x before y.

Accommodating the collection in Euclidean space

This was set up as a class exercise, and the next challenge was to look at a new morphing construct. Our curator has demanded a third hybridisation in the z direction to fill up the rows and columns of empty shelves above the Flatland collection, and has requested that *pyramid DNA* be the next

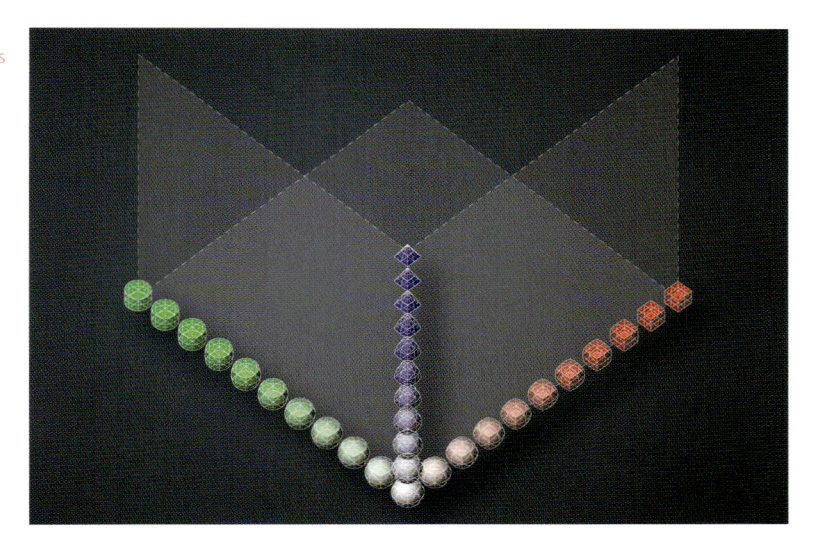

Genotype (sphere) at 0,0,0 with the three Cartesian axes hosting three phenotypes: cube at x, cylinder at y, and pyramid at z.

phenotype drawn from our Phileban solids. How might we adapt our existing hybridisation script without a massive rewrite?

We have found that the fragmentation of the sphere into six contiguous surfaces has worked adequately for the cube and cylinder variants. Whether we need points as vertices or not – so far only the cube has demanded them – we have established that they do need to be defined, as does a series of representative midpoints. We have tackled the curve through three points not necessarily defining an arc by placing three rather than one intermediate point between the end points forming a set of five. By sidestepping the geometrical problem of an arc needing to become a straight line at some point, a polyline through five points allows us accurately to define an arc, partial ellipse, parabola, hyperbola, or a straight line. Our fresh complexity, however, is that a pyramid has only five surfaces, and although we could invisibly construct the cylinder's extruded surface as four cotangent quarter-circle extrusions seamlessly joined, with the pyramid we have to lose a surface. Again, conceptually this seems a much smaller problem to cope with relative to the computational demands of making an entire face disappear. We can envisage a top face of a cube reducing in size at each iteration while the base face stays resolutely put becoming the pyramid base with similar dimensions and position as the cube base. We accept at some point the top face will reduce in dimensions angstrom by angstrom, such that it is no longer visible to the naked eye, and out of sight becomes out of mind. We are unlikely to be bothered much by the internal shenanigans accommodating a disappearing face if it cannot be seen. Unfortunately, the computational aspects are not so relaxed, and indeed we cannot simply disappear the surface at a point where it no longer *seems* to exist when, within the strictures of dimensions, it has not been rubbed out entirely. Nor should it be, for were we to reverse the algorithm and seek a pyramid-to-cube transformation, there must be at least a vestige of a sixth face hiding within the five-faced pyramid. Our script is fundamentally corrupting because although the visual representation of the pyramid works, relying as it does on the limits of human acuity, our coding reveals that under the bonnet, we did not produce a pure pyramid, only the semblance of one.

The class now has to perform one last step in their project: coding to a common purpose with no one in charge. Having filled up the west wing of the gallery with our hybrid objects from floor to ceiling thereby pulling our collection out of Flatland, our ambitious curator has insisted we not only occupy the hypothetical east, south and north wings (-x and -y axes) as well, but also the basement level below (-z axis). He or she does not want similar objects for this is a collection taxonomically ordered by shelf, by row and by column. Having set off on our journey working with the complete set of six Phileban solids, our constructed world alas is deficient because we are working from one genotype towards six phenotypes, which requires a set of seven unique objects. We will have ended up completing our collection

Invited in to the set of six Phileban solids is a hyperboloid of revolution.

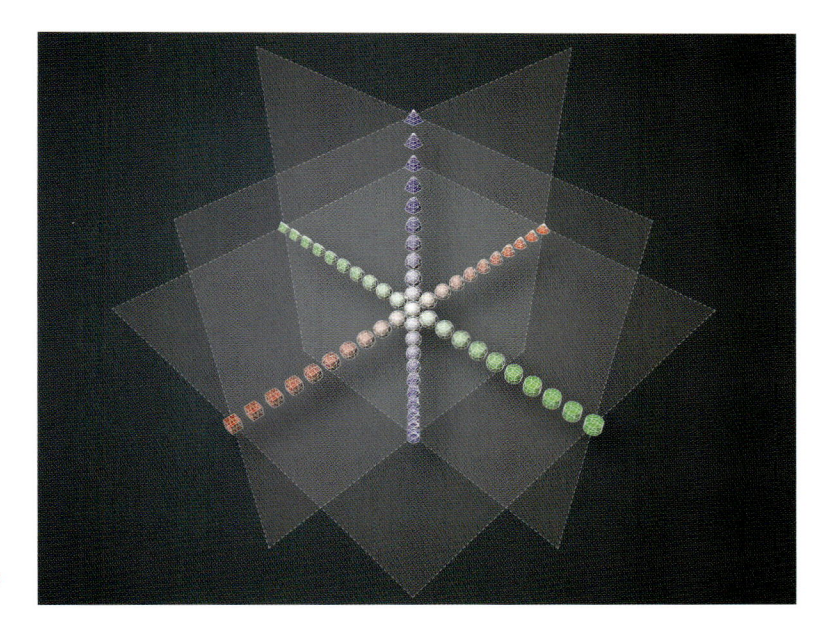

Genotype with three Cartesian axes hosting six phenotypes. One of the overall set of seven objects has to be invited in from outside the closed set of six Phileban solids.

of unique but related objects, our 'constructed world', but our conceit has left us vulnerable, for we have destroyed the purity of a complete family set of six Phileban forms by introducing a foreign phenotype, and this cannot be resolved by any means other than looking beyond the family. Already potentially embittered by the lack of cleanness in the scripting generally, what with the retention of phantom surfaces, arcs made as polylines from five points rather than being mathematically derived curves, we have now opened ourselves up to the vagaries of choice, for the sixth phenotype could be anything: our world is an incomplete set with regards to our construct, and there is no innate quality that sponsors the missing member. We might just as well choose the hyperboloid from Chapter 6 as any other.

Fortunately the task of working individually using a common approach and set of conventions distracts us from dwelling overly on any demoralising untidiness, for there is a lot to sort out. We have to develop together a naming convention so '*point 1* for me is *point 1* for you too', and not, say, 'your *vertex 4*'. We need to agree priorities such as *x* first, then *y*, then *z*. We need to agree on '+' before '-'. Generation of lines must involve using the same algorithm and sequencing, and we must be in accord as to which of the various surfacing approaches that are available to us is the most appropriate.

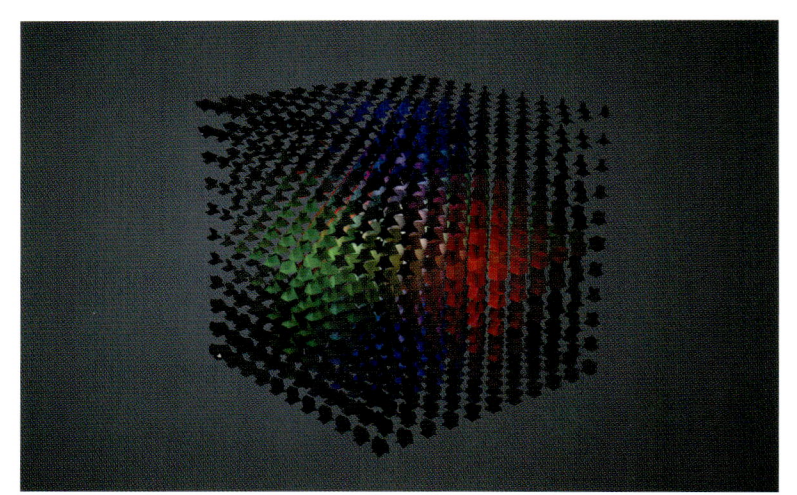

Set of hybrid morphs: sphere into cube, cylinder, pyramid, cone, prism, and hyperboloid of revolution.

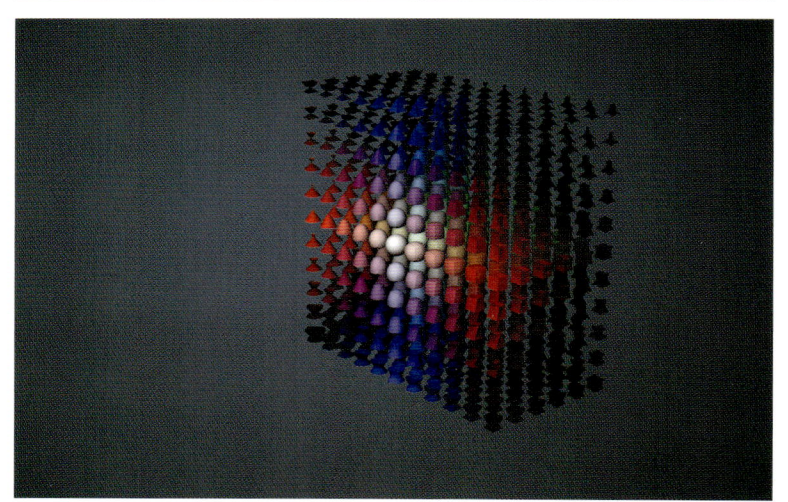

Morphs towards six phenotypes, but only in a x+ direction.

In other words, we derive a meta language regardless of the actual scripting language. Our World is a shared construct and our individual pieces of code need to mesh together seamlessly as one augmented nested script. This allows any user to choose any object from a set of seven to act as a genotype trending gently towards any of six phenotypes arranged in a Cartesian grid, thus ensuring that the collection is intact and coherent.

The genotype has six phenotypes morphed following positive and negative Cartesian axes.

Our World, 1998/2010: the complete collection of 10-step morphs from sphere to cube, cylinder and pyramid.

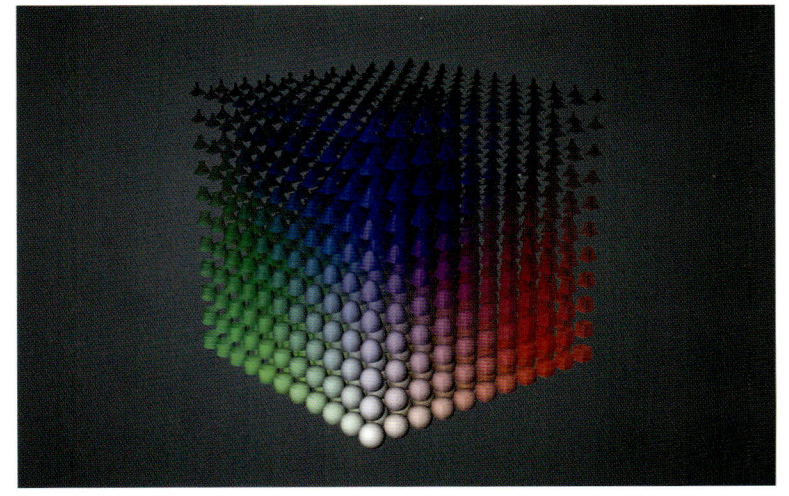

Of course, the joy of scripting for design is that we will not be satisfied through simply meeting the curator's conceit, that of completing their entire collection for them through our coded procedure. Irritated perhaps by the imperfect code and the corrupted family set (just as well we did not choose the set of five Platonic solids …), it is time to disrupt further and break the machine. This turns out to be very easy. Firstly, let us tinker with the stopping problem.

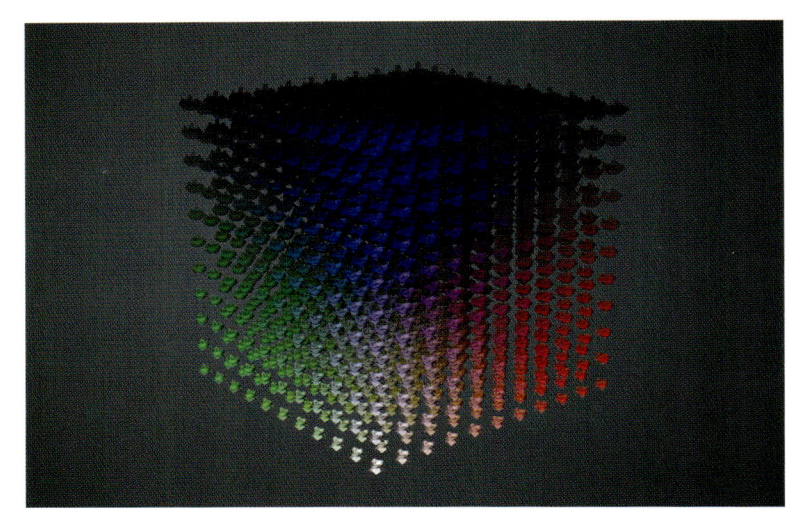

Our World, 1998/2010: taking the 0.7 sphere->cube->cylinder-t>pyramid->hyperboloid phenotype and making it a genotype for a full morph, the family of 5th-dimensional morphs produces results unlikely to be easily predicted by the mind alone. If every phenotype became the genotype for the next world, the 10-step morph would generate more that 7 quadrillion (7,355,827,511,386,640) individual objects.

Our World, 1998/2010: string showing scripted outcome with a premature genotype (-x) and overgrown phenotype (x+). Example shown in bottom right while top left shows a 4D morph (sphere to 0.7 cube, 0.7 cylinder, 0.7 pyramid, and 0.7 hyperboloid.

In our perfect world, the algorithm that morphs the sphere to a pyramid stops as soon as the shrinking of the top face has reached the tolerance of the software to produce the smallest possible surface, and not get confused. But what if the *pyramidisation* does not just stop so cutely, and instead presses on into cyberspace? And why should we presume a perfect sphere – what if we were to start it off as an immature genome, brought prematurely nto our world?

Scripting allows us to anticipate our genotype as a protoplasmic zygote, that point where cell division is barely under way and dabble with progeria, or advanced and premature ageing. Computationally we are exploring effects cerebrally that are otherwise hard to predict. It seems that we can all readily describe the effect of morphing a sphere to a cube for example, and accurately sketch the resulting hybrid at midpoint. So too in the main can we sketch that same hybrid sequentially morphed partly into a second phenotype such as the cylinder. Beyond this our conceptual abilities seem to be much more challenged, and the relative ease with which our script can generate Our World as a 3D collection is appreciated.

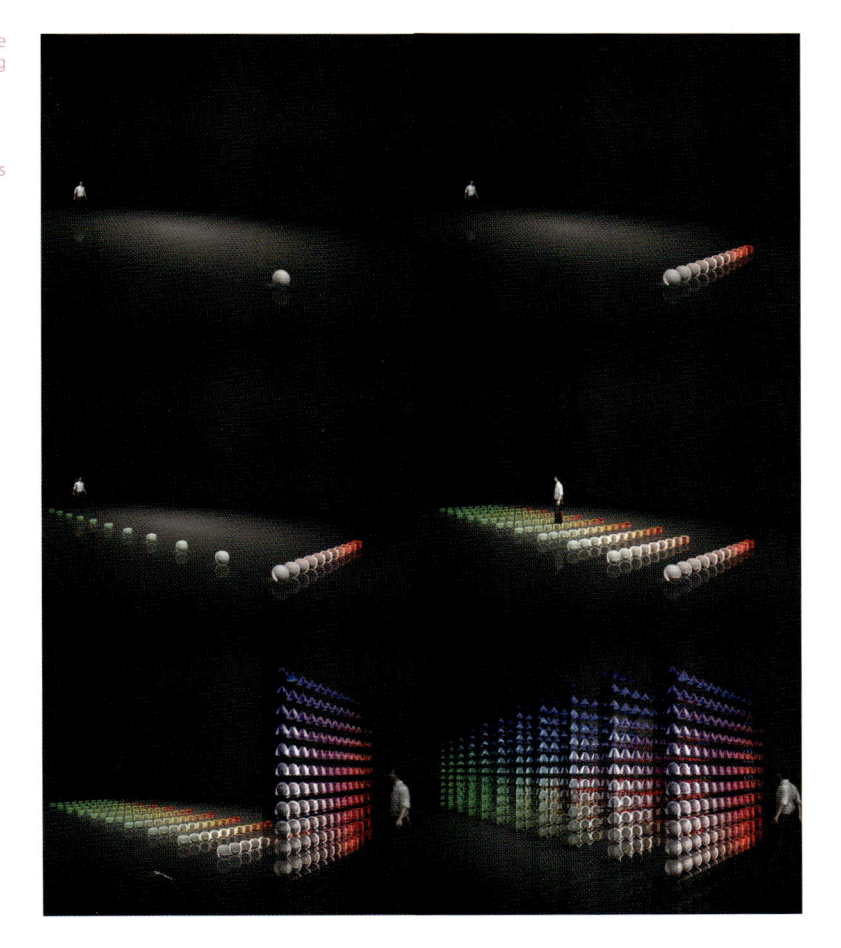

Our World, 1998/2010: The Curator's Conceit – building up a 'complete' collection, in this case, one room of the gallery holds just 1/8 of 'Our World' generated from the six 'Phileban series + 1' phenotype morphing sequence (sphere->cube->cylinder->pyramid). The rest of the collection is housed in three adjacent rooms, and on the floor below.

Because the algorithm is operationally sequential, however (sphere -> cube -> cylinder -> pyramid, for example), we are not necessarily confined to three dimensions. Buoyed up perhaps by our incursions into cyberspace beyond the cosy confines of Our World, we can confront our curator with the ultimate disruption by providing them with collections that are not otherwise limited to the neat confines of their shelving system. The scripter has no such operational restrictions and there is nothing to stop our script producing a 4th, 5th, n^{th} generation of hybrids while remaining highly aware that in doing so it is impossible to show the resulting collection physically in any meaningful way. The sphere -> cube -> cylinder -> pyramid sequence can be genetically morphed to include hybrid vigour using some *prism DNA*, for example.

Our World, 1998/2010: glimpses into the collection.

Where might this work sit as critique?

Our World is a demonstration of the museographical futility of the curator's approach, were he or she to attempt to organise rich collections of objects where direct comparison between morphological variants is required. It is also a visual demonstration of the arbitrariness with which we define groups, families or worlds of related members, and of the potential artificiality of that membership when it is based only on qualifying physical characteristics. Generating anything outside the norm is difficult to encode with precision unless we can envisage exactly what the outcome will be. To move beyond the design of a desired and deliberate sequence of actions, subversion and coding seems to be limited to relying on 'moves' such as the playful inclusion of the random function, working to a set of entirely arbitrary rules, or mimicking natural systems. In contrast, qualifying characteristics, when

Our World, 1998/2010: glimpses into the collection.

known, are easily coded within the script with the result that our worlds can be readily defined as a series of scripted actions. The distinction between generative design and intentional design is rather fuzzy conceptually, but with scripting it is either one or the other.

Our metaphor using a collector-curator-commissioner was at once satisfied with a collection that initially fitted their brief perfectly. We discovered that we could also frustrate their ordered needs using the same code to produce families of objects that came from n-dimensional operations. In pondering the architectural significance of this, I was reminded of Flann O'Brien's *The Third Policeman* in which we are offered a literary version of the same n-dimensional construct, one that disrupts all that we think we know about our various worlds. This is to say, while we perceive a world of three dimensions and act accordingly, we know that this is an artificial condition, and the scripted world we create can have an infinite number of dimensions, a condition made very clear in *The Third Policeman*. Our World transgressions reach beyond the human capacity readily to conceive of them and, as a result, offer visual references to much of the weirdness that is *The Third Policeman*. Inadvertently, each supports the other: the novel gives far greater context and value to what was originally a straightforward class exercise in collaborative scripting, and the development of constructed cyberspace worlds of objects that resulted gives a visual armature to what is otherwise confined unillustrated between the covers of Flann O'Brien's extraordinary narrative.

Discussing *The Third Policeman* is exquisitely challenging when the interests of anyone who has yet to read it are taken into account, as I am doing now, because the fundamentally pivotal event by which such a fantastic tale can be properly unfolded is only revealed by a crucial piece of information disclosed at the novel's conclusion. The reader struggles to make sense of the novel through most of its passage. The eventual denouement succeeds in clarifying what up to that point are fascinatingly inexplicable interfolds of time and space achieved with considerable literary dexterity. It is not a simple matter of drawing diverse threads together as the conclusion to a mystery, but instead a revelation of another world of thought, actions and consequences. For the reader who has not guessed the novel's prevailing situation the ending is a compelling reason to reread the book and reread it yet again, which bizarrely echoes the main message. I have yet to meet anyone who has guessed the essential point, although it may be hovering close by as one reads, and the temptation should be avoided to read the publisher's note placed at the close of the book (in some editions) where the ending is given away for reasons unknown.

So, how to relate *The Third Policeman*'s various eccentric tableaux to Our World without giving the book's plot away, yet make the connection all the same?

Fortunately I can make some associations by taking material directly from both projects without too much interjection through the remainder of this chapter. The minimum of a plot summary is required all the same in order to locate the story and orientate some of the relevant Our World material, and here it is.

The Third Policeman

> *Human existence being an hallucination containing in itself the secondary hallucinations of day and night ...*[5]

The main protagonist of *The Third Policeman* is an individual orphaned early on, a would-be thief, a murderer and a scholar of the life and works of the fictitious philosopher de Selby. He chronicles these circumstances in an autobiographical account. We do not know his name, and it transpires that he does not know it either. Together with his friend John Divney he assists in dispatching a wealthy elderly farmer, Philip Mathers, ambushing him on a lonely and foggy road – their motive is to rob him of all the wealth he has squirrelled away in the large house that he inhabits alone. Divney strikes the first blow with a bicycle pump (the bicycle is an absurdly recurrent theme throughout the account), but the narrator delivers the more lethal ministrations using his spade, the one with which he had previously dug a deep hole nearby and alongside the moorland road in anticipation of the events for which they were the precursors. While he is burying the victim, Divney is strangely absent, returning just as the grave is being tidied up. He explains that he had gone to the old man's house, located the black box containing his wealth, and hidden it for retrieval later once the presumed fuss resulting from Mathers' unexpected disappearance has died down. Ironically, there is no subsequent hiatus to deal with at all, as it is assumed that Mathers has just taken himself away from the community – he was a not-much-loved reclusive neighbour.

As a suitor Divney's motivation for enriching himself is to make himself a better prospect for his intended, whereas the narrator simply wants to fund developing his scholarship on de Selby, fuelled by his near-lifelong mission to catalogue the entire works as the *de Selby Index*. This would be the first ever compiled, and demanded resources additional to the income from his inherited farm and pub that had anyway been grossly mismanaged by the older Divney on behalf of the narrator while the latter was still at school.

The book was written in 1940 but only published posthumously in 1967, two years after O'Brien's death. The fictitious philosopher was advancing theories in modern physics that we might well regard as somewhat alternative to the findings of Galileo (1564–1642), Newton (1643–1727) and Einstein (1879–1955). There are many impeccable scholarly interjections throughout the book furnished as referenced footnotes, especially in Chapters 7 and 9 towards the end of the book, where they begin to dominate the main text in terms of page extent. The footnotes include epithets from de Selby and the conflicting arguments of his commentators, who with their various pseudonyms, even begin to register doubts as to each other's existence. De Selby's interpretation of 'atomic theory', for example, would have us believe that an individual who makes heavy use of a bicycle will, in time, become part human, part machine in proportions that vary with the degree of exposure.

De Selby is described by our narrator as someone who, with a habit of pointing out fallacies in existing conceptions and having demolished them, quietly presents his alternative design. For a further taste of the absurdity of de Selby's theories and the way they ride roughshod over the empirical evidence of human experience, let me take as examples his analysis of 'existence' and the 'phenomenon of night'.

Existence, claims de Selby, is a permanent hallucination known as life. Standing on a point of a 'postulated spherical earth', while one would appear to have four directions in which to move, namely north, south, west and east, in fact there are only two meaningful cardinal directions, for if one keeps moving either north or south the result is the same, as it is for west–east. De Selby postulates further that since one always returns to the same spot on a spheroid regardless of which circumferential path s chosen, so there can only be one 'route' were the world a sphere. His 'logic' continues in this vein with a resulting contention that the earth is 'sausage shaped', not spherical. A world of entirely new sensation and experience would be discovered if only a way could be found to travel in a different direction, i.e. along the barrel of the sausage. These geographical considerations, along with associated theories such as gravitation, being the one directional line of oblivion denying the freedom that lies in an upward direction, do not evoke any particular scepticism about the robustness of de Selby's logic in our narrator.

Night is the accretion of 'black air', composed of micro fine black particles of such volatility that any incandescence such as a match or a candle consumes the surrounding black air instantly, letting light back for as long as the flame continues to burn. Like the tides, night–day is a cycle of volcanic black air eruptions blanketing the world with darkness until the inky miasma gradually disperses allowing in the light of day. De Selby's explanation becomes more elaborate as he firstly attributes this inky miasma not only to volcanic eruptions but claims it is supplemented by

The Third Policeman, 1998/2010: Black Air (extrapolated from 'Our World').

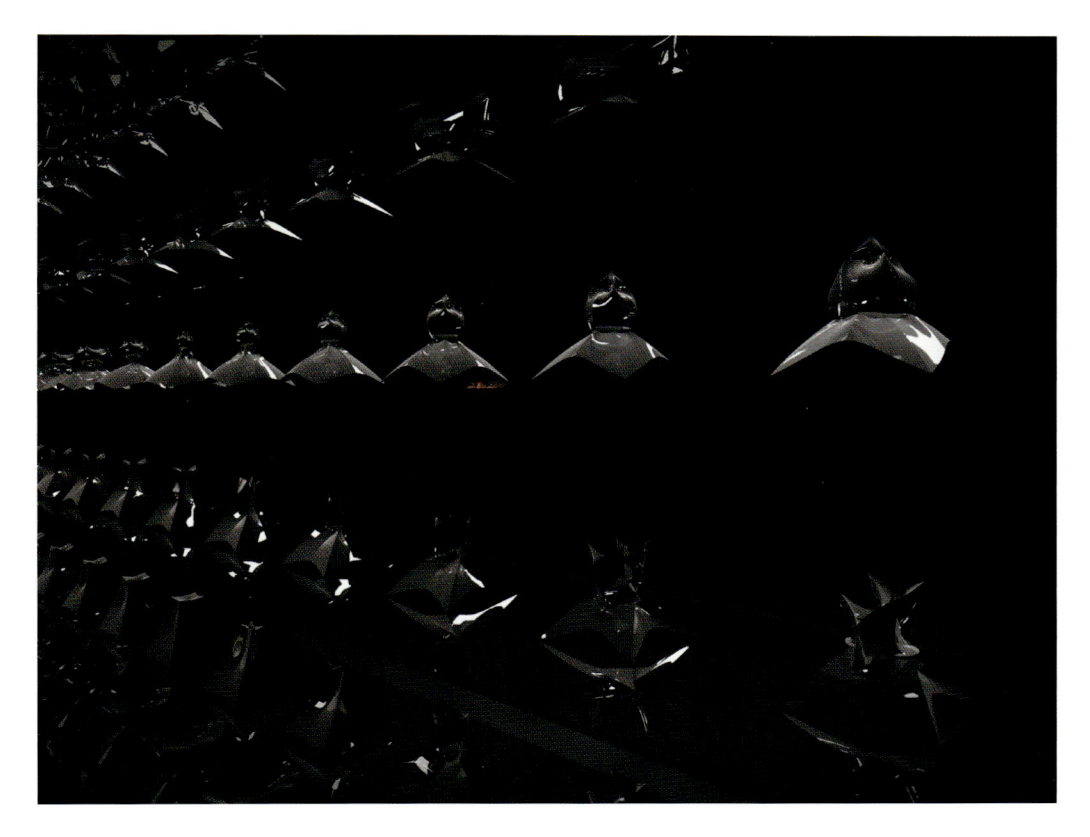

'regrettable' industrial emissions, and then that sleep is merely a series of fainting fits resulting from semi-asphyxiation.

In *The Third Policeman* our narrator embarks on a strange journey punctuated by bicycles, police stations and policemen, and peppered with odd encounters with even odder people. The narrator narrowly escapes execution against a backdrop of frequent references to a mysterious subterranean apparatus that manufactures eternity, governed by a highly sensitive mechanism supervised by the mysterious Policeman Fox, the third policeman whom we meet only at the end of the novel. This third policeman is neither seen nor heard by his colleagues, being always on his beat, never engaged in interrogating suspects yet always taking notes. The only tangible evidence that he exists at all is that he signs the 'book', but only when the whole world sleeps.

When not on his beat the elusive policeman is otherwise ensconced in his police station situated within the interstices of a partition wall inside Mathers' house, slightly wider than the 1-foot-wide staircase used to enter it. Policeman Fox has a 'great fat body', and each of the stairs (1-foot cubes) has to be negotiated by climbing sideways. The police station itself is comprised mostly of a table that can be used only by people squeezed into niches along its length – the ultimate intrusion into the poché. The narrator enquires, without result, the reason for the station's location within the walls of another house.

We, the reader, do have some idea of the circularity of the narrator's journey by the book's end: for him, the book's principal protagonist, each end is only a fresh beginning, which is what makes the book darkly humorous, but starkly chilling beyond the humour. It is this aspect that probably serves to make the message darker still. Written during the Second World War, in 1940, and despite Graham Greene's favourable reading having led to acceptance and publication of O'Brien's immediately prior and first novel, *At Swim-Two-Birds* (1939), *The Third Policeman* was considered too weird by publishers on either side of the Atlantic for them to proceed with it at that time. Apparently *At Swim-Two-Birds* had not sold well, and whereas his first publisher had thought his next book should be less fantastic, O'Brien made *The Third Policeman* more so. Quite why O'Brien subsequently claimed that the manuscript had been lost, blown out of the back of his open car boot page by page while driving in Donegal, when it had in fact sat for decades on his sideboard close to where he ate every day, is not clear.

The novel simultaneously compresses and expands both time and space in ways that an animator can only dream of being able to do, and reminds us of the power of literary evocation of the supernatural, which seems to be more potent than conventional visual explorations of both time and space in this regard – the power of the imagination: with the visual we seem to polarise between the merely descriptive or decadently abstract. Collage, perhaps, offers some possible intermediary position between, but fundamentally it is the narrative overlay within the pictorial that connects a written and visual account of apparently familiar constructs in a world that we have never experienced.

If O'Brien's imaginative flights were too outlandish for publication in 1940, it certainly did not hold readers back 27 years later, and it is one of those novels so rich in detail that it seems capable of being reread any number of times, each time affording fresh insights. It is this attribute, its deliberate incompleteness (completeness in a novel does not necessarily mean completeness of the story) that drew me to similarities with some of the implicit narrative aspects of Our World. It is not that Our World seeks to illustrate *The Third Policemen*, albeit abstractly. Rather, it is the novel that offers spatial and temporal insights into the implications of Our World. Starting with 'colour', here are some challenges to the spatial colourist with

The Third Policeman, 1998/2010: Rare Colour (the genotype for the fifth dimensional morph sequence from 'Our World').

a deficient palette complete with a synaesthetic factor of difficulty that Our World seeks to complement. The narrator learns of the consequences for someone looking at a card inside a box despite being expressly forbidden to do so. Claiming that it was the colour of the card that caused this action, he is unable to explain what the colour was, except to say that it was not a colour that a man carries around with him in his head.

> 'I saw colours often on eggs,' I observed, 'colours which have no names.'[6]

The Third Policeman also provides a curatorial and taxonomic view of colour, classification and temperament. Early in the novel, in a conversation that takes place between Mather and the narrator, winds are identified not only by their cardinal origins but also by their colours, a skill claimed to have been lost to humankind in more recent times. Longevity is determined by the direction of the wind during birth with the original and subsequent birthdays marked by the addition of a new gown (in the colour of the birth wind) on each occasion. The gowns are made from diaphanous gossamer so filmy that they can only be seen at their edges when held to the light. As they numerically increase as a series each birthday they intensify in colour and, when eventually and inevitably combining to produce black, they herald the wearer's death day. Some colours are therefore better than others. Pink, for example, tends towards purple and subsequently to black

The Third Policeman, 1998/2010: Birth Winds. In the passage describing the phenomenon of birth winds, Flann O'Brien mentions deep purple, shining silver, hard black, amber, 'a reddish-yellow half way between silver and purple, a greyish-green which was related equally to black and brown' among others, including a colour 'something that ordinary eyes could not see at all'.

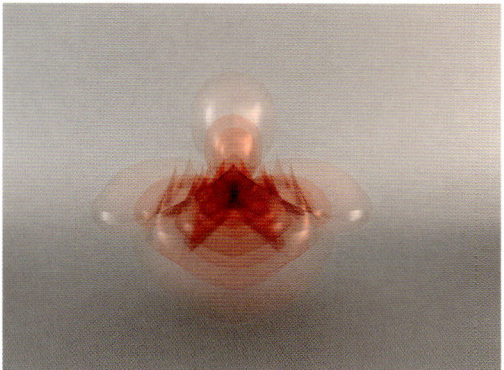

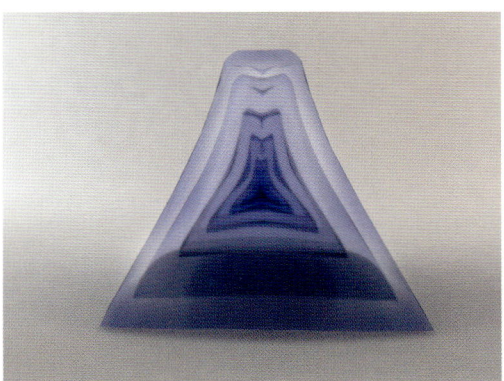

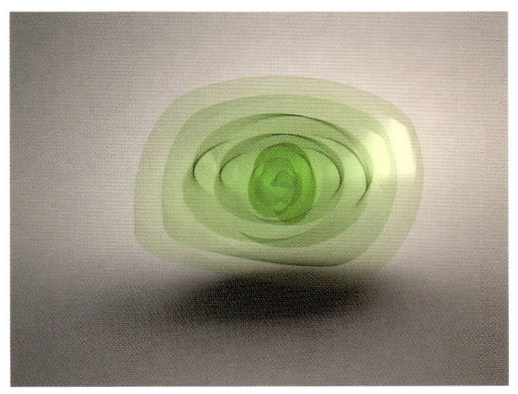

The Third Policeman, 1998/2010: Birthday Gowns (coloured by the winds blowing at the time of birth).

in fewer years than say yellow, a luckier wind to have been born by. Each annually provided attire is worn over the previous one. As each birthday occurs, therefore, the previous gowns must stretch, ultimately perhaps, to a size a hundred times their original. Thus, the colour will dilute to become many times 'rarer' than as its outset. Describing Sergeant Pluck and Policeman MacCruiskeen as having been down in the barracks for hundreds of years, Mathers says:

> 'They must be operating on a very rare colour, something that ordinary eyes could not see at all.'[7]

Here are some examples that attest to O'Brien's genius in delving into space–time dilemmas with comic flair. In the first, the opening to Chapter 4, the narrator grapples with de Selby's statement on the nature of 'journey'.

Referring to the many such statements of de Selby that can be described as striking, he says:

> 'I do not think that any of them can rival his assertion that "a journey is an hallucination".' [8]

The assertion is premised by de Selby's definition of human existence as a succession of infinitely brief static experiences. De Selby is said to support this proposition through an examination of a number of old cinematograph films which probably belonged to his nephew. He then claims that there is no essential difference between when one is at the beginning point of the journey, called point A, and what happens at any single stage during it. Indeed, de Selby describes each moment of a journey as a series of resting points, of which there are an infinite number infinitesimally close to each other, yet not so close that further resting points cannot be inserted between them. Close, but not equidistant, and a principle that can be applied indefinitely. Progression is an illusion resulting from the inability of the human brain – insofar as it has hitherto developed – to accept this series of rests and therefore we describe it as motion. But, says de Selby, since a body cannot achieve two positions simultaneously, this is a nonsensical notion and as 'conclusive' proof he cites any photograph.

A little further on, he again draws on the cinema as a metaphor for space and time as a linked series of contestably discrete events. The narrator, asked whether he has experienced a visit to the cinematograph, says he never has, and goes on:

> '… but I believe it is a dark quarter and little can be seen at all except the photographs on the wall'. [9]

The narrator's consternation at the imploding of dimensions is demonstrated by his description of seeing a house, which he finds both extraordinary and astonishing. In Our World, non-uniform scaling offers the means to deplete an object of 'at least one of the customary dimensions' referred to below, but cannot provide the meaning of the transformation itself. For the narrator, what he sees seems at first as if it were a very poorly painted billboard. Whilst that would not in itself concern him, he has an innate and strong sense that this is the house he has been seeking and that there are people inside. Indeed, he is convinced that this is the policemen's barracks.

> '*I had never seen with my eyes ever in my life before anything so unnatural and appalling and my gaze faltered about the thing uncomprehendingly as if at least one of the customary dimensions was missing, leaving no meaning in the remainder.*'

As he fearfully approaches this house, its appearance seems to change. It did not acquire the shape of an actual house and its outlines were uncertain as if he were seeing it through water. As he comes closer still, he begins to see that it has a back to it, but this too is discomforting, since he can see both front and back at the same time, yet he is approaching it from what he thinks must be the side and, seeing a small window, he knows this must be so. Thus, he concludes that there must in fact be some space for rooms behind the frontage. Mesmerised and anxious, the narrator describes himself as timorous and dry-throated:

> '… *the whole morning and the whole world seemed to have no purpose at all save to frame it and give it some magnitude and position* …'[10]

O'Brien deals with space, scale and artifice via an intriguing adventure into the infinitesimal and unseeable. The narrator has taken up Policeman MacCruiskeen's offer to show him a '*medium fair example of supreme art*'.[11]

From the dresser, MacCruiskeen takes a beautifully made ornamental box, which he places on the table for the narrator to inspect. At first, it seems unremarkable but as the narrator looks more closely, he notices some extraordinary properties. It is actually a small chest, about 12 inches high:

> '… *but it was diminutive in a very perfect way as if you were looking at a full-size one through the wrong end of a spy-glass.*' [12]

The chest has shiny brass corner pieces of superb workmanship, is carved and decorated on every side and is described by the narrator as having all the qualities of true art.

There follows a dialogue about the chest, in which MacCruiskeen explains that it took two years to make and the narrator states that it is the most beautiful thing he has ever seen. The narrator wonders whether there might be something inside. MacCruiskeen tells a story of how he had pondered what would be suitable to keep inside it. He considered letters from Bridie (a former confidante, we are led to presume), but decided that since these letters contained 'hot' bits it would be sacrilegious to do so. For a variety of reasons, he also decided that his studs, cash, certificates, things he found on the road, his razor and all manner of other items were equally unsuitable. Ultimately, MacCruiskeen satisfies his conscience by arriving at the only solution to this conundrum, which was to place inside this first chest, another, identical save for being of slightly smaller dimensions. Opening the chest that sits on the table, MacCruiskeen extracts a second chest and places it beside the first. The narrator is so moved by looking at it that he has to find a chair to sit down. Whistling so as to project an air of nonchalance, the narrator asks what is inside the second chest and, being invited to guess, confesses to being almost afraid to do so.

At this point MacCruiskeen delivers a delightful non sequitur:

> 'You may have come on no bicycle,' he said, 'but that does not say that you know everything.' [13]

The second box contains a third, and the third contains a fourth. As MacCruiskeen continues to extract a new chest from each that preceded it, he is forced to use smaller and smaller knives with which to remove each one, until lined up on the table are twelve, the last about the 'size of half a matchbox'. So small is this last one that the narrator can barely discern the detail of carving, but he knows with certainty that it will be exactly the same as the others.

> 'That last one,' said MacCruiskeen, putting away the knives, 'took me three years to make and it took me another year to believe that I had made it.' [14]

Opening the smallest of the twelve chests, MacCruiskeen works with a pin until he has extracted a thirteenth. He works away quietly until it seems that there are twenty-eight of the chests, and the last looks no bigger than a speck of dirt, except that the narrator can discern a shine. When he looks even more closely, however, he can see that next to this is an even smaller thing that he describes as like something you take out of an eye on a windy day. The narrator believes that there are actually twenty-nine perfectly made chests, identical except for the fact that their scale progressively diminishes.

Returning the pin, MacCruiskeen takes from his pocket something that is too small for the narrator to see and returns to the table where he works quietly on the smallest of the chests. The narrator watches and, observing this, the policeman hands him an enormous magnifying glass, through which he can see that there are now two more chests beside the last that he was barely able to make out with his naked eye. The last he describes as being half a size smaller than ordinary invisibility.

MacCruiskeen explains that number twenty-two was crafted fifteen years previously and that he has made a new one each year since. As the chests become ever smaller, six years ago they were already becoming impossible to see, even with the aid of the magnifying glass. MacCruiskeen tells the narrator that the last five that he made have been seen by nobody. He says that the one he is currently working on is almost as small as nothing and that more than a million of them could fit inside the first that he made. MacCruiskeen wonders when this work will ever finish.

Finally MacCruiskeen tells the narrator that the musical instrument, which the narrator was unable to hear, was an ingenious invention of his own design. The notes it produces are of such a high frequency that no human ear, other than MacCruiskeen's, can hear them. Asked what he makes of it all, the narrator replies:

'I think it is extremely acatalectic …'[15]

The Third Policeman, 1998/2010: Policeman MacCruiskeen's collection of miniature chests (extrapolated from 'Our World').

The Third Policeman, 1998/2010: Detail of the miniature chest collection. MacCruiskeen explains that number twenty-two was manufactured fifteen years previously and that he has made a new one each year since. As the chests become increasingly small, six years prior they were becoming impossible to see, even with the aid of the magnifying glass (extrapolated from 'Our World').

At the end of my 1967 edition of *The Third Policeman*, in the 'Publisher's Note', the page that may not be read before the book itself is read for the first time, there is a 'note from the author' which refers to the narrator's soul, Joe:

Elsewhere, the author wrote:

'Joe had been explaining things in the meantime. He said it was again the beginning of the unfinished, the re-discovery of the familiar. The re-experience of the already suffered, the fresh forgetting of the unremembered …'[16]

Creating outside the box

For the scripter this chapter is a creative call to arms for it is a reminder that we do not need to be constrained to a physical interpretation of the world that we design for. It is a reminder also that while designers are always thinking 'outside the box', there are other non-visual media creatives who do so too and, in the case of Flann O'Brien, with considerable poise. The verb 'to script' means to adapt a story for broadcast or film. On this basis Our World might be linked to *The Third Policeman*, however precariously, as a means to endorse the use of scripting for the nurturing of architectural ideas beyond the physical constraints that otherwise limit the definition of the built world for which we design.

(This chapter is adapted from my *Beyond Animation* [17])

1 A building that physically responds in real time to a change of circumstances such as environment, weather and use.
2 Brian O'Nolan (Irish name: Brian Ó Nualláin) was born in County Tyrone in Ireland and wrote satirical columns for the Irish Times as well as several unusual novels including *At Swim-Two-Birds*, *The Third Policeman* and *An Béal Bocht*. He used several pseudonyms including Flann O'Brien and Myles na gCopaleen.
3 The difference between Fuller and Le Corbusier lies not in the ideal importance which they attach to mathematics but in the symbolic role it plays. In Fuller's domes the forms are identified by their lines of force, resembling those High Gothic structures where a framework alone defines the volumes which it encloses, and seeming to exemplify Fuller's philosophy of the forms of art being absorbed back into the technical process. In Le Corbusier, the plastic act is hypostatised. His forms are, as it were, congealed in space, as in a solid graph. In both, the Phileban solids play an essential part; in both, the aesthetic and the discipline are identified. But whereas in the case of Fuller the formulation and the identification take place on a supersensuous level and the aesthetic is transmuted into the act, in the case of Le Corbusier the act becomes solidified in the sensuous object.
2(1):59-65; doi:10.1093/bjaesthetics/2.1.59
© 1962 by British Society of Aesthetics; see also A Colquhoun, 'The Modern Movement in Architecture', *British Journal of Aesthetics*, 1962; 2, 59–65 at 63
4 Flatland refers to *Flatland: A Romance of Many Dimensions*, an 1884 satirical novella by Edwin Abbott Abbott. Ostensibly a means to provide a commentary on Victorian social hierarchy and culture, its more enduring contribution has been as a very readable treatise on dimensions.
5 De Selby in Flann O'Brien, *The Third Policeman*, MacGibbon & Kee (London), 1967, preface.
6 Ibid, Preface, p 159.
7 Ibid, p 33.
8 Ibid, p 52.
9 Ibid, p 60.
10 Ibid, p 55.
11 Ibid, p 72.
12 Ibid.
13 Ibid, p 74.
14 Ibid, p 75.
15 Ibid, p 72.
16 Ibid, p 207.
17 MC Burry, 'Beyond Animation', *Architecture + Animation, Architectural Design,* Vol 71, No 2, Academy Editions (London), April 2001.

10 Performative scripting

This final worked example gives an overview of a discernibly deepening engagement with performative architecture worldwide. Buildings that physically adapt to changes in environmental circumstances are part of an emerging architecture for which real-time-responsive performance is seen as a major opportunity. As sensor and actuator technology catches up with digital computation, the imagined near future will become closer to achievable reality. Drawing on a number of influences, most notably the natural world, it seems that we are ultimately on a quest for an architecture that has the same degree of responsiveness that organisms manifest with their highly evolved active adaptation to shifts and alterations to both cyclical and unexpectedly sudden changes in their environment. At its simplest this means buildings with sensors that track the movement of the sun advantageously in the way that a sunflower first opens up to receive the sun's rays at daybreak, then follows those rays during the course of the day. Buildings might be designed to do the same, nor is this an entirely 21st-century idea. In the Italian province of Verona, for example, the revolving house Villa Girasole ('sunflower house', constructed 1929–35) was the inspiration of the structural engineer Angelo Invernizzi in collaboration with the architect Ettore Fagiuoli.

Active rather than passive performance

The word 'active' is key to the principal argument in this concluding chapter. It seems strange that so much of modern architecture is now subject to environmental performance requirements that are enshrined in regulations as if, without the legal obligation, we are disinclined to make the sensible decisions necessary to keep energy consumption to a minimum. This has not always been the case, and there are notable passive models of climatically responsive and environmentally friendly buildings that have formed very valuable parts of a vernacular architectural culture. A perfect example is the *masia*, an isolated farmhouse that can be found all over rural Catalonia, in northeast Spain, whose ancient territory and influence extends well into the Pyrenean foothills in the south of France where Catalan is still spoken today.[1] Typically the *masia* accommodated the beasts on the lower floor, the workers (vassals) slept on the uppermost floor, while on the middle level social functions such as dining and community prayer were accommodated along with the feudal landowner's family sleeping arrangements, effectively the *piano nobile* – traditionally the 'noble floor' that sat above the defensible (rusticated) ground floor avoiding the dampness of the lowest floor, and offering views and access to the passing breezes. Ideally, the house (more a manor house in scale

Vernacular Catalan manorial farmhouse (*masia*), Garrotxa, Northern Catalonia, 1500s.

but accommodating everyone associated with the agricultural enterprise) stood facing the south, preferably on a slope for maximum solar exposure. In this way, animals could move back up to their stables and byres from the pastures near the rivers and creeks below at close of day. Due to this clever use of the topography, the animals might reach the dwelling by a completely different route than their human cohabitants, who access the principal floor by another doorway at a higher level.

Many *masias* are located in regions with extremes of temperature: cold winters and hot summers, and day-to-night extremes too. Among the most distinctive characteristics of these south-facing buildings are deep and elegant porticos at the first (principal social) level along the length of the facade. In summer, the porch provided relief from the intense heat of the sun, while in winter the much lower midday sun angle would ensure the rays would help warm up the wall behind. Such a porch is also a very effective suntrap. Another characteristic is the spatial and structural division of the building by two internal walls parallel to the side walls. This means that there are four parallel walls with three parallel spatial alignments, something that is not usually visible from the outside but is very important in terms of typology. The reason for this configuration is the need to span such a wide building efficiently. As a feature of a typology, it allows two conclusions to be drawn. The first is the absolute nature of the type feature. Whether the *masia* is located far north in the Pyrenean valleys servicing the needs of high-altitude pastoralists, or to the south in the heat of Tarragona where the occupants might be growing grapes and olives, the tripartite division remains typologically evident. More intriguing still is the way that this particular feature links the *masia* back to Roman imperial occupation, and the discernible influence of the northern Italian farmhouses of that time finding its way to the Roman colonies two thousand years earlier.

What has all this to do with scripting?

One of several cusps of change for the architectural profession is a move from the passive to the interactive. By this I contend that permanence, immutability, typological consistency, adherences to a paradigm are constructs that will not necessarily survive as securely as would have seemed a certainty at one time. I have argued in earlier chapters that a designer's sensibility towards the animated is perhaps an instinct that has always been there, only to have been challenged by the limitations of the constructional and representational repertoire before the digital age. Whether it is the

Baroque or Gaudí, Michelangelo and the Laurentian Library (1525) or van Doesberg's insistence on the need to move rapidly to non-Euclidean spatial thinking as early as 1924,[2] there is evidence of a desire to escape the strictures of type. My account above of the development of the *masia* as a pluriclimatic and topographically flexible archetype lends itself to scripting. A topographical plan with intelligible features such as contours, roads and rivers, can be tied to a spreadsheet with cells that are linked intelligently both to and from the plan. In this way 'northern Catalonia, sheep farming, low economic output' could be interpreted by comparing these inputs with the local features on a point selected on the plan automatically, offering a performance-optimised solution. It is unlikely that a computed solution would be very different from an actual example of such a farmhouse, were it situated at the appointed location. Equally, the same algorithms would adapt just as well to 'southern Catalonia, olive oil producers, cashed up', providing a solution embellished by features that a kinder climate, less challenging topography and better economic base can offer.

Such a scripted response could be used to test the historical and anthropological components in my brief history of Catalan farmhouses, just as *Possible Palladian Villas* no doubt offers historians new insights into Palladio's theoretically unfulfilled portfolio.[3] The script might be labelled 'performative modelling', but I argue that in this instance this is passive, historicist and not necessarily progressive. What are the design opportunities here?

Let us summarise the value of such scripting as follows: scripting a *masia* for all possible situations so that a new variant of retro-architecture might have its day, a banal encoded set of features that shows how a simple manorial house design can conform to site specificity, diurnal and seasonal shifts in light and weather, geographical location and orientation. We could call this the '*Para-masia*', acquiring its features for any given instance from the relevant dataset for its location. The user picks a site and the script intelligently does the rest … Designed to house animals, serfs and the landowner and their families, the model adapts superbly to most kinds of terrain and climate, in fact, and therefore through the script. The archetype is so 'strong' that it can be distilled to a set of essential features. It was not so long ago that this would have been considered as a successful phenotype in its own right. Is that the best use of a scripter's time, a scripter who wishes to explore possibilities?

Towards actively performative design scripting

The tension here is between the analyst, the synthesist and the hybrid thinker who claims to use the former to direct the latter. In this chapter I would like to end the book on a progressive note, by considering a more forward-looking practice-oriented focus by adopting performance in an active sense. By working through an example tuned to a sensible analytical approach such as the 'dial a Catalan farmhouse', I would succeed in a 'case-closed' finale, whereas I shall do the opposite here and steer the reader to a 'work in progress' conclusion, to support my proposition that in the world of actively performative architecture these are indeed early days. The final project for this scripting primer is *Dermoid*, which offers a view of a future that can only be determined through a digitally scripted mode of design enquiry. Hoist a little by my own petard, as any future-gazing designer who is not a science fictioner places themselves at risk of being, here is a scripted future-gaze that is based on computable material performance at one level, and an optimistic presumption that amazing new materials await us just around the corner. Dermoid is simply a fantastically adaptable architectural skin, yet to be invented, supported by a reciprocal frame truss that appears to be well within our computational reach, but in fact presents significant computational challenges. Prior to discussing the project, here is some conceptual background to the central proposition: architecture that performs actively in response to changes in the external environment.

Performative botany as model for performative architecture

As a high-school botany student, I learned about the world of mosses (*Bryophyta*), and the subtleties of this particular histology have remained with me ever since, not least as a model for how our future buildings might perform active internal climate modification.

We were asked to investigate one in particular: wall screw-moss (*Tortula muralis*). This is the moss that we see around us in most temperate and cooler climates around the world – those green clumps that signify dampness wherever we come across them, on the shady sides of masonry buildings or deep in the woods on boulders, decaying branches and up the sides of trees. Apart from its brilliant green it is an otherwise unprepossessing component of the ecosystem, but on closer investigation, microscopic in fact, a fantastically intricate world of microclimate adaptability emerges. Perhaps it

Botanical detail of moss.

is this discovery of worlds within worlds that made the reference to Policeman MacCruiskeen's collection of Russian Doll boxes within boxes in the previous chapter so engaging when I first read it.[4] The richness of what is there in front of the observer whose visual acuity is instrumentally unaided is tangible only to the mind through prior knowledge. Those strange sparse little orange hairs (seta) that rise out of the moist green mass support the spore capsule heads clear of the leaves which, when conditions are right, allow the wind to disperse their minuscule packets of genetic material. Being in moist locations, however, the spores will only find wind-borne conveyance in a dry breeze. While the capsule heads are developing, they are protected by little 'Noddy' hats (calyptra) that come away as soon as the capsule reaches the first stage of maturity. The capsule (calyx) that contains the spores is still closed off by a diaphragmatic cap (operculum): in the drying breeze this contracts and eventually detaches itself from the capsule too at the time the moss is ready to spore. The capsule remains tightly closed off still by a whorl of sepals (peristome): tiny little 'teeth' pointing inwards from the capsule rim. Humidity keeps the sepals closed, and the spores safely dry inside their vessel, but when a warm breeze wafts by, they react by opening up allowing the mature spores to be released. Once the humidity rises again the sepals react and fold back to their closed position until favourable conditions resume. The relevance of this description will become clearer later in the chapter. Before that, let us consider the impacts of technology and computation and a systems approach to thinking about design.

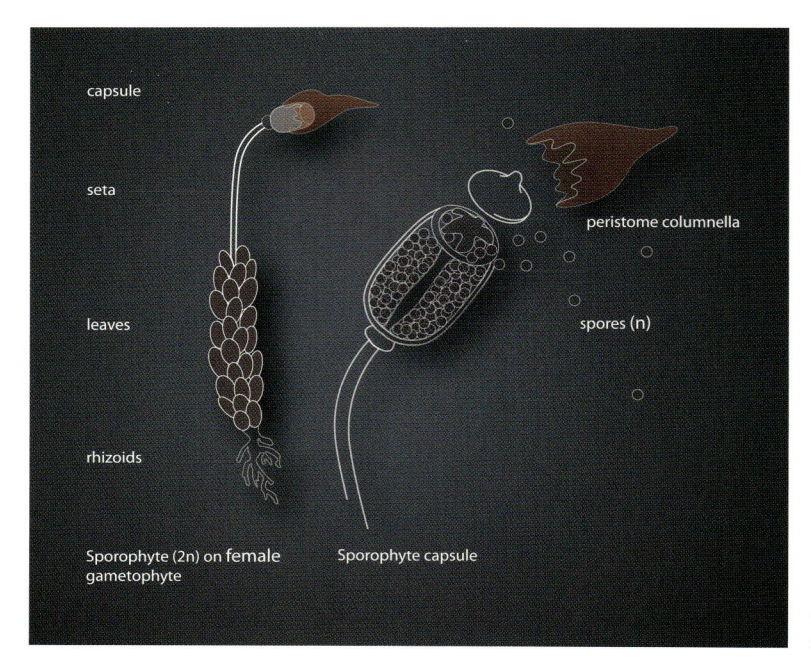

Tortula muralis (wall screw-moss).

On technology and computation

The history of architecture and engineering education and practice – including the differences between the Anglo-Saxon and Southern European contexts – is one of separation between the art and science of building. At its simplest, architects have the ideas and engineers ensure that they go on to be structurally viable. This has developed into a linear sequence: ideas are nurtured in the studio, then filtered through to the technical problem solvers, whose advice is subsequently received back and acted upon, the design is refined, and the cycle repeated iteratively depending on the degree of complexity. With notable exceptions, there is usually little creative dialogue between the two parties at the early conceptual stage, however much heads will be scratched together later in the process at formally convened meetings. The relationship between materials scientists, product developers and architects is even more remote. The materials and systems available to architects and engineers are ever more sophisticated, client demands too, so what does this traditional professional interdisciplinary relationship mean for buildings demanding innovation at all levels?

Antoni Gaudí, Sagrada Família church, Barcelona, Spain, 1882–ongoing: device that Gaudí used to load test the compressive strength of stone empirically on site.

Gaudí standing next to a stone load test in which the testing machine appears to have failed.

One consequence is that invention is largely reactive; instead of finding solutions the team solves problems, which is hardly a design strategy at its most creative. If we can move the actors around a little, and reframe their respective challenges, vitally different professional roles emerge. Let us take the situation where deeply thought-through alternative structural performance, a minimal use of material and inventive construction techniques are merged as a single opportunity for holistic innovation; a situation Gaudí set up most notably for Colònia Güell chapel in 1896. The core to tying all three together today is the availability of computation of an order not possible with the abacus, slide rule, or calculator. Gaudí, of course, resorted to inventing an analogue computer in the form of a hanging model, but the project had an initial design phase lasting eight years, and the following six years were spent building the crypt, itself one of the world's most remarkable interior spaces, at which point the project was abandoned. Since Gaudí's time, and relative to the effectiveness of Gaudí's analogue modelling techniques despite the years in its construction, digital computation of this order has been somewhat held back. The obstacle today is a combination of what still remain long calculation times using software highly specific to discrete professional domains, and with insufficient holism to allow the decision-making that presumably characterised Gaudí's working style.

Given that the building professions may have more demands placed on them such as achieving even more with even less, faster construction and tighter management, the problem is essentially the same for the design team as it has always been. As has happened previously in history, the combination of circumstances external to the professional environment, such as the move from Romanesque to Gothic in medieval times and the arrival of the Industrial Revolution in the 18th century, all impact on the way the professions go about their business. The transition from analogue design processes to, firstly, digital assistance through computer-aided design (CAD), and subsequently to computer-aided architectural design (CAAD), is one such externally driven mega-shock for which architecture has yet to make the necessary transformations. Such transformations are disruptive, but advantageous at least in the long term all the same. Scripting combined with emerging computation power is narrowing the gap between the designers' and engineers' respective roles. This is not to argue for a convergence of disciplines: in fact the contrary. We are at a time when specialisation is even more necessary as knowledge deepens but our respective practices can converge from operating sequentially to collaborating in real time. 'Operating sequentially' refers to designer as dreamer and engineer as problem solver, which necessarily means a sequence of interactions and propositions over an extended time frame. Emerging digital tools allow feedback to take place in real time enabling dreamers and pragmatists to make decisions together – and I am not besmirching engineers as pragmatists here; I am simply conceding that pragmatists are essential design team members. This shifting professional relationship is not socially driven, but digitally enabled through rapidly extending computational facility and combined with new communication technologies and software interoperability. We can investigate nature's solutions, understand the processes as a system in operation, mimic them within design and today compute solutions never previously possible.

Nature as master?

At the beginning of this book I looked at our propensity as architects to swarm towards particular approaches to design coupled to or helping establish a cultural *Zeitgeist*. As architects we would like to lead, but typically it is more viable to hitch onto the coat-tails of avant-gardists coming from another discipline. Most of our built work is ultimately framed within a highly intensive capital framework; it is hard not to be held back by regular doses of fiscal reality and our professional responsibilities as architects and designers. It is for this reason we should not feel overly disconcerted to see the currency of the late-1990s 'blob' debate that emerged within architecture upstaged by the equivalent 1950s debate (at least in relation to freeform) within the plastic fine arts.[5] The turbulence that abstract sculptors such as Henry Moore caused in the art world half a century ago seemed to find its echo when architects such as Frank Gehry, Zaha Hadid and Greg Lynn gained prominence in the 1980s and 1990s. The desired technical possibilities of emerging architecture may, for the first time, align more credibly with what was formally unrealistic futuristic thinking about architectural performance. On the one hand, the urgencies of global environmental and economic challenges have reached a higher level of community consciousness with a public who are beginning to demand more action. On the other hand, new computational capability and emerging material science are trending towards potential solutions that are far more viable than they have ever been in the past.

The near-parallel trajectories between how we might see architecture performing in material fact, versus science fiction-inspired optimism, are appearing to converge in some areas. Currently, most forward thinking within architectural scripting is heavily located in the province of biomimetics. This is not surprising, given the essential paradox between our powers of inventing entirely new situations and circumstances being far greater than our powers to foresee technology beyond what we already know. We can imagine extraordinary buildings of the future made by machines extruding mixtures of miracle materials with precision, speed and economy, but we cannot envisage the extraordinary machines that will actually do this, other than those based on technology that we already know about. I imagine that prior to the invention of the steam engine, speed would have been conjectured as something society might benefit from without any mechanical sense of how it would be achieved. Art often succeeds in presciently showing us what novelty lies ahead, but seldom the means by which it will be achieved – I am thinking of Leonardo da Vinci's design for a flying machine (c 1488), for example.

In looking outside architecture for some clues on how we might do a better job with performance, it is hardly surprising that we therefore seek guidance from nature, there being no other 'system' available for us to study for convincing prototypes. The intellectual migration for architectural thinking from object-related thinking (building form) to one of systems (building performance) is well on its way, and scripting naturally offers a means to queue jump millions of years of evolution, by computationally filling in for time's selection of the fittest solutions. It is on this basis that Dermoid is proffered in this chapter as an example of a thought experiment seeking to establish where we have got to thus far through empirical data capture and interpretation through scripting. As a stepping stone, the rate of change between what we can do now compared with a decade ago tells us that we

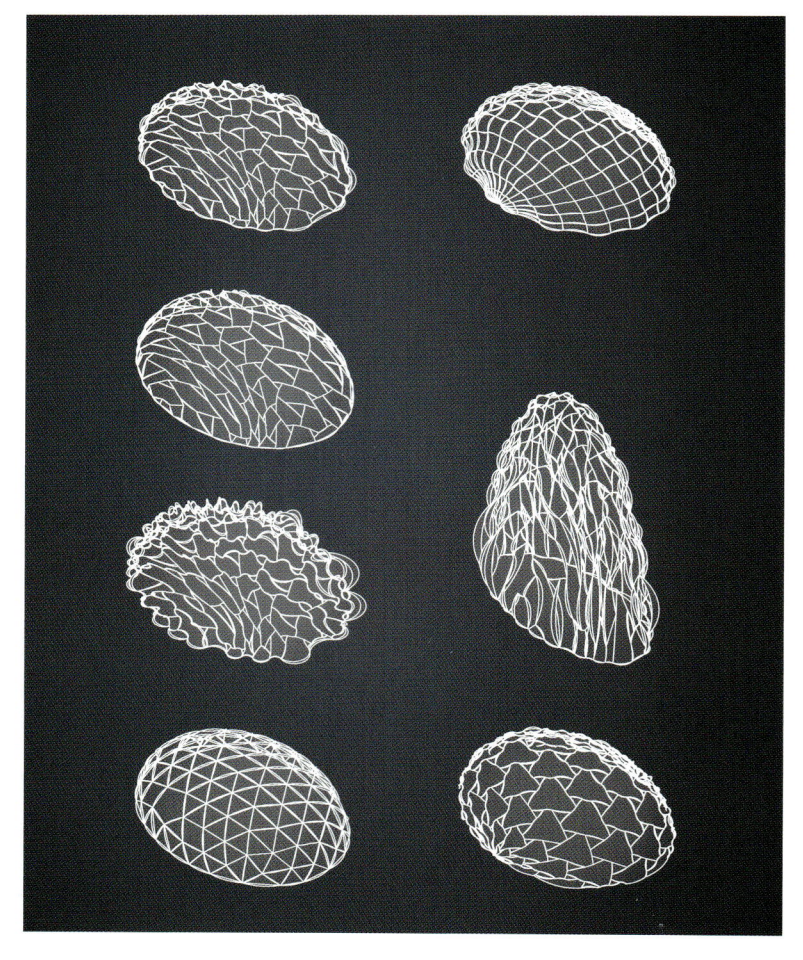

CITA-SIAL, Dermoid, Copenhagen, 2010: populating the surface of the ellipsoid with reciprocal frame trusses. The ellipsoid extends the earlier thought experiment in Chapter 8, the surface chosen for the factor of difficulty it represents with constantly changing double curvature.

CITA-SIAL, Dermoid, Copenhagen, 2010. Dermoid is an inhabitable paramorph scripted to be parametrically variable in all its attributes, including the breathing and insulating skin.

have only just begun the journey, despite the difference in potential seeming worlds apart in just these ten years. This rate of change forces the concession that this is work in progress, with no false conceit that it is anything more advanced than hesitant first steps.

Dermoid

When we combine new digital design practice emerging from studio with that coming from the digital fabrication suite, we can see exciting opportunities for major reform to architectural practice. It is with this in mind that we ran a series of workshops at CITA at the Royal Danish Academy of

Fine Arts School of Architecture in Copenhagen commencing in 2009, and ongoing at the time of writing.[6] The component of the workshop written up here, Dermoid, is essentially a thought experiment tested in studio. Up to this point I have characterised the typical architectural project as an inter-professional engagement between architects and engineers based on linear series of technical, environmental and financial questions and answers. How feasible is it to recombine these sequential dialogues into an informed conversation conducted in the same space at the same time? In other words, through rapidly accelerating computational thinking and action, how practical is it for more of the crucial design decision-making to be made around a table in real time, rather than have the dialogue stretched over weeks and months in the traditional input–output model?

The research framework we adopted for the studio has been an amalgam of 'interdependent design'[7] and 'early stage'[8] doctoral research at SIAL at RMIT University in Melbourne, Australia, part of our research into the evolving architecture–engineering nexus, and one of the research streams at CITA led by Professor Mette Ramsgard Thomsen and dubbed (by her) as 'new tectonics' within a conceptual model of 'the active material'. We believe that both this research framework and its conceptual support propel the vitally important tests of new models of material engagement for the future. The overriding motivations for exploring these new models are summarised as a quest for better design with improved performance using less materials more cleverly,

CITA-SIAL, Dermoid, Copenhagen, 2010: understanding material properties in order to propagate appropriate performance-oriented parametric reconfigurations for each of the Dermoid's structural elements.

thereby reducing costs of procurement, maintenance and use. The underlying challenge for Dermoid is to test addressing these ambitions without compromising design quality.

The principal ingredient for the project is that of an enriched feedback loop between material choice and testing for appropriateness and design selection. We commenced with experiments looking at the performance of thin strips of plywood in novel configurations. Loads were applied, measurements taken and graphs plotted, providing us with real data to drive the structural parameters interactively that govern the performance of the material under load used in design conditions. In this same space we therefore ran material tests, the results of which allowed for immediate deployment within the design. What makes this different from Gaudí, for example, famously photographed testing the bearing strength of masonry under load at the Sagrada Família church?

The difference is now having tests and applications of results in the same space. Although the Gaudí example is nevertheless the exception and not the rule, it is the real-time design testing associated with computation today that is the essential difference. Only in the last few years has software such as Rhino 3D™ developed tools that parametrically link data to 'options machines'. Using Grasshopper™ for the example above, a slider bar allows the user to calibrate

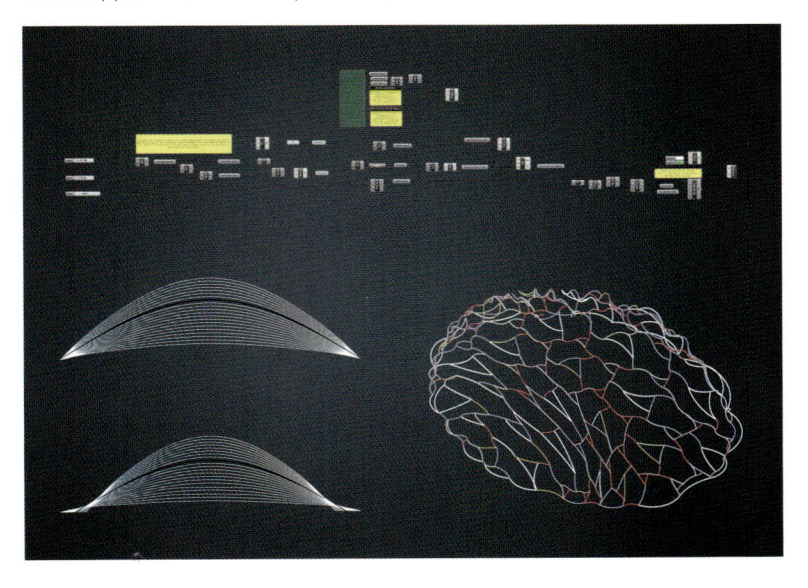

CITA-SIAL, Dermoid, Copenhagen, 2010: parametrically variable structural layout using feedback from empirically obtained performance data.

CITA-SIAL, Dermoid, Copenhagen, 2010: load testing and measuring the performance of curved plywood trusses in which the flange and web are notched together without glue or mechanical fixing.

CITA-SIAL, Dermoid, Copenhagen, 2010: analogue and digital research into material performance at CITA.

the forces required to bend the plywood to a desired configuration or, having configured the plywood visually to the desired position, the designer can read off the forces that would need to be applied. As computational power increases in years to come, the implications of this real-time feedback loop will become manifest in the quest for leaps in performance.

The context for the computationally enriched feedback loop is a large structure that is designed and built with known materials, used in novel configurations and supporting an intelligent skin that automatically responds to climatic variables and user desires. The skin is made from materials not yet invented, actuated by unknown devices in response to the very well-known human comfort needs. The *parti* for the project, completely artificial, was to take the ellipsoid from Chapter 8 and test its viability using reciprocal frame trusses. This particular structural strategy was chosen because along with the elegance of a mutually self-supporting structural system using short timber lengths (a constraint from using plywood), the digital design representational challenges are legion.[9]

In terms of scripting, obviously essential to this task, there were six discrete principal pathways followed in conjunction with each other:

1 parametrically responsive engine used to configure the ellipsoid form and reconfigure it to a non-regular geometry;

2 interactive panelling of form into structural modules;

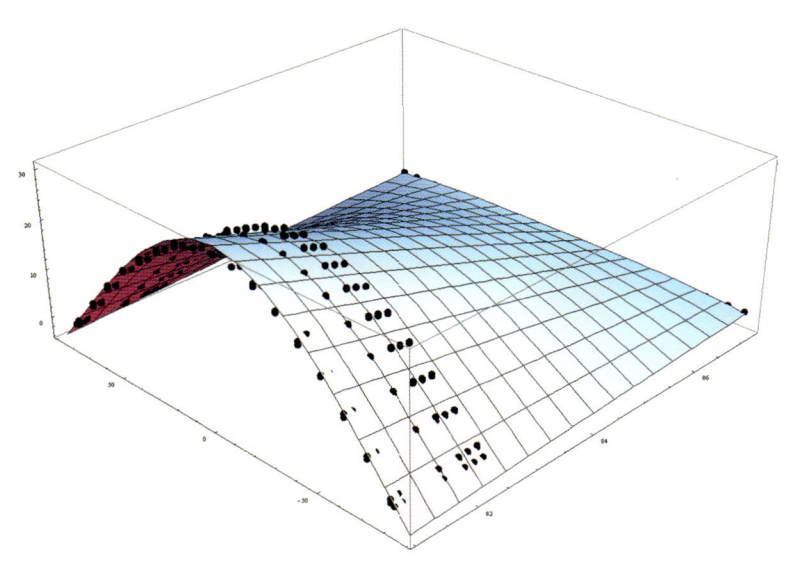

3 performance-adapted design of individual components based on structural criteria;

CITA-SIAL, Dermoid, Copenhagen, 2010: data from the structural load tests were plotted mathematically in order to provide meaningful inputs to the structural frame's parametric scripting.

4 performance-adapted configuration of individual components based on constructional criteria;

5 structural performance of Dermoid as a system;

6 performance-adapted configuration of Dermoid skin based on performance criteria.

CITA-SIAL, Dermoid, Copenhagen, 2010: each structural element is parametrically variable responding to local structural performance requirements.

The illustrations for this chapter tell their own story, so I shall conclude with some notes on the scripting used for each pathway.

The choice of the ellipsoid as the genotype is highly appropriate for such thought experiments. It has a clearly understood geometry with the possibility of three distinct curvatures around the x, y, and z axes when comprised of three different ellipses. This means that despite being a regular geometry, its components have little opportunity for standardisation, which is an attractive degree of difficulty. The scripting used here needs to allow the user to reconfigure the form from a low and wide 'auditorium' space or a tall 'steeple' ellipsoid to a freeform that is derived from the ellipsoid. We used this project to benchmark the relative merits of Processing, MAYA™, Rhino 3D™ with Grasshopper™, Digital Project™, Generative Components™ and Open Cascade (open-source libraries).

The choice of the reciprocal frame truss as the structural rationale, while elegant as a configuration, is extremely inconvenient in all other respects. The ends of each module either lap over the next or are seated by half-housing techniques, all of which are bespoke to

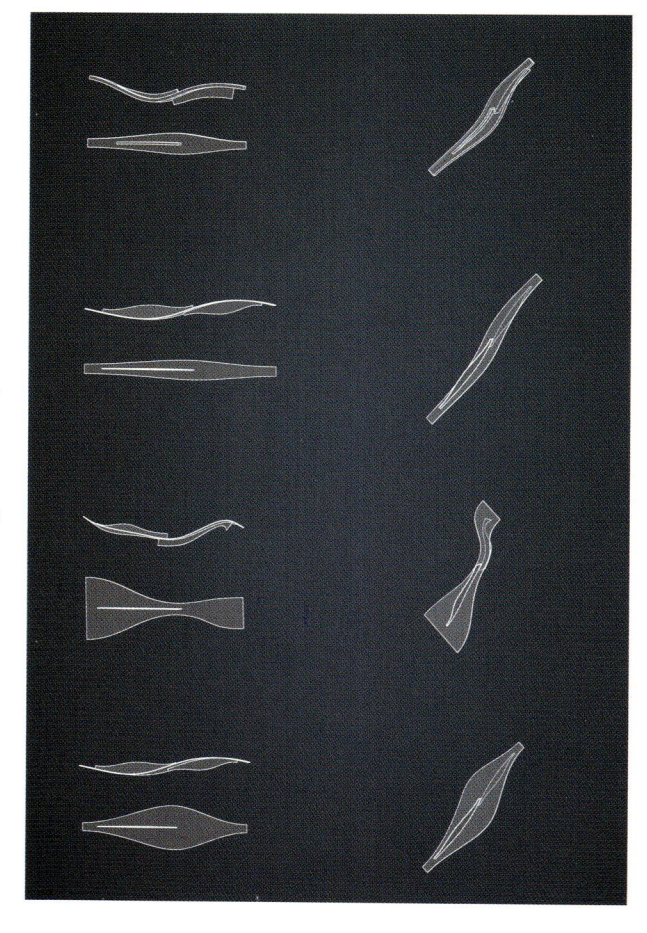

CITA-SIAL, Dermoid, Copenhagen, 2010: reciprocal frame truss made from web and flange elements sized individually to meet performance requirements.

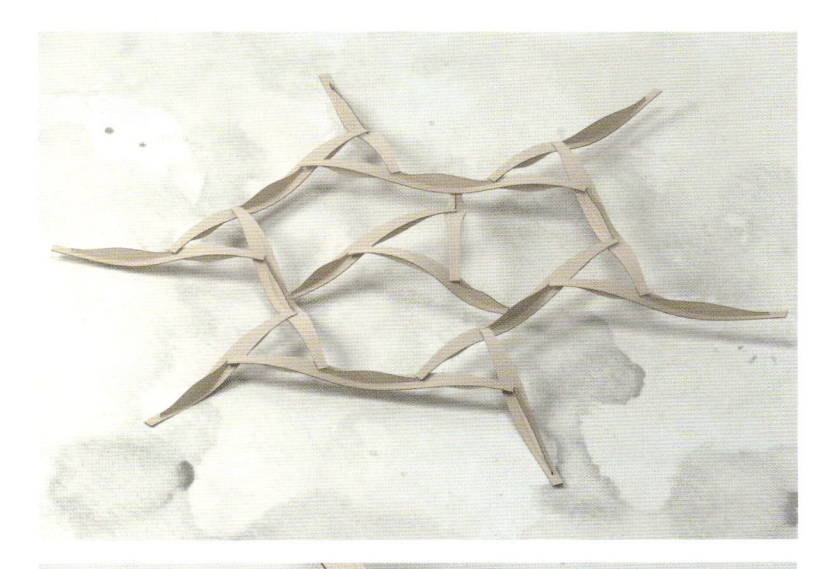

CITA-SIAL, Dermoid, Copenhagen, 2010: detail of connection and Dermoid skin.

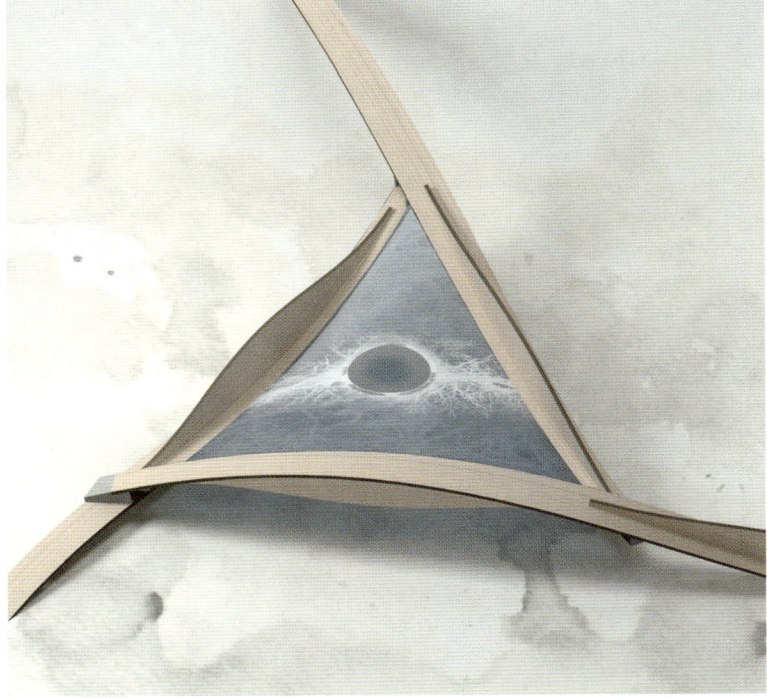

CITA-SIAL, Dermoid, Copenhagen, 2010: the breathing insulating skin is phosphorescent.

each situation. Plywood at least offers the possibility of localised bending, which is the technique we adopted, but this is an extreme challenge for the scripter, which gave this approach its merit.

The possibility of calculating the structural performance of Dermoid as a system in real time such that every member (which has every dimension made parametrically changeable) is individually sized and curved is remote. As a configuration, this was as complicated a structure as we could contrive for the purposes of the investigation. In terms of new knowledge, we can make the following claim. Each element has its material characteristics built into the script such that any viable set of parameters can be varied at will. The internal feedback loop for each structural and constructional member is therefore comprehensive and intact having been derived empirically and built into the script. As a complex system it seems unlikely that it can be optimised using currently available technology for real-time decision-making. This is not what is principally at stake; the contention here is that at least theoretically with the right degree of computer power, the feedback loop as a totality can be scripted bi-directionally with the feedback loop for each element.

CITA-SIAL, Dermoid, Copenhagen, 2010.

The Dermoid skin was beyond the scope of our workshop but it is core to this chapter in terms of signalling future directions for scripting tied to inventions of materials and systems. The hypothesis is that with scripting we have the possibility of adapting form around parameters that range between an *a priori* take such as a contrived geometry (as in the ellipsoid used here), to free form, to form responding to feedback from an adaptive criteria set. By this I mean that we will be able to migrate from *conforming* to a dominant paradigm (regardless of cultural and practical considerations) to being directly *informed* by the immediate physical and environmental circumstances through real-time computation. We have the possibility of interactively configuring the structural envelope around given performance criteria, for example, and we can constructionally adapt to any situation scripted to accommodate real-time performance feedback. Finally, we can postulate on how a skin adapted directly from natural systems might play out visually and performatively through scripted parameters. In short, scripting affords a level of speculation without which we would be stuck with Gaudí's dilemmas, and his successful failure at Colònia Güell chapel.

Value judgement

The chapter draws from two examples: the unscripted Para-masia, an environmentally performative archetype with a 2,000-year-long tradition, and Dermoid, an environmentally performing responsive enclosure actively

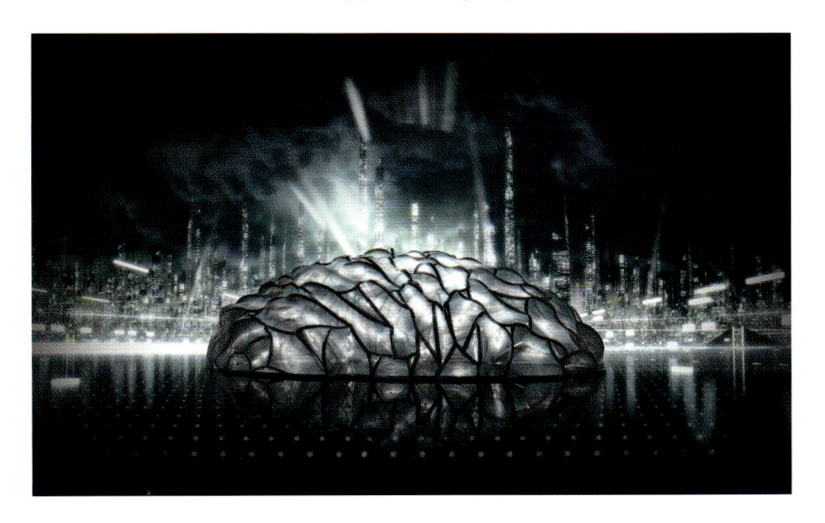

CITA-SIAL, Dermoid, Copenhagen, 2010.

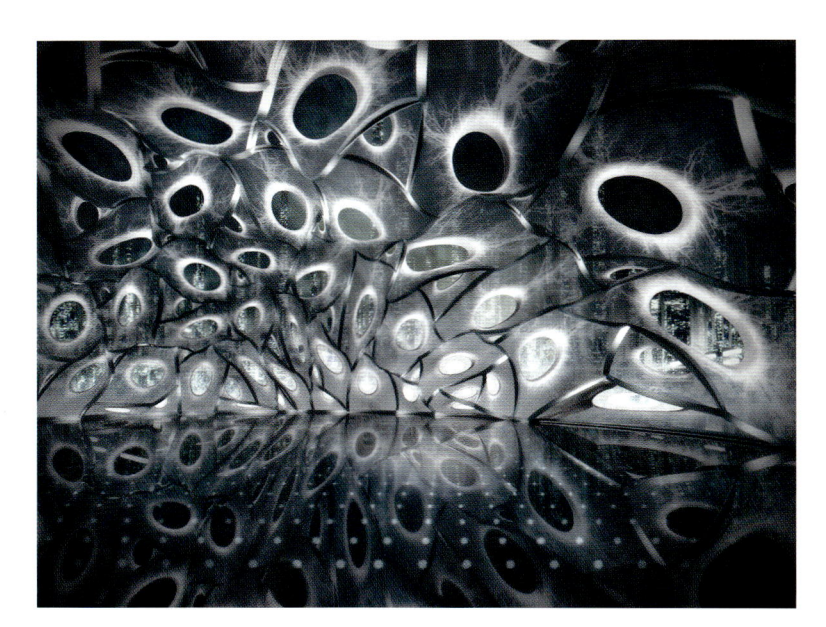

CITA-SIAL, Dermoid interior Copenhagen, 2010.

affording maximum comfort for the least use of materials. I have argued that in terms of progressive design investigation, Dermoid warrants the time invested more than seeking interesting evidence of a universally effective farmhouse model through scripting. Is such value judgement necessary?

While it is a touch provocative to hypothesise future environmental performance attributes of architectural skins and the underlying structural epidermis using unknown materials and technologies, it provides the necessary degrees of freedom to allow us to dream as designers and to speculate without constraint. Scripted to mimic familiar cutaneous structures, driven by systems yet to be invented, this project is offered as a fitting counterpoint to some of the earlier worked examples that form the foundation of *Scripting Cultures* in terms of scale and motivation. On the one hand, scripted consideration of both Para-masia and Dermoid could connect the past to the future; on the other hand, focusing on the future alone in the way I have accounted for here could question the viability of my argument appearing as anything other than wishful thinking. We are, after all, facing more immediate challenges and we could sensibly constrain ourselves to scripting for tried and tested materials and methodologies already well understood. The temptation to script extraordinary variety completely beyond known economic realities, and optimistically pretend that the commissioning cavalry is within earshot, blurs the distinction between avant-garde architecture and science-fiction fantasy; it could be read as self-indulgence and, given the flocking towards the futuristically motivated secondment of biomimetics, as collective indulgence. Ultimately, how much of a test of actual usefulness should we feel obliged to apply to our scripting?

References

1 J Moner, J Riera, A Pla, 'The rural househouse: "Masia", typology and setting' *Lotus International*, 23, 1979/II, Electa (Milan), pp 34–8.
2 Proposition 9 in Theo van Doesburg, *Towards a plastic architecture*, 1924, extracted from: Ulrich Conrads, *Programs and Manifestoes on 20th-century Architecture*, MIT Press (Cambridge, MA), 1970, p.79.
3 See George Hersey and Richard Freedman, *Possible Palladian Villas*, MIT Press (Cambridge, MA), 1992.
4 See discussion of Flann O'Brien, *The Third Policeman*, MacGibbon & Kee (London), 1967 in Chapter 9 above.
5 See: EH Gombrich, *The Story of Art*, Phaidon (London), 1950, 2nd edn.
6 CITA and SIAL. See project credits.
7 Dr Paul Nicholas, *Approaches to Interdependency: early design exploration across architectural and engineering domains*, PhD Thesis, RMIT University, 2008.
8 Dr Dominik Holzer, *Sense-making across collaborating disciplines in the early stages of architectural design*, PhD Thesis, RMIT University, 2009.
9 The reciprocal frame is first written about by Philibert DeLorme (c 1514–1570) where he specifically deals with 'construction at little cost' by ingenious use of short lengths of timber, effectively a laminated construction *(Nouvelles inventions pour bien bastir et à petits frais* – 1561). A more recent account of the system is: Olga Popovic Larsen, *Reciprocal Frame Architecture*, Architectural Press (London), 2008, 1st edn.

11
Cultural account: scripting and shifts in authorship

To be writing about scripting in 2010 has been an interesting experience. *Scripting Cultures* is a primer, a 'small introductory book on a subject', but scripting is still a big soft-boiled topic rendered small only by the lack of real take-up of code writing in design relative to opportunity. I have endeavoured to show that scripting design is potentially as creative a design domain as any other for exploring ideas.

The editorial preface to the 2006 issue of *AD* foregrounding computer programming, software and design tantalised its readers by stating:

> *So much more than a development of architects' technical skill bases, it [computer programming] is set to have a huge impact on the culture of architecture. At such a nascent stage, the ultimate cultural repercussions of a new programming era are only to be guessed at.*[1]

Scripting, as opposed to its more hard-core sibling computer program writing, has been around for as long as there have been computer users – seven decades: the first programs to access memory were written in the 1940s.

However much designers access digital technology as part of their practice, in the main they do not script; yet many who do so achieve spectacular results, but they are still the exception, and not the norm. Why is this, and what will persuade the uninitiated to look at scripting as a skill worth adding to the others they deploy when thinking about design using contemporary media?

This primer is seeking both to enthuse the sceptic and honour the enthusiasm of the expert. The first half of this book captures, at least in part, the spirit of many who are pioneering. The second part, the five projects, presents the ascendency of idea and 'problem decomposition' as a skill over and above code writing. Having solicited the informed opinion from a range of contemporary scripting maestros, I received an embarrassment of riches – close to 40,000 words of thoughtful and erudite answers to my 'questions of the day'. Regretfully, I have had space only to quote highly selectively from these responses in Chapter 3, but I have contextualised the excerpts with the briefest of retrospective gazes over a key selection of the early pioneers in Chapter 4, and reflected on two decades of digital design projects from my own ambit in the remainder of the book. The insights gained thereby suggest that this is a shared journey, albeit one on which we have not really moved past first base. There is a palpable sense too that scripting is not a style fad but an operational fundamental. I contend that scripting has the potential to turn much of existing practice on its head; many design practice orthodoxies are already being challenged, and they will ultimately yield simply by being insufficiently competitive in an exacting market.

dECOi Architects, One Main: office renovation, Cambridge, MA, 2008. An office refurbishment that deploys numerical control machining of sustainable plywood to demonstrate the versatility and efficiency available from CAD-CAM design-build processes.

Just as log tables supplanted the abacus, the slide rule the log table, the calculator the slide rule, cold clumsy CAD finally exiled the drawing board and instrumental technical drawing tools from almost all offices worldwide. Once scripting becomes more accessible at least at a practical level, we will have new potential to share our design thinking across diverse design professions as well as with one another in fundamentally different conversations. Design culture will alter and scripting culture will shift accordingly (or is it the other way round?). This chapter brings these thoughts together and offers some concluding provocations.

Cultural account

As we have many design cultures, so too a variety of cultures is emerging internally within scripting. These range from the purely pragmatic, such as automating routine office processes – scripting to save time – to being more imagination-oriented, such as scripting to support speculative design enquiry, and the many variations that lie in between. It is likely that the meaning of the term 'scripting' will morph over time, but at this stage it serves as a convenient label that helps define a particular class of designer.

Those who have quietly got on with scripting for office productivity in the sense of writing the applications that streamline routine operations are largely unheralded in comparison with those who script to more conspicuously exhibitable effect. Particularly within the larger offices, the role of the efficiency facilitators is highly respected but their existence can rapidly lead to a dependency culture: too few of their non-scripting colleagues are able to access their talent for training purposes as the pressure of practice means that neither teaching nor learning can be factored into busy workloads. There are notable exceptions to this – Foster + Partners is among the important exceptions with their early establishment of the office's Specialist Modelling Group.

Once a practice can step back a pace from the hurly burly of prioritising getting building plans out the door and accommodate more sharing knowledge and skills with greater commitment, new divisions of labour will emerge. This shift in priorities will allow certain colleagues to dedicate a scripting focus to the documentation stage as well as to speculation

dECOi Architects, One Main: office renovation, Cambridge, MA, 2008. The project replaces the combinatorial logic of ready-made components typical of late-industrial process with a seamless and non-standard protocol of customised fabrication. A formal aesthetic emerges from these processes.

in early design, apportioned around their own predilections and office responsibilities. As I write, without an office input of this nature (that is, specifically inducting existing staff into scripting), scripting will only move a practice forward by a combination of talent engaged to provide a superior kind of IT role, as is the norm, and the enthusiasm of fresh appointees with prior knowledge of scripting. The situation whereby a scripting junior architect has difficulty in persuading a non-scripting senior colleague that writing code rather than drawing details is a better use of their time is not entirely unknown.

The ardent non-scripter probably needs to be acknowledged as part of scripting cultures as they play an important cultural role. However inadvertent their behaviour, their passivity or active discouragement holds back progress in several respects. How many scripters have been at least partially galvanised into writing code after participating in really stupid office procedures? Why practices will accept software as a productivity tool on the one hand, but not look at scripting on top of that same software in quite the same terms remains a mystery. I do not believe that scripting needs to adopt a counter-culture role, as it is likely we will see more young agile collectives outperform more established but dyed-in-the-wool practices in both competitions and the market.

Paradoxes to be challenged

Nobody who scripts like an angel could ever consider precluding coding and design computation while they continue to use the computer in design. As the essential counterpoint to the expert scripter, any non-scripter reading this account who cannot imagine themselves scripting may never be entirely convinced that scripting is essential. This remains the principal paradox and impasse: critics with strongly negative opinions about scripting who have never themselves scripted. This primer has highlighted several other paradoxes too that still need much thought in order to ensure that scripting will progress from code writing to a more loose-fit engagement with design computation.

In Chapter 2 I discussed the irony of software designed to emulate traditional practice in order to make its incursion more palatable. In general architects have been reluctant to move too far from their comfort zone, which is why we still have CAD material being abstracted by engineers into different and incompatible software packages to those used by architects, and returning material that then has to be abstracted back to the project by the architect. This is not inevitable, but it seems that the simplifications undertaken to get Building Information Modelling (BIM) to work in a very complex bespoke industry help maintain the construction sector's relative lag in progressiveness compared with the aircraft manufacturing industry, for example. The construction sector has for decades supported the comfortable familiarity of the digital equivalents of their analogue modes of operation rather than fully embrace opportunities to fundamentally modernise.

Another paradox is the exactness of scripting languages and the wooliness of some design thinking: they are essentially incompatible. This difference in precision and the highly anomalous process of 'designing by typing' is probably the single greatest turn-off to anyone reluctantly setting about learning to code. Developments like the Processing language and the emerging visual interfaces with code such as Grasshopper™ do point to less instrumental alternatives coming closer to hand.

A third paradox raised in Chapter 3 is that while we script by typing in code, the more talented the designer and the more complex the design, the more likely that they will need to work with a specialist scripter. This appears to be tenable so long as the designer has previously scripted him- or herself at a sufficiently sophisticated level to be able to work closely with their colleague. Similarly, the specialist scripter must have some design sensibility, otherwise too many blind alleys will be explored inadvertently. How we educate computer scientists to have the requisite design thinking remains a challenge not easily addressed within the typical contemporary tertiary education system.

Another paradox is that of the swarm. In the short history of scripting, instead of design becoming more plural as so many exciting and viable alternative approaches present themselves, through the agency of scripting we flock to a particular methodology of the day, for want of a better term. Each time an intriguing new plug-in is helpfully included in software, once it is discovered its 'grooviness' causes it to spread like wild fire across the globe for expert but not necessarily thoughtful application. Perhaps this is inevitable, but there is an interesting question to be resolved here about the 'effect' chasing a yet-to-be-identified worthwhile cause, compared with the effect solicited through the deep understanding of a situation.

In Chapter 3 I also observe that most school programmes lag behind the prevalence of exhibition and published design, which is at least partially supported by scripting, code writing and software customisation. Having said that, there is obviously a view abroad that despite the huge leaps in computer performance and access to much more user-friendly software the results are not commensurate with opportunity in terms of creative endeavour. I see this rather differently, however. This level of critique is usually made on the basis of 'in the beginning there were computers …'. With the several examples extracted from my Sagrada Família church projects outlined in Chapters 6 and 7, I aimed to show that scripting tools can have nothing to do with thinking algorithmically. Rather, if a designer can think in those terms, scripting is a natural ally. I am shy of equating human creativity levels with the power of our instruments: 'try harder!' could be demanded of those of us who are not performing at the level of Gaudí, even with our new instruments and implementation skills. Such masters remind us of the difference between idea and concept.

Shifts in authorship

The most interesting paradox of all for me is the difference between the generations of secretive designers obsessed with the worry that others will steal their ideas (an interesting proposition that I have never fully understood), and a generation of Internet-savvy sharers of information, including snippets of code. Could it be that this largely younger generation have worked out that it is how well you work with an idea that counts as much as propagating the idea itself?

Conceptual development from an idea has been a clearly defined process in my experience. Whilst many in a team might have the same idea, someone will have had it first. From that point, once the idea is shared, its development into a concept will almost certainly involve other people. How those people are organised within the team, that is, the hierarchies, traditionally evolved around experience. Involving scripting as part of the design team effort is likely to completely change roles and status. Scripting has the potential to flatten hierarchies fundamentally, and the teamwork around constructing code that works as integrated snippets from a number of authors is extremely motivating. The complexity of involving computer coding within a project mirrors the increasing levels of technical specialisation already changing many of the traditional roles within practice. Together they point to design teams paralleling the film industry more than the model of the signature architect and the largely anonymous team.

It is this aspect of scripting that offers great potential especially to the small practice. Small practices that include scripting talent now have more opportunity than ever before to compete with larger practices; they have affordable technology at their disposal and less of the institutional inertia that can evolve within larger practices. In other words they can be more agile. Office procedures in one kind of practice might continue to support the abstraction of the architects' details into shop drawings by specialists ending up in the hands of fabricators whose staff have to rebuild the material as 3D numerical control sequences to drive their automated machinery. This sequence increases the scope for mistakes, and involves fee erosion along the way. A more flexible practice might consult directly with the fabricator and script output from their own 3D models in a format immediately readable by the fabricators, so saving time and money and significantly reducing the risk of error.

Unfortunately, I may be getting a bit ahead of myself. My assessment of scripting and practice is more about optimism and potential than actuality, although many examples of small practices short-cutting through innovative and highly efficient file-to-factory protocols have been emerging over the past few years. The single most experienced scripting-for-design leader whom I consulted for this book, Hugh Whitehead of Foster + Partners Specialist Modelling Group gave me this opinion around authorship:

> *At present scripters tend to be of the 'lone gun' mentality and are justifiably proud of their firepower, usually developed through many late nights of obsessive concentration. There is the danger that if celebration of skills is allowed to obscure and divert from the real design objectives, then scripting degenerates to become an isolated craft rather than developing into an integrated art form.*

I believe that we, practitioners and educators alike, all have a role to ensure that the shifts in authorship I describe above tend towards Hugh's 'integrated art form'.

Quo vadis?

A culture of openness to scripting as the logical extension to software use will probably work best for all at this point in CAD's evolution. Crucially, I believe that scripting must not be identified as a movement with the potential to be discriminated against – an exclusivist force that must be thwarted. A movement's call to arms is hardly necessary for the scripting enthusiasts as there are many opportunities to exhibit and be published in ways that publicly describe scripted creative paths as alternatives to practice still locked into the late 20th century. Practices unwilling to make the necessary learning investment in scripting may well feel that they have been provided with insufficient evidence of the potential dividends, but this need not lead to any intransigence towards its take-up. Established designers with little apparent need to enhance their skills, or to increase the scope of their accomplished repertoire, ought not to let their own lack of experience with scripting, or even an unspoken fear of young colleagues and their seemingly voodoo scripting skills, limit opportunities for development.

In reviewing the terrain, we all seem to be waiting for a natural language and a seamless physical interaction system to appear, one that does not require the designer to prematurely declare priorities in order to comply with the strictures of computing logic, nor to be forced to interact so palpably with a black box. Ultimately designers would much rather not supplant the doodle with computer language and keyed-in input, regardless of whether they can code or not. Both scripters and non-scripters desire the equivalent natural interface for their creative intellect with any tool they work with; the fact that we are unable to define what we imagine to be the ideal scripting tool in terms sufficiently clear for the toolmakers to furnish such a miracle environment emphasises our shared condition of being mere babes in this context. We know what we want but we are unable to define it: if we could, we would make the ideal tool for ourselves.

Most likely the best way forward to encourage design innovation in this arena comes down to redefining education and the role of design schools. Practice in association with progressive school programmes would benefit from learning to be more critical in their engagement with CAD and counter its manifest deficiencies. By mastering their tools through deep customisation they will be less supine in the face of software engineers' predication of computer programs based on a singular view of how designers design. If the senior designers' creative role has moved to one of managing design rather than undertaking design at the proverbial drawing board, they might further equip themselves with sufficient knowledge to be able to mix a new cocktail, blending their sagacity born of experience with the alternative creative design approaches offered by the emerging generation of highly creative scripters.

Whether for a city, a block, a major building or a house, we are used to conspicuous design leadership. When we look at the outcome from a talented scripter and contrast the 'design process' with that which often leads to signature buildings, inevitably we have to reconsider authorship. What if the 'signature architect' assumes a role more as 'creative director'? What if the creative team declares a new identity of its own? What if all the consultants including the clients were enfranchised and more conspicuously credited within a broader description of and participation within the design process?

As a society we demand overt if not charismatic leadership, and this seems unlikely to change, especially given the culture of hero designer promulgated through the media. Scripting may well provide the route to rethinking how the team is composed, how it interacts, how it reaches decisions, and how it communicates them. There is nothing about contemporary practice or its declared expectations to suggest that these shifts are anticipated. Reviewing the work and opinions of my selection of scripters making the most waves today, it seems abundantly clear that a significantly alternative shift in design practice is already afoot, even if many practices and schools do not recognise it.

To be 'conservatively progressive' serves society adequately but only up to a point; to address emerging global issues comprehensively with the best technologies at our disposal is almost a separate matter. With the tools we already have, the scripter potentially has the upper hand. If we can accelerate the invention of the much-desired miraculously invisible scripting agent to facilitate wider take-up, then so much the better. From my research, the best possible arena appears to be schools with active engagement with progressive practices, where each adopts clear pathways to inform the other of their ongoing learning and discovery through digital design.

Informed opinion from active scripters asserts that coding is an essential part of their design repertoire, and that this extrapolates beyond the gifted individual to the talented team. Design schools would do best to ensure that all students emerge with sufficient scripting experience at least to reject scripting if not actually take it up with the advantage of knowing what it is that they reject. More progressive still would be to accept the importance of the many scripting cultures, grasp the scripting nettle with both hands, and help find the way forward by supporting scripting more prominently as an essential component of 21st-century design education.

References

1 H Castle, *AD* Special Issue: *Programming Cultures*, editorial preface, Wiley (London), July–August 2006, p 4.

Glossary

Boolean operations
Boolean operations, named after the mathematician George Boole (1815–64), have three logics relevant to the use of the term in this primer when applied to solid geometry. The first is the union of two solids, the second the intersection of two solids and the third the subtraction of one solid from another. In terms of their relevance to scripting, Boolean operations can only be performed with a minimum of two solids 'A' and 'B' at least partially intersecting in space. In the first, *union*, 'A' is fused with 'B'; *intersection* calls for the identification of the material that is common to both 'A' and 'B'; with *subtraction*, the result of what is left when 'B' is subtracted from 'A'.

Clerestory
Formerly applying specifically to a wall with windows that rises above the roofline of a lower adjacent aisle, as an architectural term the clerestory describes the upper levels of Roman basilicas or the naves of Romanesque or Gothic churches. In modern usage, the term is used to describe any high windows above eye level that let in light and/or fresh air.

Crossing
A crossing, in ecclesiastical architecture, is the junction of the four arms of a cruciform (cross-shaped) church. In a typically oriented church (especially of Romanesque or Gothic style), the crossing gives access to the nave on the west, the transept arms on the north and south, and the choir on the east.

Diurnal
Is the antonym of nocturnal and means active during the day.

Doric (order)
Relates to a style of architecture that features fluted columns with a rounded moulding at the top and no base. Originating in Greek and represented later in Roman architecture, the Parthenon in Athens is probably the best-known example of the Doric order.

Euclidean geometry
A mathematical system of geometry based on a number of 'simple' axioms and presented by Euclid, the 3rd-century-BC Greek mathematician referred to as the 'Father of Geometry'. According to the principles of Euclid, for example, geometry allows only one line parallel to another to pass through a given point. Modern teaching of algebra and number theory is still based on these principles.

Euclidean space
In Euclidean space the axioms and postulations of Euclid apply in both two and three dimensions, and any two figures on a plane or objects in space are equivalent if one can be transformed into another by any sequence of translations, reflections and/or rotations.

Genotype
This is the genetic makeup of an organism rather than its physical characteristics. A genotype contains the full hereditary information and represents its exact genetic makeup. Observed changes from this original such as morphology, behaviour or development result in a phenotype.

Helicoid
Shaped or coiled like a spiral, it is so called for its similarity to the helix. However, at every point on the helicoid there is a helix contained in the helicoid that passes through that point. Discovered by Jean Baptiste Meusnier in 1776, it is the third minimal surface after the plane and catenoid.

Hyperbolic paraboloid
A combination of a hyperbola and a parabola, these are often referred to as 'saddles'. A horizontal cross section produces the hyperbola, whilst a vertical cross section is parabolic. Seen commonly in roof construction, the form

is distinguishable by being concave around one axis and convex around the other.

Hyperboloid of revolution
The most recognisable place to note structures representing a hyperboloid of revolution are cooling towers of power stations, especially nuclear ones. It is a quadratic surface obtained by rotating a hyperbola about the perpendicular bisector to the line between the foci (one-sheeted) or by rotating the hyperbola about the line joining the foci (two-sheeted).

Masia
Rural Catalan farmhouse, often built to be easily defended, accommodating the landowner and family, farm workers and families and, in some cases, livestock.

Nave
Generally considered the 'body' of the church for worshippers, the nave is the central approach to the high altar. In larger churches and cathedrals, it may be flanked by aisles. However, whether Romanesque, Gothic or classical it will extend from the main entry through to the chancel.

Organicist
Perhaps containing a sense of holism, organicism emphasises a concept of society or the universe as analogous to an organism where all parts have to work together in order for the whole to function. As applied in an architectural context, an organicist seeks to integrate design seamlessly with its place and purpose.

Parametric
Using a finite number of parameters, parametric design is based on a set of equations. Parametric design software includes parametric data embedded within 3D objects, such as height, depth, thickness, weight and possibly specific attributes of materials.

Phenotype
A phenotype is the result of a genotype influenced by environmental factors interacting with hereditary factors carried within its genetic code. Whilst a genotype is pure heredity, a phenotype represents what that heredity produces.

Piano nobile
Literally translating as the 'noble floor', *piano nobile* is the principal (sometimes assumed as the first) floor of a large house. The origin of the term may lie in the elevation of this floor such that it affords finer views, cooling breezes or perhaps the avoidance of the damp and odours commonly afflicting the lower floor(s).

Stereotomy
Stereotomy refers to the cutting of stone into smaller components. Stonemasons between the 10th and 13th centuries, without the benefit of geometry, converted stone into complex shapes producing vaults, helical stairways and arches. In later centuries stereotomy became a more rigorously applied science based on descriptive geometry.

Triforium
An arcaded storey in a church between the nave arches below and the clerestory above. In Romanesque and Gothic buildings it is either a spacious gallery above the side aisles or it may be a modest passage confined within the thickness of the walls.

Scripting tools

Software name / scripting tool	Producer	Scripting language
3ds Max	Autodesk	MAXScript
ActionScript	Adobe	ActionScript is a scripting language developed by Adobe
C#	Microsoft	Multi-paradigm programming language encompassing imperative, declarative, functional, generic, object-oriented (class-based) and component-oriented programming disciplines
C++	Developed by Bjarne Stroustrup at Bell Labs in 1979 as an enhancement to the C programming language	Compiled general-purpose programming language

Software name / scripting tool	Producer	Scripting language
Catia	Dassault Systèmes	Visual Basic and C++ programming languages, and it has an Application Programming Interface (API) called CAA2 or CAA V5, a component object model (COM) interface; formulated for use in engineering
Digital Project	Gehry Technologies	Visual Basic and C++ programming languages, and it has an Application Programming Interface (API) called CAA2 or CAA V5, a component object model (COM) interface; a hybrid version of Catia, adapted for use in architecture
Flash	Macromedia	ActionScript
Generative Components	Bentley Systems	The software has a published API and uses Visual Basic
Grasshopper	McNeel	Graphical algorithm editor tightly integrated with Rhino3D and therefore can work in association with RhinoScript, Visual Basic on top of a Java Application Server
Mathematica	Wolfram Research	Can be made to work in conjunction with other software

Software name / scripting tool	Producer	Scripting language
Matlab	MathWorks	High-level technical computing language and interactive environment for algorithm development, data visualisation, data analysis and numeric computation
MaxScript	Autodesk	Bespoke scripting for 3ds Max
Maya Embedded Language (MEL)	Autodesk	Bespoke scripting for Maya
Microstation	Bentley Systems	VBA, MDL, BASIC, JMDL
Perl	Written by Larry Wall and a cast of thousands	High-level programming language suited for quick prototyping, system utilities, software tools, system management tasks, database access, graphical programming, networking and programming for the web
PHP	PHP is free software released under the PHP License	General-purpose scripting language originally designed for web development using dynamic pages

Software name / scripting tool	Producer	Scripting language
Processing	Open source	Sits on top of a Java Application Server
Processing (Java)	Open source	Teaches the basics of computer programming in a visual context serving as the foundation for electronic sketchbooks
Rhino3D	McNeel	RhinoScript (Visual Basic)
RhinoScript	McNeel	RhinoScript based on Microsoft Visual Basic Script (VBScript)
RhinoScript (Python)	Open source	More powerful scripting tool based on Python
RhinoScript (VB)	McNeel	Adequate scripting tool based on Visual Basic
VBA	Microsoft	Visual Basic Programming language for use with Microsoft Word, Excel, Access
VBScript	Microsoft	Designed as a 'lightweight' language with a fast interpreter for use in a wide variety of Microsoft environments

Recommended reading

R Aish, *Smart Geometry Architectural Exploration*, Taylor & Francis, 2008

B Aranda, *Tooling*, Princeton Architectural Press, 2006

C Balmond, *Informal*, Prestel, 2007

C Ceccato, *The Architect as Toolmaker: Computer-Based Generative Design Tools and Methods*, Architectural Association, 1998

M Coates, *Programming.Architecture*, Routledge, 2010

F De Luca, M Nardini, *Behind the Scene: Avant-garde techniques in contemporary design*, Birkhäuser, 2002

J Frazer, *An Evolutionary Architecture*, Architectural Association, 1995

I Greenberg, *Processing: Creative Coding and Computational Art*, Friends of ED, 2007

M Hansen, *Bodies in Code: Interfaces with Digital Media*, Routledge, 2006

M Hensel, A Menges, *Techniques and Technologies in Morphogenetic Design*, *Architectural Design (AD)*, Wiley, 2006

N Leach, D Turnbull and C Williams, *Digital Tectonics*, Wiley, 2004

J Maeda, *Creative Code: Aesthetics + Computation*, Thames and Hudson, 2004

J Maeda, *Maeda @ Media*, Universe Publishing, 2001

J Maeda, *Design By Numbers*, MIT Press, 2001

Chapters by M Meredith, Aranda\Lasch and M Sasaki in T Sakamoto, A Ferre, M Kubo (eds), *From Control to Design: Parametric/Algorithmic Architecture*, Actar, 2008

W Mitchell, R Liggett, T Kvan, *The Art of Computer Graphics Programming: A Structured Introduction for Architects and Designers*, Van Nostrand Reinhold, 1987

W Mitchell, *The Reconfigured Eye: Visual Truth in the Post-Photographic Era,* MIT Press, 1992

W Mitchell, *The Logic of Architecture: Design, Computation, and Cognition,* MIT Press, 1990

C Reas, *Processing: A Programming Handbook for Visual Designers and Artists*, MIT Press, 2007

SHoP, Sharples, Holden, Pasquarelli, *Versioning: Evolutionary Techniques in Architecture*, *Architectural Design (AD)*, Wiley, 2003

M Silver, *Programming Cultures: Architecture, Art and Science in the Age of Software Development*, *Architectural Design (AD)*, Wiley, 2006

K Terzidis, *Algorithmic Architecture*, Architectural Press, 2006

MS Watanabe, *Induction Design*, Birkhäuser, 2002

Index

3 metals 114
3 satin sheets 115

A
Acconci Studio 33
Acconci, Vito 33
Adobe ActionScript 36, 37
Aegis Hyposurface ™ 110, 111, 112
agency 86
agent-based swarm intelligence 85
Aish, Francis 33
Aish, Robert 33, 44, 61, 63, 69, 104
Akos, Gil 33
AKT Architects 23, 33, 43, 44, 58, 69
Alexander, Christopher 84
algorithms 8, 24, 25, 58, 64-6, 75
 definition 79-81
 evolutionary 79
 flocking 85
 genetic 31, 79, 80, 141, 143, 167
 shading 193
 surface 192, 195
 surface perturbation 109-13
 swarming 85-6
Andrasek, Alisa 33, 45, 51
applets 28

Archigram 53
Artificial Intelligence (AI) 15
Atlas Titan machine code 52
AutoCAD ™ 28, 29, 111
AutoLISP ™ 29, 82, 111

B
Ball, Keith 110
Balmond, Cecil 18, 27
Banham, Reyner 196
Baroque 227
Basic (programming language) 141
Beekham Tower, New York 16
Beer, Stafford 51
Bellemo, Michael: *Shoal Fly By* 171, 172-3, 175, 183, 184, 185, 188
Bergós, Joan 102
BIM (Building Information Modelling) 15, 250
biomimetics 78, 107, 233, 245
Biothing 33, 45, 46
 Fissure – Agent Wall 45
 Seroussi – Mesonic Fabrics 46
Birmingham Hippodrome Theatre 109, 110
Boole, George 147
Boolean operations 86, 97, 100, 131-6, 142, 145, 147,
148, 152
Borromini, Francesco 92
Bratton, Ben 66
Bridges, Alan 84
British Museum courtyard roof 92
Building Information Modelling (BIM) 15, 250
Burry, Jane 122, 123
Burry, Mark 105, 107, 108, 118, 119
 Paramorph I 105, 107

C
C, C#, C++ 36
CAAD 231
CAD 28, 30, 35-6, 48, 105, 232, 247, 249, 253
 history of 14-17
CAD-CAM 21, 247
CADDS5 ™ (Computervision) 104, 141
Cage, John 51
Campo, Matias del 33, 55, 60, 66
Cartesian geometry 92-4, 95, 136, 156, 201, 203, 204, 205
CEB Reas 33
Ceccato, Cristiano 33, 77-8
 Form Evolution 62
CITA 21, 33, 53, 57
CITA-SIAL 234, 235, 236,

237, 238, 239, 240, 241, 242, 243, 244
Coates, Paul 33, 62, 63, 80-2, 84
   Shape Grammar 83, 84
Collins, Mark 33, 46, 57, 60, 155
Colquhoun, Alan 196
complexification 75
computer-aided architectural design (CAAD) 231
computer-aided design *see* CAD
contractor space 183, 186, 187
Corbusier, Le 196-7
Crick, Francis 80
cube, morphing of sphere to 192-6
cylinder, morphing of sphere to 198-200

D
da Vinci, Leonardo 233
Darwin, Charles 80
dECOi Architects 114, 247, 248
   Aegis Hyposurface ™ 110, 111, 112
Deconstructivism 19
Dermoid 228, 229, 234, 235-43, 244
design exploration 38-9
design productivity 38-9
Digital Project™ 62, 240
Doesburg, Theo van 94, 227
Douglis, Evan 33
   Helioscope 47, 48
Dunlop, Grant 105, 107
   Paramorph I 105, 107

E
Eastman, Chuck 84
Ednie-Brown, Pia 33, 55
education, scripting 41, 43-9
Einstein, Alfred 212
ellipse, drawing 177
ellipsoid 184, 186, 187, 188, 234, 239, 240, 243
essential scripting 40-1
Euclidean geometry 20, 94
Euclidean space 93-4, 200-11
evocative surface 155
evolutionary algorithms 79

F
Fagiuoli, Ettore 224
Flatland 199, 200, 202
Fleming, Alexander 80
Fleming, Ulrich 83, 84
flock 85
Fontanals, Josep Ràfols i 167
Form Z ™ 36
Fornes, Marc 33, 66
Foster + Partners 33, 52, 92, 108, 114
   Specialist Modelling Group (SMG) 108, 248, 252
   Smithsonian Courtyard Roof, Washington DC 52
Frazer, John 33, 51-3, 64, 76-7, 78, 79, 80, 81, 82, 84
   circular cathode ray tube 80
French curves 176
Fry, Ben 74
Fuller, Buckminster 196-7
Future Systems 53

G
Galileo 212
Gaudí, Antoni 23, 24, 28, 90, 92, 94-104, 108, 109, 114, 115, 116-23, 124, 227, 231-2, 237, 251
   Casa Vicens 130
   Colònia Güell 92, 130, 133, 134, 231, 243
   La Pedrera (Casa Milà)156
   Pabellones (Finca) Güell 130
   Teresianas Convent 166
   see also Sagrada Família Church, Barcelona
Gehry, Frank 233
Gehry Partners 113
Gehry Technologies 33, 53, 54, 62
Generative Components™ 36, 62, 240
generative scripting 67, 75-7, 210
genetic algorithms 31, 79, 80, 141, 143, 167
Gero, John 84
Glanville, Ranulph 84
Goulthorpe, Mark 33, 47, 66, 69, 109, 110, 113, 186
Grasshopper ™ 62, 237, 240, 251
Greene, Graham 214
Greg Lynn FORM 114
Grovsmedje, Copenhagen 176

H
Hadid, Zaha 233
Häring, Hugo 20
Hasegawa, Toru 33, 46, 57, 60
helicoid 100, 144
Hensel, Michael 33
history of Computer-Aided Design 14-17
HTML 36
hyperbola 28, 29, 82, 132, 135, 136, 139, 201
hyperbolic paraboloid 118, 119, 120, 130, 133-4, 144, 155, 156, 162, 165, 166, 167, 169
hyperboloid of revolution 28, 118, 119, 120, 130, 132, 134-6, 138, 141-5, 202, 204

I
ICD 40, 42
Ihnatowicz, Edward 51
IM Pei 92
initiation to scripting 33-6
Invernizzi, Angelo 224
Iron Python 36
ITKE research pavilion 40, 42

A
JavaScript 36
Johnson, Jason 33

K
Kaijima, Sawako 23, 33, 43, 44, 58, 69, 92
   Topology optimiser 43
Kaplicky, Jan 53
Kilian, Axel 33, 51, 57
   Vaults, particle spring library 44
Klein, Felix 94
Knight, Terry 84
Knippers, Jan
   ITKE research pavilion 40, 42
Kokkugia 33, 58
   Micro 49
   Swarm Matter 49
Kvan, Tom 33, 47, 61, 85, 87

L

labDORA 33, 45, 67
  gross topology tower 50
Laurentian Library 227
Leach, Neil 33, 54, 64, 66, 67
Liggett, Robin S. 87
Louvre pyramid, Paris 92
LUA 36
Lynn, Greg 183, 233
  Slavin House 187

M

Macapia, Peter 33, 45, 67
Mackintosh, Charles Rennie
  Willow Chair 85
Macleod, Cat 171
  Shoal Fly By 171, 172-3, 175, 183, 184, 185, 188
Maeda, John 73, 74, 84
Maher, Andrew 105, 107
  Paramorph I 105, 107
March, Lionel 84
masia (Catalonia) 225-7
Matamala, Juan 153
Mathematica 37
mathematics, role for 58-62
Mather, Tom 84
MATLAB 37
Max/MSP ™ 62
MaxScript 37
Maxwell, Iain 33
MAYA ™ 37, 240
Maya Embedded Language (MEL) 37
Meldahl, Ferdinand 176
Menges, Achim 33, 65
  ITKE research pavilion 40, 42
Meredith, Michael 18, 33, 54, 57
MESNE 33, 51
  Resonant Frequency 54
Metzger, Gustav 51
Michalatos, Panagiotis 23, 33, 43, 44, 58, 69
  Topology optimiser 23, 43
Michelangelo 227
Mille-feuille 113
MinusArchitecturestudio 33
  Catch & release 57
MIT 59, 60
MIT Media Lab 73
Mitchell, William J. (Bill) 14, 82-3, 84, 85
Mode 33, 58, 69
Modern Movement 18, 19-20, 113,196
Monge, Gaspard 92
Moore, Henry 233
MOS 33, 54, 57
  Sand 58

N

Neumann, John von 84
Newton, Isaac 212
Nicholas, Paul 33
non-Euclidean geometry 20, 94, 227
non-parametric design 18
non-uniform rational B-spline (NURBS) 171, 175, 178, 180, 186, 187
numerical control 95
NURBS 171, 175, 178, 180, 186, 187
NURBS-to-arc methodology 186, 188

O

Objective-C 37
O'Brien, Flann
  At Swim-Two-Birds 214-15
  Third Policeman, The 191, 192, 210-22
Oosterhuis, Kas 186
Open Cascade 240
organicism 97, 119, 129, 159-61
Our World project 80, 190-223
Oxman, Neri 33, 54
  Carpal Skin 60
  Subterrain 59

P

Panagiotis, Michalatos 92
Para-masia 227, 243, 244
Paradox [there are many reported on throughout the book]
parametric design software 18
parametricism 18-19, 22, 105, 117
paramorph 104-9, 126, 148, 157, 235
Parsons, Ronnie 33
Pask, Gordon 51, 76, 84
Perl 37
Peters, Brady 33, 64
Phileban solids 157, 196-7, 201, 202, 203, 207
PHP 37

Pigram, Dave 33
Pisca, Nick 33, 53, 54, 62
Platonic solids 196, 197, 205
point-and-click digitiser 174
point-cloud scanner 174
polyline 28
Postmodernism 19, 21
Pound, Ezra 51
primitives 157
problem decomposition 189
Processing (Java) 37, 62, 74, 240, 251
Proxy 33, 46, 57, 60
  Stabile 61
pseudocode 34

R

real absence 128-36, 154, 169
Reas, Casey 33, 37, 51, 55, 74, 75
  Process6_Puff_4 70
  Tissue-B01 69
Rhino 3D ™ 37, 62, 120, 174, 178, 188, 237, 240
RhinoScript (Python) 37
RhinoScript (VB) 37
Rhl 37
Riiber, Jacob 53
  Lamella Flock 53
rules, need for 22-4

S

Sagrada Família Church, Barcelona 24, 28, 90, 95, 96, 97-9, 101-2, 104, 105, 109, 114, 174, 231, 237, 251
  liquid stone 169
  nave roof 167-9
  Passion Facade 116-23, 124
  rose windows 126-50, 152-69
  triforium *columnetes* 162-6
'salami approach' 183, 186
San Carlo alle Quattro Fontane 92
Schumacher, Patrik 18, 27
Schork, Tim 33
Scott, Alex 110
scripting critique 49-50
scripting languages, choice of 36-7
scripting tools 36-7
shareware programs 28
Shelden, Denis 33
Simon, Herbert 15

simplexity 75, 92-3
Sketchpad 84
Smithsonian Courtyard Roof, Washington 52
Snooks, Roland 33, 58
SOFTlab 33, 57
  Alice 63
  Shizuku 64
SPAN 33, 55, 60, 66
sphere, morphing into cube 192-6
sphere-to-cylinder morph 198-200
Steadman, Phil 84
Steinfeld, Kyle 33
stereotomy 121, 175, 177
Stiny, George 84
Stockhausen, Karlheinz 51
StudioMode
  Parsing Populations 65
  RK4Tile3 66
Subirach, Joan 119
Supermanoeuvre 33
  Protosynthesis 67
Sutherland, Ivan 84
swarm 85-6
Swiss Re London headquarters 108
Szivos, Michael 33, 57

T
Tamke, Martin 33, 53, 58, 65
  Lamella Flock 53
teratoid 152, 161, 162
THEVERYMANY 33, 66
  Echidnoids 68
Thompson, D'Arcy Wentworth 80, 155
Thomsen, Mette Ramsgard 21, 33, 55, 236
  Thaw 57
triple points 137
Turing, Alan 84

U
UNIX 141

V
VB, VBA 37
VB Script, 180
Villa Girasole, Verona 224
virtual presence 128, 153, 159, 164, 169
Voronoi 86

W
wall screw-moss (*Tortula muralis*) 228-30
Water Worlds, Salt Water Pavilion, Neeltje Jans, Netherlands 186
Watson, James 80
Web 2 35
Whitehead, Hugh 33, 61, 252
Wiener, Norbert 51
Wilkins, Maurice 80
Wood, Peter 110, 141, 180

X
'Xhyper' 141-3, 148

Y
Yessios, Chris 84

Z
Zeeuw, Gerard de 84

Picture credits

The author and the publisher gratefully acknowledge the people who gave their permission to reproduce material in this book. While every effort has been made to contact copyright holders for their permission to reprint material, the publishers would be grateful to hear from any copyright holder who is not acknowledged here and will undertake to rectify any errors or omissions in future editions.

Cover image model: Mark Burry, Scripting support: James Wojtek Goscinski, render: James Loder

l = left, r = right, t = top, b = bottom

All images and diagrams are by the author, unless otherwise stated.

p 16 Courtesy Gehry Technologies; p 21 © Mette Ramsgard Thomsen; p 56 © Mette Ramsgard Thomsen, photography Anders Ingvartsen; p 23 & 43 © P. Michalatos & S. Kaijima @ AKT; p 40, 41 Institute for Computational Design, Prof. Achim Menges and Institute of Building Structures and Structural Design, Prof. Jan Knippers; p 44 Example of a form finding exercise of multiple linked arcs using an application written in processing by Axel Killian using a particle spring library by Simon Greenwold; p 45 Design+Computation: Alisa Andrasek + Jose Manuel Sanchez; p 46 MESONIC FABRICS / 2007/09, biothing with Ezio Blasetti, Alisa Andrasek Ezio Blasetti, FlowerPower custom written plug-in: Kyle Steinfeld with Alisa Andrasek, photo: Georges Meguerditchian, Permanent collection Centre Pompidou; p 47-8 Reproduced by permission of Evan Douglis; p 49 Kokkugia; p 50 Design Peter Macapia, Rhino Scripting, Robert Baker, Francis Bitonti, Mathematica Matthew Howard, design interns Day Jimenez, Martial Marquet, Andres Mendoza; p 52 © Foster and Partners, photo Brady Peters; p 53 CITA - Martin Tamke, Jacob Riiber and Stig Nielsen, Knippers Helbigg Engineers – Hauke Jungjohann, Trebyggeriet.no, hsb-SYSTEMS gmbh, Hans Hundegger Maschinenbau GmbH, Prof. Christoph Gengnagel/ TU-Berlin Chair of structural engineering, photo: Anders Ingvartsen; p 54 © Mesne Design Studio; p 57 Catch & Release Part 2 minusArchitecturestudio Design: Jason Scott Johnson, Scripting: Sam Alcorn Fabrication: Wil Marquez Catch & Release; p 58 MOS, Michael Meredith, Hilary Sample; pp 59, 60 © Neri Oxman, Architect; p 61 Mark Collins & Toru Hasegawa, Proxy; p 62 © 2010 Cristiano Ceccato; p 63-4 Reproduced by permission of Softlab Michael Szivos; p 65-6 Mode; p 67 Project Team: Dave Pigram, Iain Maxwell, Matthew Hall, Jared Olmstead, Susan Teal; p 68 (t & b) Reproduced courtesy of The Very Many; p 70 Image courtesy of Casey Reas, Gallery DAM (Berlin and bitforoms gallery New York); p 79-82 © John Hamilton Frazer; p 83-4 © Paul Coates; p 85 (t & b) Courtesy of Tom Kvan; pp 93, 100, 101 (t & b), 102 (t & b), 106, 119 (l & r) Diagrams © Mark Burry; p 95 Diagram © Mark Burry and Dominik Holzer; pp 96, 97, 116, 127, 157, 231 (l & r) © Expiatory Temple of the Sagrada Família; pp 98, 99 (t & b), 109, 128, 129, 131, 132, 133, 146 (bl, bc & br), 153, 161, 164 (b), 166 (r), 168 (tl), 176, 225, 236, 238 (t & b) © Mark Burry; p 103 Models by Mark Burry, renders by Grant Dunlop; p 104 Original video: Duncan Burry; pp 105, 107 Parametric models: Mark Burry, Andrew Maher, Grant Dunlop; p 108 Parametric model: Mark Burry; p 110 Design team: Mark Goulthorpe, Mark Burry, Oliver Dering, Arnaud Descombes, Gabriele Evangelisti; pp 111, 112 Design team: Mark Goulthorpe, Mark Burry, Oliver Dering, Arnaud Descombes, Gabriele Evangelisti. Photograph: Mark Burry; pp 113, 114, 115 Scripting choreography: Mark Burry, code snippets: Peter Wood, Render: Grant Dunlop; pp 118, 134, 135 (t & b), 136, 137, 138 (t & b), 139, 140, 155, 156, 158, 177 (t & b), 181 Drawings © Mark Burry; pp 120 (t & b), 121, 122 (b) Scripted model and prototype: Mark Burry; p 122 (t) Parametric model: Jane Burry;

p 123 Parametric model: Jane Burry, Render: Grant Dunlop; p 124 (t & b) Parametric model: Jane Burry, CNC cutting: Jordi Barbany (Granits Barbany); pp 142, 145 Scripted parametric models: Mark Burry; p 143 Scripted parametric model: Mark Burry, coding and building of Xhyper: Peter Wood; pp 144, 146 (t), 149, 150, 168 (b) Scripted parametric models: Mark Burry, renders: Grant Dunlop; p 147 (t & b) Parametric model and scripts: Mark Burry; pp 159, 160 Scripted models and renders: Mark Burry; pp 162 (t), 162 (bl & br) Model: Mark Burry, Scripting support: James Wojtek Goscinski; pp 163, 164 (tl & tr) Model: Mark Burry, Scripting support: James Wojtek Goscinski, Modelling support: Michael Wilson, Renders: Grant Dunlop; pp 165 (l), 165 (r) Parametric scripted model: Mark Burry, render: Grant Dunlop; p 166 (l) Courtesy of Javier Lopez Bravo; p 168 (tr) Models: Mark Burry; pp 171, 172 © Andrew Maher; p 175 (l & r) Screen capture: Andrew Maher; pp 179, 180 Screen capture: Mark Burry, Scripting: Peter Wood, Diagrams: Mark Burry; p 182 (t & b) Screen capture: Mark Burry, Scripting: Peter Wood; pp 183, 187, 188 (t & b) Models: Mark Burry, scripting Peter Wood and James Wojtek Goscinski, renders: James Loder; p 183 (r) Model: Andrew Maher, Lee-Anne Khor and Rebecca Naughtin, scripting Peter Wood, render: James Loder; p 184 Model: Andrew Maher, Lee-Anne Khor and Rebecca Naughtin, scripting Peter Wood; p 185 Photograph Andrew Maher; p 186 Drawing: Mark Burry, scripting Peter Wood and James Wojtek Goscinski, render: James Loder; pp 193, 194 (t & b), 195, 197, 198, 199 (t & b), 200, 201, 202, 203, 204 (t & b), 305 (t & b), 206 (t & b) Models: Mark Burry, Scripting support: James Wojtek Goscinski, drawings: Michael Wilson; pp 207, 208, 209, 213 Models: Mark Burry, Scripting support: James Wojtek Goscinski, renders: James Loder; p 215 Lighting and photography: Andrew Miller, Model: Mark Burry, Scripting support: James Wojtek Goscinski, rapid prototyping: Brad Marmion; pp 216, 217 Models: Mark Burry, Scripting support: James Wojtek Goscinski, renders: Grant Dunlop; pp 221, 222 Models: Mark Burry, Scripting support: James Wojtek Goscinski, scene setting and renders: James Loder; p 229 Photograph DeaPeaJay http://creativecommons.org/licenses/by-sa/2.0/; p 230 Drawing Saskia Schut; pp 234, 235, 237, 240, 241 (t & b), 242 (t & b) Scripting and drawings: Daniel Davis and Alex Pena de Leon; p 239 Mathematical graphing: Daniel Davis and Alex Pena de Leon; pp 243, 244 Scripting: Daniel Davis and Alex Pena de Leon, renders: James Loder; pp 246, 248 dECOi Mark Goulthorpe, Mathematics Prof Alex Scott (Oxford University), Gabe Cira, Matt Trimble (Scripting), Millwork Contractor Shawn Keller (CWKeller)